A GRINGA'S STORY

LANDING
IN THE
HEART OF
MEXICO

A Memoir

COLLETTE SOMMERS

LANDING IN THE HEART OF MEXICO
A GRINGA'S STORY

iUniverse books may be ordered through booksellers or by contacting:

iUniverse
1663 Liberty Drive
Bloomington, IN 47403
www.iuniverse.com
1-800-Authors (1-800-288-4677)

Because of the dynamic nature of the Internet, any web addresses or links contained in this book may have changed since publication and may no longer be valid. The views expressed in this work are solely those of the author and do not necessarily reflect the views of the publisher, and the publisher hereby disclaims any responsibility for them.

Any people depicted in stock imagery provided by Getty Images are models, and such images are being used for illustrative purposes only.
Certain stock imagery © Getty Images.

ISBN: 978-1-5320-7854-5 (sc)
ISBN: 978-1-5320-7853-8 (e)

Library of Congress Control Number: 2019911052

Print information available on the last page.

iUniverse rev. date: 10/07/2019

CONTENTS

ACKNOWLEDGMENTS

I could not have found a better group of women who would dedicate themselves to the sometimes tedious and always time-consuming task of assisting me as readers and editors of this book. None of these women had taken on a task like this before, yet they were eager to get started and carried me through to the end. Each of them has enhanced this book in substantive and unique ways. Each one of them has been a friend and/or family member to me over the years. I cherish them and offer them my deepest and most humble thanks. (They have allowed me to use their first names in this acknowledgment.)

Leandra understood the vision of the book early on. She is responsible for the addition of a much more intimate account of my relationships with my mother, father, and sister. She somehow knew that these relationships shaped my personality far more than I had realized. I am grateful to her for the increased depth of character I reveal in this book. Her eyes were like lasers, finding little things that mattered hugely. Her Hispanic background made her so valuable to me, as she noticed spelling and grammatical things, like how to spell *rebozo* and some sentence-structure problems I had overlooked as well.

Kerry, a writer herself and an amateur stand-up comedian to boot, knew so much about my story, as she is a co-worker as well as a friend. Working a full-time job yet being a faithful reader and great giver of important feedback, she has given great encouragement to me as I battled to finish my story.

Irina has been my cheerleader over many years, urging me to keep working on my book and volunteering to read it several years ago, when I hadn't even arrived at the stage of self-editing. I provided her with less than a quarter of the chapters and then left her waiting until just months ago. At that point, I was able to form a readers group and was fortunate that Irina happily agreed to be a member. She was very candid in her review of my book, and pointed out various discrepancies and grammatical issues that I needed to resolve. My favorite edit she graced me with was making me aware that a kilo is equal to 2.2 pounds, not 3!

Marge, another co-worker and friend, is also an avid reader. She told me often that my book was an important one. She even told me that in the future she would love to go to Mexico with me to see all that she envisioned in the book. This fact brings me incredible satisfaction, knowing that I have brought something new to her world that she otherwise might not have experienced.

Elizabeth has faithfully exhibited a kindred spirit and has offered many encouraging comments. She has, from the start, been very enthused with the idea and importance of the book. She has been soul food for me.

Liz has graced our meetings with a very clear, objective look at various elements of the storyline and structure of the book (it must run in the family). She also has a Hispanic background, so she offered several corrections to my Spanish words as well. She so quietly and gracefully phrased her keen suggestions and corrections that I effortlessly absorbed them and wrote them down.

Alicia is quiet, yet one of the most enthusiastic readers I've encountered. She has consistently made me feel so (virtually) important when she's told me she can't wait to read the next chapters. This is what a writer craves—someone who is hungry for her work. Her husband even got into the act and gave me sage advice, both culturally and factually. I thank him as well as Alicia for being a reader.

INTRODUCTION

I was an opportunistic American teenage girl growing up in Southern California in the 1960s. A proud member of the rebellious hippie love-in generation, I availed myself of every opportunity that attracted me—inviting friends over for pool parties, driving a choice of cool cars my father had, surfing, getting involved in cheerleading and student government, speaking out and going to rallies against the Vietnam War, dating and dancing all night to the Beatles and the Rolling Stones at various venues. But there was an experience ahead of me that I could not have imagined. Eager to learn about the world, I started my journey away from home at a foreign university, where a whole new world would open up to me.

Without fear of the unknown, I bought a ticket to Mexico City, where I lived and studied and discovered much more than I'd ever dreamed possible about the Mexican culture. My heart and mind would be stretched beyond the borders of my birth country, and the final task for me would be to understand why it all mattered so much.

AUTHOR'S NOTE

The characters and events in his book are factual. I knew each person well and am still in touch with most of them. I have protected their anonymity, however, by using fictitious names throughout the book (except for the readers mentioned above). After all, this is my story about people who changed my view of the world—my involvement with them and my observations of them. Every human has a different perspective of the events in their lives. I chose to make this memoir emphatically mine by writing from my point of view yet recognizing that others I've written about could have perceived things differently. I respect that.

A TRIBUTE TO MY PARENTS

I am indebted to my parents for their adventurous spirits. They taught me to reach out and grab life. I credit them for the adventures I have had in my life, some of which are recorded in this book. Whether every adventure was advantageous or not, I grew from each and became more enriched, understanding and empowered. Thank you, Mom and Dad, I know you're watching from above!

1

SEEDS OF WANDERLUST

As job-desperate teenagers in 1943, both of my parents came to Southern California, though not together. They had not yet met. Their hometowns in Oklahoma held no promise of decent jobs, and they were eager to make their own life.

They each had relatives and friends who had already escaped the poverty of rural Oklahoma and moved to California. My father stayed with a cousin; my mother with a friend of her family. Each situated themselves in a little suburb of Los Angeles called South Gate, living just a few miles from each other. Within a month, my father was hired by an oil refinery, and my mother began working at a steel manufacturing plant. Slowly, they began to make their own ways.

Their new lives were in stark contrast to their pasts. My father's family had eked out a living on a dirt farm all of his life. He was young, dark, and handsome and had a tremendous drive to better his life. My mother was raised in a little town by a single mom, whose economic resources were very limited. Abandoned by her father when she was nine years old, my mother had to go to work in a boarding house after school, making beds and washing dishes. Her two brothers earned money doing odd jobs. All three of them supplemented their mother's inadequate income as best they could.

Within a few months of living in California, my parents were introduced to each other by my mother's friend, who knew my father's cousin. They fell in love and were married six months later, eloping to Las Vegas. They scraped together just enough money to put a down payment on a little house they had found in a nearby town called Lynwood. I still have a precious photograph of them lying on the sand in Long Beach, side by side, propped up on their elbows, smiling for the camera. They seemed so carefree and happy. Little did they know that just one year later, my father would receive his draft notice from the US Army. World War II was well underway, and he would ultimately be shipped to London, then flown to Cherbourg, then be obligated to march (or board army vehicles when he got lucky) through Normandy, parts of Belgium, a vast swath of Germany, and then to Paris, which was almost destroyed but was a secured city when he arrived.

When he returned home from the war, my father and thousands of other fortunate veterans would begin their young adult lives as major contributors to the economic boom of Southern California. My sister, Lynn, was born in late 1945. Two years later, I was born (a curly-haired, chubby little girl). I realize now how mechanically talented my father was, as I look back at photographs of the amazing remodel and addition he built onto that previously humble little house. He even built a playhouse for my sister and me that was a perfect duplication of our house—doorbell, siding, front door, and all.

Dad noticed that wherever Lynn went, I toddled along. So he solidified our relationship by welding a fabricated seat onto the back of my sister's tall tricycle. Lynn would put me in the back, hop on, and pedal me around the yard and out onto the sidewalk, taking us on adventures around the neighborhood. By the time I was three, we played more around the house, as I didn't want to be in the back seat anymore. Sometimes we were deeply involved in making mud pies and decorating them with various flowers and plants we'd found around the yard. We ran through the sprinklers on hot days, inviting the neighborhood kids over, and then Lynn took me with her to their houses (with my mother's permission).

2

PLANTING OF SEEDS

When I turned five, my mother had a birthday party for me. She invited the neighborhood kids and I was so excited as they arrived. This was my first big birthday party, I felt so amazed that everyone came to celebrate just me!

Among the gifts I received, I remember being most enchanted by the little butterfly net that my best friend gave me. When the last tail had been pinned on the donkey, and the last of my guests had left, I ran into our house to retrieve the net from the gifts my mother had carefully placed on my bed. I couldn't wait to explore our backyard and hoped I would capture my very first specimen.

I felt a sense of adventure and independence as I hid behind the tall bushes that bordered our fence, waiting for my opportunity. In a matter of minutes, I spotted an orange-and-black butterfly, flitting around the very bush I was hiding behind. I crouched down and moved around the bush, just below where it was resting. Net in hand, poised for adventure, I slowly reached up and whisked the net over the beautiful creature. I had it!

As it tried to fly away, it only went deeper into the net, giving me the chance to pull the net toward me and block the opening with my hand. I will never forget the deep sense of wonder I felt as I stared at its delicate body. Suddenly, the idea came to me that the God I learned about in Sunday school had brought this creature to me to tell me that I too would explore His big world one day. I carefully slipped one hand into the net and touched its fragile, fancy wings. I noticed the "fairy dust" that clung to my fingers. I knew it had come through a heavenly window.

After what seemed like an hour of repetitive inspections, I decided that my captive was too beautiful to be imprisoned. It deserved its freedom. I unlatched my protective grip over the net and allowed the butterfly to escape. It flitted up, up, up with gossamer strides, flying so powerfully yet elegantly into the sky until it left my sight. How I yearned to go with it and travel the world from on high.

That night, I was awakened by my own screaming: "Mommy! Mommy!" My mother ran to my side. "I was flying with that butterfly!" I exclaimed. She patted my head, gently indulging me. I felt so ecstatic, but my mother's attempt to calm me overcame me. "I'm going to find my dream again …" I mumbled as I fell back into a deep sleep.

Many times afterward, as my mother kissed me good night, she would ask if I was going to find my butterfly dream again. Her sweet encouragement coaxed me into welcoming sleep, since it became my precious opportunity to fly with the butterflies.

Late the next summer, I found a chrysalis hanging from a small branch on a bush in our neighbor's yard. The neighbor saw me gazing at it and asked if I would like to have it. She carefully cut off the little branch with a pair of gardening clippers and gently handed it to me with instructions. "Now, have your mother put it in a glass jar and poke holes in the lid because in a few days, a butterfly will come out of that little bed that it's sleeping in, and it will need to breathe."

I carried it home, walking slowly so that nothing could happen to it. My mother greeted me as I came inside and cheerfully followed our neighbor's instructions. (How many millions of parents have done the same thing for their children all over the world?) My mother suggested that we take it to school the next day, so that I could share my discovery with my classmates.

The next morning, the teacher welcomed my treasure, and during sharing time, I stood before the class, showing them the little "butterfly bed" that I had found. The teacher explained the process of metamorphosis to the class in a very simplistic way, saying that a caterpillar had changed into the little bed, called a cocoon, and that inside the little bed a butterfly was growing that would soon come out. I agreed to keep the jar in the classroom until the weekend so that the class could see it if it emerged.

After our lunch hour on Friday, when we returned to our classroom, one of my classmates yelled, "The butterfly is coming out! Look!" The whole class gathered around the teacher's desk, captivated by the process that was taking place before our eyes. A leg, then two legs, then a wet wing, then two wet wings, then its feelers. Finally, every leg and wing had freed itself of that little bed, and its new form unfolded slowly as it flexed its wings and began to dry. It was a beautiful orange with black designs on its wings.

I was so proud of my contribution to the class and so excited to bring it home to my parents and playmates that day. My eyes didn't leave it, but on Sunday afternoon, my mother coaxed me to release it. She said it needed to go "discover the world." With my best friend at my side, I reluctantly opened the lid. As I held the jar sideways, the cautious butterfly crawled across the jar, finding its way to the opening. Ever so slowly, it started fanning its beautiful wings. Just then, off it went, flitting up and gradually over our fence. "Goodbye, sweet butterfly," I called after it. It circled back for a few moments, as if it had decided to come back. But its wings pumped and pumped, and it flew over our other neighbor's fence and then higher and further, until it was out of sight. I was sad yet envious of its freedom to fly over the world, wherever it chose. I was fascinated to think that one form of life could change into another form of life. How dazzling, the mystery of what went on inside that tiny shelter.

The seeds of wanderlust had been planted in me when I witnessed the birth and ultimate escape of that first captive butterfly. Little did I know that experience would become my personal metaphor.

3

COSTUMES, DANCING
AND FLYING

My mother and father were very talented. Mother expressed her art through sewing. She made matching dresses, pants and tops for Lynn and me. She dressed us in our fancy matching dresses for special occasions, like Christmas and Easter, until we were ten and twelve. We were often referred to as twins, since even our play clothes matched!

We were so blessed to have a mother who involved us in a variety of activities. She took us to dance lessons when I was five and Lynn was seven. She made us incredible costumes for the performances that came along over the three years that we danced. One of the costumes involved meticulously tailored Victorian dresses, with the peplums and collars and outrageous hats that were popular from the 1830s until the turn of the twentieth century. Our dance studio was to perform on stage at the Shrine Auditorium in Los Angeles for the then-governor of California, Goodwin Knight. Lynn and I would dance to the song "You Wore a Tulip, and I Wore a Big Red Rose." We both loved the hubbub and the gratification of dancing in front of an audience. Looking back, I am certain that my self-confidence grew exponentially during those years. I do have to thank my sister, however, because she was much more talented than I and so patient with her younger sister, practicing and practicing till we had our dance synchronized to perfection.

In 1955, when I turned eight, my father bought a new home for our family about fifteen miles southeast of our home in Lynwood. My sister was ten, and I was eight. The town was given a Spanish name—*La Mirada*.

Within a year of living in La Mirada, our mother went to work as a bookkeeper for a friend of our father's. Lynn and I became latchkey kids overnight. We walked together to school each morning, but I walked with some of my classmates after school, as I got out an hour earlier than she did. I started enjoying the independence of visiting neighborhood friends from my class after school. Sometimes I would rush home, eat cookies and milk, put on my play clothes and go out looking for whoever was home. Lynn, on the other hand, wasn't enjoying herself nearly as much. She would come home and find me gone and didn't know what to do with herself. Many years later, she divulged that when I became independent from her, she went into a long-lasting depression. She didn't really have any classmate friends in our neighborhood, so she was lonely and had lost her full-time relationship with her sister. It is extremely sad for me to look back, knowing this now.

Lynn and I also noticed a change in our parents' relationship. They didn't communicate much, unless it was necessary, and a heavy tension hung over the house. Lynn and I became the entertainers when we were all home together, whether eating dinner or finding things to do in the living room to break the silence. We managed to have lots of fun playing our records, dancing, singing, and, of course, watching Disney shows on television. It also was a treat to watch shows like Lawrence Welk, Red Skelton, and numerous others I don't remember now, but I relished all of us being home together. Even if our parents didn't talk to each other, they did talk to *us*. I was enchanted when the opening of Walt Disney's show started, as my sister and I sang along to "When You Wish upon a Star." There were no cell phones to distract us!

Our parents were very adventurous and socially active people. They now had two girls who were old enough to go with them on various excursions, or they could leave us with trusted friends. My dad was the first to get his pilot's license; my mother followed. They joined a flying club in Seal Beach near an old munitions compound owned by the US Navy. On weekends, all of us would drive to the little airport, and Lynn and I would go on air races with them to various western states. We got to visit a large number of historical monuments and enjoy some amazing views of mountains, the Grand Canyon, and beautiful lakes across the country. I'll never forget one trip to Las Vegas to see the Blue Angels perform an air show. It was thrilling to watch them crisscrossing the sky, swooping down so low to the ground and then straight up into the clouds. It was thrilling. Afterward, we got to take a photo with all of them. I kept that picture in my room for several years.

Bowling became the rage in the 1950s, and our parents (like a multitude of others) started bowling in at least two different leagues. They became very accomplished bowlers, evidenced by the number of trophies that lined our living room shelves. Lynn and I started bowling too, in a youth league. We were so proud of our own personal bowling shoes and bags, and our balls had our names carved on them. Our parents were generous people, and as I look back, we were what many would call spoiled. The difference was that we didn't take anything for granted. We were always stunned when they gifted us with things, and we respected their love for us.

4

MISSIONS, SPANISH AND MEXICO

School was always interesting to me. I loved learning; I was inquisitive. My father said that I didn't talk till I was three, and then I never stopped asking questions! One particularly interesting subject for me was the Spanish influence I noticed almost everywhere we traveled in California. My third-grade class included a wonderful introduction to the history of California. That school year, I learned that Spain—and later, Mexico—actually owned California for a total of more than 185 years. Slowly, I began to realize that all of the streets in our neighborhood had Spanish names. Our street was named La Barca (the ship) Drive. Even the name of my grammar school was a Spanish word—*Escalona* (terraced). I had learned my first Spanish words from my own neighborhood. My class studied the history of the twenty-one California missions that had been developed by the Spanish government. As part of our study of California, we were required to build a scale model of our favorite mission. This assignment was repeated in all California schools, as it is to this day in many of the California school districts, to commemorate the era of the Spanish settlers. I decided to construct the Mission San Juan Capistrano, built in 1776, which was approximately twenty-five miles southwest of La

Mirada. It was the closest mission to our school, and thus it was a standard field trip for surrounding grammar schools.

Although we used scraps of cardboard and homemade paste to build our missions, we learned that the real mission walls were made of adobe (mud mixed with straw). As I grew up, I noticed that the architectural style of the missions was repeated in many of the big homes that I saw on our Sunday drives. These glaringly white haciendas with their red-tile roofs in turn inspired the style of many newer custom-built homes in the '50s (as they do to this day). They dotted the canvas that surrounded my life, glistening like brilliant diamonds in the California sunshine, huddled among the acreage of citrus trees that had been the wellspring of the economy for nearly fifty years. When the trees were heavy with ripened oranges and lemons, they seemed to shout "Pick me!" as you drove down the two-lane roads that meandered through Southern California. Aqueducts of cool water crawled over the landscape. They were not only beautiful, with their swirling, azure rivulets, but they served as vital lifelines to the orchards.

5

A WATERSHED MOVE

In the summer of 1960, my family moved another fifteen miles away to a rural town called Yorba Linda. The town was named after Don Yorba, who had been a local Spanish landowner in the late 1800. *Linda* means pretty or beautiful in Spanish. Again, this town was made up of numerous Spanish-named streets, such as Alta Vista (lofty view) and Buena Vista (a good view) of the surrounding area, two of the streets over which the school bus carried my sister and me to school in a neighboring town called Placentia, derived from a Latin word meaning "pleasant place to live"

Our home was a custom ranch-style house on a half-acre in a rural setting across from a small lake. There was a huge undeveloped area of land around the lake, of which our neighbors availed themselves for riding their horses. My sister and I loved feeding the horses, brushing them, and ingratiating ourselves to their owners so we too could ride them.

The stands of eucalyptus trees sheltered the orange trees in our yard and those of our neighbors from the relentless Santa Ana winds (strong, dry winds that mostly blew in the autumn and winter). During the winter, smudge pots were placed among the orange trees. The pots burned cheap oil and bellowed black smoke from their chimneys. The oranges were thus blanketed with a cloak of smog that protected them from freezing.

I remember so vividly when dad mowed the lawn on Saturdays. He rode his tractor-mower for at least an hour, rolling up and down the slope on which our house was built. He scooped up the cuttings into a huge heap. The dark-green blades of grass exuded a distinct acrid fragrance. The smell reminded me of my grandparents' farmland in Oklahoma. It was a faraway place but one that blessed me with so many earthy experiences that I treasure to this day.

I entered junior high and my sister entered high school at the end of that summer. We didn't realize at the time how fortunate we were to be living in such a beautiful part of the country. As we became more familiar with our new schools and acquired a number of friends, we thrived in this verdant rural community. We were blessed with friends from a variety of backgrounds—some whose parents were wealthy country-club socialites, some whose parents worked in the service industry, and still others whose families made their living picking farm produce and caring for other people's orange and avocado groves.

I was so happy to have friends from such a broad spectrum of backgrounds, but I had an affinity for my Hispanic friends. Their culture was so warm and friendly, and their food was so delicious! Many of their parents had been born in Mexico and had stayed true to their historic roots. Prior to high school, I'd had no exposure to Mexican, Hispanic, or (as they are referred to now, "Latino") people or their history. I was learning their culture now through my friends.

In later years, I learned that there was a difference between the terms *Mexican* and *Hispanic*. Mexican refers to a person who was born in Mexico (their nationality); Hispanic is their ethnic identity (more often a mixture of indigenous races from Mexico, in general, mixed with Spanish heritage). It made perfect sense because even though I was of German, French, and Irish/English descent, no one had ever referred to me by any of my inherited ethnicities. I was a Caucasion American. Thus, my Hispanic friends were Hispanic Americans.

Often on Friday nights, two of my Hispanic American friends (who were twin sisters) invited me over for tacos. Their mother was an incredible cook. She very competently managed to prepare delectable meals for ten to twenty family members and friends at a time. The tacos were spicy, crunchy, and full of aromas I had never experienced before. After my introduction to Mexican food, I knew I would never stop pursuing it.

The Yorba Linda and Placentia communities provided an almost utopian environment for youth. Not only were these beautiful, rural settings, with their abundance of mature, shady fruit trees, but the people who settled there were genuine and kind. Most women were stay-at-home moms, ready to volunteer at the schools. The orange groves were our playground, the irrigation canals were our rivers, and the trees were our hiding places. Life seemed to bloom for anyone who was willing to put forth an effort.

Most importantly, I had a large group of wonderful friends, a nice car that my father had so kindly bought for me, a swimming pool (again, my father was generous), more than a hundred 45 rpm vinyl records to keep up with the Top 40 music charts and the freedom to take off on weekends to go to the beach to work on a tan, surf, or just spend time visiting friends and finding adventure with them.

Dad decided to buy a boat for water skiing and a mobile home at a campground alongside the Colorado River. We began making trips out to the river and learned to bait fish, catch fish, and cook them to boot! What we most enjoyed was the water skiing, but it was rather tense because we fell so many times. My dad had to circle back around, wait for us to grab the ropes, and start all over again. Lynn was better at it than I was, and she learned to ski on one ski. I was barely able to stay up on two.

I lived a teenager's dream for six wonderful years, from junior high through high school. I did well academically and was never without a boyfriend. I became a member of the drill team in my first year of high school and then a cheerleader for the remaining three years. I was involved in student government and was a member of the Honors Society. As my last semester of high school began, I felt gratified that I had made the most of my school experience. My sister had married the summer after her senior year, so I had a bedroom to myself for the last two years of high school. But I knew that my playful youth was coming to a close. I was becoming a young woman. It was time for some serious focus on my future.

6

MY FIRST YEAR
OF COLLEGE

It had always been my plan to attend college—to be the first woman in my family's history to obtain a college degree. I decided to make an appointment with the academic counselor to discuss my college prospects. I trusted his wisdom, as he had been my algebra and geometry teacher in my freshman and junior years, and I looked up to him with great respect. He was kind but firm and a wonderful teacher who made the students feel confident. He had researched colleges for upcoming graduates, and the first one he suggested to me was in San Diego.

Going away to college was a big step for a woman at that time. Yet San Diego was only a two-hour drive from my home, and I hoped that would sit well with my parents. He showed me the brochure from a private college called California Western University (CWU). It was in a little town called Point Loma (another Spanish name meaning hill point). What caught my eye immediately was that it was positioned on beautiful cliffs overlooking the ocean. I tried to focus on the academic offerings, however, and the counselor more than convinced me that I would have a wide array of majors to choose from. My dream was to major in Spanish, with a minor in international business. I had thoroughly enjoyed the four years of Spanish I had taken in high school and loved being involved in student government. To top it off, I cherished my Hispanic friends and their culture. It all seemed to add up to the ideal career for me. My counselor agreed.

After school that day, when my father arrived home, I broke the news to him. My mother wasn't home from work yet. There was no point in waiting for her to join the conversation, as she and my father had pretty much stopped communicating with each other over the past two years. At some point, my mother had told my father that she wanted a divorce, and now she had (inconveniently) decided that she was going to move out of our house the day I graduated. She had rented a little house in the next town, which she had finally disclosed to me. I didn't want to be living with one parent and going to college near my hometown. I knew it wouldn't be pleasant, having to interact with each parent separately and dividing my time between them.

My father looked at the brochure the counselor had given me and seemed proud of me for demonstrating my desire for independence. He also had tears in his eyes, as I would be leaving, and he knew my mother would be as well. It was a very tough moment, one that I will never forget. I gave Dad a warm hug and explained how often I would come to visit on the train that ran daily from San Diego to nearby Fullerton. That made him smile, and I felt relieved, knowing I had demonstrated my love for him in a very sincere way by being sensitive to what he was experiencing. "I will stay with you too, Dad. I'm not going away for good."

I called the university to have an application sent to me. In February, ahead of the game, I sent my application to CWU. By mid-May, I had received my acceptance letter. Too excited to wait, I decided to visit the university grounds to see for myself the seemingly picturesque campus the enclosed brochure had attempted to capture. I asked a close high school friend to go with me, and two days later, we were on our way.

The two-hour drive went by quickly, and it was apparent upon our arrival that the brochure had not misrepresented the beautiful setting. The whole campus was built in a crescent shape that edged a very tall cliff, overlooking a fringe of secluded beaches. The long dorm buildings were lined up about one hundred feet from the edge of the cliff. Each had an enormous study hall at the center that jutted out over the ocean. Inside, the study hall revealed a panorama of continuous floor-to-ceiling windows that framed the ocean. Since the beach area wasn't visible from the center of the room, it gave the illusion that we were afloat on the open sea. Obviously, I was dazzled. That window to the world that I had envisioned when I caught that butterfly came back to me. I was full of wonder!

After gawking for some time, my friend and I took a walk around the campus, taking in the lay of the land. We walked up the two-lane road that we had taken down to the dorms. The first building up the narrow road was an old, wood-sided two-story house that had been converted to the Registrar's Office. We walked in and were given a warm welcome. The clerk handed us a map of the campus and encouraged us to take in various points of interest. As we followed the map, we checked out all of the buildings, which were all painted white and surrounded by neatly groomed, beautiful green lawns. With the ocean view, it was easy to imagine being on a Greek island. At the end of the circular route, we came upon a Greek amphitheater, which confirmed the architectural intent. Although I was impressed by what I saw, I enjoyed even more the complimentary glances we received from the male students (and each glance was reciprocated).

On our last walk along the edge of the campus, working our way back to my car, we gazed at the sun's reflection off of the beautiful turquoise water with the waves breaking below. A soft, warm breeze reminded us that it was spring. High school graduation was just around the corner, and I could hardly wait. Going away to college had been a dream of mine since I was twelve, and now it was going to come true.

Graduation finally arrived. Our grad night party was held in the high school gymnasium. The efforts of the parents' club had transformed the gym into a wonderland, with parachutes floating above our heads to form the "sky" and ornamental trees and blooming plants surrounding the dance floor. A small stage was set up on the basketball court floor in front of the bleachers, and all of us were excited to see what would transpire there. To say the night was blissful would be an understatement, as we were entertained by a hypnotist, a magician, and an incredible comedian. The music was perfectly chosen, and the grand finale was dancing and general carousing. All of our parents picked us up at the school at 2:00 a.m., as school policy prohibited students from driving home that late. Since my mother had taken custody of me, she picked me up and took me home with her. It was a very weird and sad conclusion to an amazing celebration.

Summer vacation began the next day, but I wasn't aware of it until one o'clock in the afternoon, when I woke to my mother's question, "Honey, are you still alive? You'd better wake up. It's lunchtime." From that moment on, I spent my summer thinking about September 1, my move-in day at CWU. I couldn't wait to get there, as I felt bridled by my life between my mother and father. It was no one's fault, but I was ready to move on. One night, I went to bed around ten o'clock. It was midsummer. I had turned eighteen exactly one week earlier. I was reclining on my bed in my new bedroom at my mother's house, surrounded by my stuffed animals and my vital link to my friends—my telephone. I was in a mood of self-reflection and eager to venture out of my uncomfortable situation. Fortunately, I had been hired by a big aeronautics company in the area for the summer, so I was very busy, and I went out with my friends most of the time in the evenings.

September 1 finally came. The summer had been fun, but I had grown increasingly impatient to begin my new life at college. My soon-to-be college roommate and I had met at the beginning of August. We had been paired up by the CWU Housing Department. After getting acquainted by phone, we met in the area where she lived (just ten miles from my home) and went shopping for the accoutrements for our room, each of us full of enthusiasm. Fortunately, she was very easygoing, and we agreed on almost every detail without much hesitation. We chose a big red area rug and red-and-white checked bedspreads. For the bathroom, we decided on white bath towels, a red wastebasket, and a red-and-white polka-dot soap dish with a toothbrush holder to match. We chose our own desk supplies, and then we were ready for our new home.

A few days later, with my car and my mother's car packed to the gills, we planned to arrive at CWU at eleven that morning. My mother would follow me in her car and help me with moving in. The two-hour drive flew by, and I pulled up in front of the dormitory. The name of our dorm was Chi Hall. The activity surrounding the dorm was lively, with pure anticipation in everyone's eyes. Girls and parents were scurrying about, carrying everything from laundry baskets to suitcases, greeting others as they passed in the halls. We joined the activity. I already felt at home; I had obsessed for months about this very day and had anticipated its arrival. I was finally going to live *my way.*

Within a couple of hours, my roommate and I (along with the generous help from my mother) had arranged the room and put away our belongings. Mom and I said our goodbyes, and I promised I would come home to visit in a couple of weeks. It wasn't a sad parting for me since it was such a comfortable distance from home. I'm sure it wasn't as easy for my parents, however. I'm certain both of them shed a few tears, independently. In later years, that day came to mind as the last of my three children left home for college. It's now referred to as empty-nest syndrome. I shed some serious tears over how my parents must have felt at that time.

My roommate and I noticed that an increasing number of dorm residents started congregating in our room. There was a short, tan blonde named Yvette from Hawaii, wearing heavy mascara. She was talking and smoking with a tall, stocky, freckled brunette, who announced that she was from Downey, my birthplace. Just then, an apparent upperclassman said, "I'm Nancy, the residents' assistant, She explained that her room was next to ours and that she was in charge of the dorm (clearly meaning the behavior of the residents in the dorm— us). Although she seemed very friendly, with a big smile and large blue eyes, she also exhibited a great deal of confidence that made it clear that no one should mess with her. (I tucked that warning into a corner of my mind for future reference.)

The fervor of unpacking had quieted down, and we all decided that dinner was the next item of importance. It was time to collect ourselves, tidy up, and walk over to the dining hall.

As the others left, I threw on my shoes and felt sure that I was right where I wanted to be—plenty of new friends, a cool-looking dorm room (with our big, bright-red rug), interesting classes, and, of course, parties to attend. I was sure that this year was going to be a major milestone in my life, an opportunity to live on a college campus, learn all I could, and experience independence.

We were all so full of anticipation, but after dinner and hours of talking, the dorm took on a more serious atmosphere, as we all dedicated our minds to tomorrow's schedule and demands. Nancy, the RA, made sure we were all going to get plenty of sleep in preparation for our first day of classes. She accomplished this by walking from room to room with a warm smile and her "don't mess with me" cautionary reminder of why we were all there.

The next morning, our alarm sounded at seven o'clock. I was up, showered, dressed, and walking out of our dorm room at eight o'clock for my physical science class at eight thirty. After that, I had an eleven o'clock English composition class. Following lunch, I would have a one-hour break and then my Western civilization class at three that afternoon. Spanish literature was the only class I would be attending on Tuesdays and Thursdays. I was going to have more than enough to occupy my mind, and I only hoped that I could keep up with it all. At least I knew that when the weekends came, I could release some of the seriousness at the (always) abundant parties or at the great tourist spots all over the county.

The San Diego area, I would learn, offered everything a young adult could want—and more. On various weekends, a group of us went out to savor the unique venues: Balboa Park, with its zoo, several Spanish-style museums, and restaurants; Belmont Park, with its scary roller coaster that jutted out over the ocean; Old Town, with its historic Spanish buildings and a museum with a miniature exhibit of the San Diego mission and all the missions as far north as San Francisco. I thought back to the life I had lived for eighteen years, just a little more than two hours north of San Diego, and realized that the two regions had the same architectural features and the same remnants of the Spanish culture—the names of highways and streets and especially the Mexican food. I was reminded, once again, of the pervasive Spanish heritage of California.

As the Thanksgiving and Christmas holidays approached, I reflected on the great friendships I had made and the quality of my professors. They each were all that I expected—friends from different parts of the country sharing their unique life experiences with me and inspiring professors who piqued my interest in a variety of subjects.

I finished my first trimester at CWU a few weeks after Thanksgiving. I had participated in almost everything that was available to me: sorority parties (though I chose not to join), fraternity parties (much more fun!), local parties, weekend trips to parties at other colleges, more outings (the beautiful San Diego beaches, trips to Tijuana on Friday nights— the famous Long Bar).

Christmas was a week away, so I went home for a short (but much anticipated) break. I got in touch with as many high school friends as possible, and we shared our very different experiences over the past four months. Of all my girlfriends, only four of us were attending college. Of those four, I was the only one who had gone away to college. I knew we would never be as available to each other as we had been in our high school years. It was a sad realization.

As the two-week break came to a close, my grades arrived. My grade point average pleased both me and my parents. Happily, I packed my suitcase, hugged my parents goodbye, and drove back to CWU for my second semester. I was ready to go back. I had outgrown my home environment, although I had so enjoyed seeing my friends and spending time with my parents.

After my first morning class, I walked over to the long lunch line at the cafeteria. I found myself standing next to a tall, thin girl I recognized from my dorm. Her name was Samantha. Although I had never said more than hello to her, I began a casual conversation—and that conversation would change my life.

She told me that she had just returned from a semester abroad in Mexico City. My eyes lit up, and my pulse began to race. She obviously noted my animated interest, saying, "I would highly recommend looking into it. I had a fantastic time! I traveled throughout Mexico." She explained that she had attended the National University of Mexico in Mexico City (also known by its Spanish acronym, UNAM). We talked about her Spanish studies, which paralleled mine. She had taken four years of high school Spanish and then one year of Spanish literature at CWU. I had just finished the first course of Spanish literature and was now enrolled in the second half. My original plan—to major in Spanish and minor in international business—was definitely encouraged by her enthusiasm. We continued talking all through lunch, and from that meeting, I went directly to the Registrar's Office to get an application for UNAM.

I concluded that CWU had been a good first step, but I was still full of wanderlust. It was exciting to know that I had another destination ahead of me.

7

THE BUTTERFLY
LEAVES THE JAR

I filled out the application for UNAM, wasting no time, as it was 3:30 p.m. now, and the next mail pickup was at 5:00. After completing the application, I placed it and a check in the return envelope. I walked straight to the dorm's mailbox and carefully dropped the large envelope inside.

I started thinking about Mexico as I walked back to my room. My pulse rapidly increased as I thought of all the reasons it was such a good fit. I'd prided myself on my straight As in Mr. Valadez's Spanish class. He always called me his *predilecta* (teacher's pet), which he pronounced very slowly—*pray-thee-leck-tah*—as if to emphasize his special affinity for me. Although embarrassing, it was also a pretty good feeling. I saw my Mexican friends as a new generation that was moving beyond the educational limits of their parents, just as I was. They were working hard to obtain a good education so that they could compete in the job market with everyone else. And they seemed to accomplish it with such grace. I had great respect for them. Their parents were always relaxed and cheerful. I secretly wished that I could be adopted into that culture, as I felt I didn't have any tangible evidence of my own cultural heritage.

Going to Mexico would be a perfect setting, a laboratory of sorts for learning all I could about the indigenous Mexican cultures, as well as the Spanish influence that had become such an integral part of the culture. I practiced my persuasive speech before calling my father. He answered my call so lovingly and cheerful that I was able to calm my nerves immediately. It went well, especially when I explained that a semester in Mexico would cost less than a semester at CWU. He hesitantly gave me his approval and asked that I call my mom (they had divorced six months prior).

My mom, I reasoned, would most likely just need to know that I would be safe, and then she'd be okay with the idea. One ring, two rings, three rings, and she picked up the phone.

"Mom, are you sitting down?" I asked.

"Yes, why?" she responded hesitantly.

"Well, Dad has already said okay [the old play-one-against-the-other tactic], and now I just need *your* okay." I said these words as if I was the decision-maker, and she was just some random person to run it by.

"Oh really? Well, whatever it is, it sounds like I'm going to need time to think about it."

I started to stammer more like the teenager that I still was. "It's … it's a … a good … good thing, Mom, really."

"Does it involve money? Risk? Good judgment?" She focused like a hawk.

"Yes, well, I guess most of those things." I now shifted to a less confident stance. "Okay, I'll just tell you what it is, and we can hang up, and you can think about it and then call me back, okay?" Then I quickly blurted out, "It's a fantastic thing—I'm going to spend next fall semester in Mexico City! Can you believe it?"

No response. In fact, I had to ask her if she was still on the line. "Yes, I'm still here. I think I'll take the option you offered. I'll be hanging up now. I'll call you back when I'm ready."

The monotonous tone of the dead line filled my ears. I lay down on my bed. The spare blanket at my feet made a great cover-up to hide my anxiety in case my roommate walked in.

Twenty long minutes went by. The phone rang.

"Okay, give me the details."

"Oh, Mom, thank you! I've read all about it. It's the National Autonomous University of Mexico, or UNAM, a school with many English-speaking teachers, many of them American. It's in Mexico City. A classmate of mine attended UNAM last semester, and she really loved it. She said it was an extremely valuable experience. I'll send you all the information and the brochure. Oh, I haven't been accepted yet, but I just sent my application a few days ago, so there's plenty of time to talk about it."

I had many more detailed discussions with my parents before I received my acceptance letter from the university. In order to quell my parents' fears, I asked Samantha to come home with me the following weekend. She was happy to have the opportunity, as she understood that my parents were uneasy about my choice. Her parents had felt the same way, and she was eager to share some real-life information with my parents that would ease their concerns.

Arriving by train the following Saturday morning, Samantha and I were greeted by my mother. The drive to Mom's home was a perfect opportunity for her to get acquainted with Samantha. As we ate the delicious sandwiches my mother had prepared, it became apparent that Mom respected and trusted Samantha, who had such a calm, assured presence. She especially loved the stories Samantha related about living as an American student in Mexico. Samantha was obviously delighted to answer, in detail, every question my mother asked. She'd brought photos to further reveal some of the highlights of Mexico. Among them were snapshots of the city high-rises, the famous anthropology museum, groups of her classmates in front of the historic Presidential Palace, and one very amusing photo of Samantha and her friends crowded into a boat among the floating gardens at ancient Xochimilco.

That evening, my dad picked us up and took us out for dinner. Samantha was as convincing to my father as she had been to my mother. We had a great time, and I was so pleased to have time with my dad. Late Sunday morning, as Samantha and I boarded the train for San Diego, my mother waved us off with a new confidence. I felt so gratified that both of my parents were now truly comfortable with my decision. I couldn't thank Samantha enough.

When my acceptance letter arrived, my housing assignment and future address were included as well. Tucked inside a separately folded sheet of paper was a tiny black-and-white photo of the couple in whose home I would be staying. More like a mug shot than a becoming photo, it didn't reveal any detail about their clothing or stature. I immediately decided not to show it to my parents—as all of Samantha's assurances wouldn't be enough to neutralize the thoughts that photo conjured up.

My move-in day was to be between September 8 and September 10. I was to send a photo of me and my flight information to the family I had been assigned to so they could arrange to pick me up at the airport. There was a brochure about safety measures to consider while living in Mexico. All the vaccinations I needed to get were listed on a separate medical record form. Emergency numbers at the American embassy in Mexico City were printed on another sheet, with various international laws for further bedtime reading. Looking back, I'm sure my parents had a few fleeting insecurities as they read the information, but they didn't say a word.

8

MEXICO HERE I COME

In the all of 1966, both of my parents decided to drive me to Los Angeles International Airport (LAX). The one thing they agreed on was unconditional support of me and my sister. I needed to arrive by seven a.m., two hours prior to my nine o'clock flight. With bags fully packed, papers in hand, vaccinations and medications accounted for, we got into the car and started my surreal adventure.

In what seemed like an eternity, we arrived at the airport. My mother had tried to make conversation on the way, but I was so tense, I just couldn't relate to her. We parked, and my father lifted my two giant suitcases out of the trunk with an "Ugh!"

Dad continued to lug my two suitcases (suitcases didn't have wheels in those days), as I carried my tote bag and purse. Mom put her arm in mine, sweetly reminding me that she was going to miss me. I appreciated her deeply at that moment, as I did have a modicum of fear.

I dream-walked beside my parents through the airport. I checked in, half dazed, and then walked back to my parents, hugging them and telling them, "I'll miss you," with my heart, while my brain was already on the plane. They accompanied me to the tarmac, where the passengers were beginning to make their way up the portable stairs to the opened hatch of the plane. As I arrived at the top of the stairs, I turned back and dramatically blew a kiss down to my parents. Unexpected tears welled up in my eyes. I knew my parents were experiencing the same tender feelings.

I waved goodbye, knowing I couldn't hold up the boarding line, and somehow found the courage to continue down the aisle. By the time I found my seat, the fear and sadness that had risen in me started to subside, and I was able to get my carry-on stashed and take my seat next to the window. Fortunately, I was seated on the side next to the building, so I scanned the crowd for my parents, who had already spotted me. We waved and waved until we knew it was time to let go. The plane's engine started up, and as we began taxiing, I blew another kiss to them, and they reluctantly turned and began their way back through the airport to the car. I was glad I had brought some tissues with me.

I was dressed in a white miniskirt and a pastel-pink short-sleeved blouse, both of which I had made. Sewing was my favorite pastime. My suitcase was full of tops and dresses I had meticulously sewn over the summer from various patterns I had used for my high school wardrobe. I took inventory of my appearance in the restroom near the gate for my flight, straightening out the wrinkles of my skirt and adjusting my blouse. My bouffant hairstyle was perfectly smoothed and set with hairspray. My clothes were well pressed, and my Mary Janes were as white as a bottle of shoe polish could make them. I placed my purse and tote bag under the seat in front of me and then buckled my seatbelt. I took several deep breaths, and closed my eyes trying to reach a sense of calm.

I awoke an hour later with my head against the airplane window. I had drooled for some time down my chin and onto my shoulder (sensing the dampness made it obvious). I thanked God no one could see my face. My eyes were still a bit filmed over with the peaceful sleep that I had just savored. Discreetly wiping my cheek, I slowly regained clarity.

I took out the magazine I had bought before leaving the airport. Since there obviously would be no talking with my seat companion (a snobbish older man, reading his newspaper), I decided to immerse myself in some of the articles that caught my interest—commentary about the Beatles' latest hit and an interview with Twiggy, the world's first supermodel (I had copied her trademark eyelashes, painting them on with my eyeliner brush below the bottom row of my own eyelashes). A friend had teased me about them, calling me "Spider Eyes." Yes, I was an authentic '60s girl.

The rest of the flight was smooth, and the hot meal they served was a welcome surprise.

"Enchiladas Suizas," the flight attendant said as she set my plate down on my tray. *Swiss enchiladas?* I pondered the combination. As I began to eat the creamy mixture of corn tortillas, chicken, and flecks of green chilies, I concluded that the sauce was made with Swiss cheese. That didn't seem right … how did the Swiss influence Mexican cooking? In any case, they were delicious.

Although three hours had passed, it seemed a short time before the captain made an announcement in Spanish. I tried my best to understand what he was saying, but I was discouraged that I couldn't understand him, even after four years of studying Spanish. But I reminded myself that people who speak in their native language speak rapidly; they don't enunciate every single syllable, just as we Americans don't. Thank God the captain followed the announcement in English, telling us (in a heavy Spanish accent) that we were thirty minutes from landing and that the weather in Mexico City was fair and seventy-five degrees.

9

MY LANDLORDS

I arrived at Mexico City International Airport, with my Pollyanna grin and open mind, ready for whatever might be. As was my modus operandi, I had filled in the details of Mr. and Mrs. Castillo with my imagination (remember—their tiny black-and-white showed nothing about them). I envisioned them as humble, of very modest means, but friendly and very glad to have the housing income from their five American tenants. Their house would be an adobe structure, with just enough space for five women to eat, sleep, and have privileges to one small bathroom (which I hoped had running water). I assumed the Castillos would arrive at the airport via taxi from their rural neighborhood, as I assumed a car would be totally out of their budget. Then again, maybe they would arrive on a donkey.

I was very surprised and shocked at the couple who walked up to greet me as I cleared customs. They were obviously *not* poor. They were dressed in very fine clothing. Señora Castillo was wearing gold jewelry to enhance her fine blue-knit suit, and Señor Castillo wore a dark suit with a crisply ironed white shirt and gold cufflinks that glimmered as he raised his arm to gesture that they were who I was looking for. He was a tall, stately man. He had fair skin and sky-blue eyes (which matched his tie). He was unmistakably of pure Spanish blood. I instinctively knew that they were not attempting to make an impression; they were too comfortable in their attire.

Señora Castillo was petite and appeared to be a blend of indigenous Mexican descent with a splash of Spanish blood. She had small, deep-chocolate eyes and long eyelashes that quivered as she spoke apprehensively in broken English: "Nice to meet you. I ahm Señora Castillo. Thees ees my hus-ban, Señor Albert" (giving me permission to use his first name).

I smiled sheepishly and answered in Spanish to the best of my ability: "Mucho gusto. Gracias por recogerme." (I'm glad to meet you. Thank you for picking me up.) I was hoping they didn't see my shock over their social standing and level of sophistication. I, of course, had to hold the words I was thinking: *Gee, I thought you would be peasants more accustomed to riding a donkey.*

Señor Albert had enlisted the help of a porter, who sweat profusely as he thrust his bulky body wholeheartedly against the five-foot-tall stack of my suitcases on his luggage cart. We ambled along after him and at last arrived at the would-be donkey—a brand-new black Cadillac that one might expect to be driven by a chauffeur. Señor Albert, however, got behind the wheel, and we drove out of the suffocating, exhaust-infused air of the airport parking structure to my first taste of the Mexican streets.

As we quickly entered the on-ramp to the freeway, I mentally exclaimed, *This is more crowded than the freeways in Southern California, but most of the cars are older than ours.* I continued with a litany of silent questions: *Doesn't anyone control the number of billboards along the freeway? Why is everyone honking? Why are all the buildings made of ugly gray cement? What are those words, of every bright color known to man, painted by hand on the sides of so many buildings? Don't they know how to make decent signs? Why are there wire cages on the rooftops? What are those big black tanks for up there? Why are there so many dogs on the roofs? Isn't there a building code here? So many taxis! It seems half the population is living without a car!* My mind was hard to stop, as it was deeply perplexed.

But as we left the freeway, I noticed the people ambling along the streets, and my negative thoughts left me. I was overcome with the similarities and contrasts. So many people were dressed just like Americans. Then I noticed a little group wearing what I assumed was indigenous clothing—bright pink flowers on one lady's smock and a bright green apron on another woman. They were cooking under a makeshift stand on the corner, covered with a tarp. I assumed they were from a little pueblo in the country. I could hardly wait to walk down the streets and see everyone up close. I started wondering what the Castillos' house would look like. *What is Mrs. Castillo's life like? Does she have servants? How will their food taste?* I jabbered incessantly to myself until we entered their neighborhood.

As we approached their house, my expectations flew out the (Cadillac) window. The streets in their neighborhood were lined with stately two- and three-story houses, with wrought-iron fences and grillwork on the windows and doors. This was a sophisticated part of the city. Mr. Castillo stopped the car in front of a white three-story house with a white iron fence and gate. He came around and opened my door for me. With another "Gracias," I slid across the luxurious leather seat and stood for the first time in front of my new home. Señora Castillo opened the gate for me, telling me in Spanish that my bags would be brought up to my room in a minute. I noticed that she had lit a cigarette the minute she got out of the car. I shyly stepped past her and waited at the front door for her to open it and motion to me to come inside. As she entered and welcomed me in, all I could say was, "Wow! This is a palace." I immediately tried to be a bit more discreet in Spanish: "Es una casa muy bonita." (It's a beautiful house.) We had entered what I would classify as a reception room, since it was obviously not set up for anything but impressing all who entered. The sofa and chairs were upholstered with an elegant silk fabric, with beige and gold trim. The carpet was white, and a large chandelier that hung from the center of the room was gilded and laden with heavy crystals that shouted, *Money lives here!*

An aproned maid approached us, ready to receive Señora Castillo's instructions. La señora told the maid to carry my bags upstairs to the living area. Then, la señora ushered me to the staircase in front of us. She was not full of conversation but was straight and to the point. She let me know that I was the last roommate to arrive, and she obviously wanted me to get to my room and get myself organized. But we were pleasantly interrupted on the second floor by one of her daughters before we got to the first of the two bedrooms for her boarders. La señora introduced her to me. Her name was Ariana. She had beautiful skin that was like coffee with just a little cream stirred in. It was so velvety and blemish-free that I wanted to touch it to see if it was real. She had large eyes the color of a California swimming pool, surrounded by thick, coal-black eyelashes that almost touched her gracefully arched eyebrows. She was wearing a turquoise blouse and a dark-tan skirt that blended with her eyes and skin, respectively. Her lips were tinted with deep-rose lipstick. They formed a gentle, natural smile. She appeared to have floated right out of an oil painting of an historic hacienda in the 1800s, but the style of her clothes brought me back to the present day.

"Bienvenidos! [Welcome!] My name is Ariana," she said with a very pleasant smile.

I was so surprised to hear her speak English that my face lit up. "How great! You speak English!" I blurted out.

"Yes, I am working for an American company, so I need to speak English every day."

I was relieved just to know I could talk to a family member in English if I needed help with anything. "Well, I am very glad to meet you, Ariana. I look forward to talking with you soon."

"It would be my pleasure," she said sweetly.

10

I MEET MY ROOMMATES

La señora led me into the doorway of a very large room that could best be referred to as a dormer. Three American girls were talking and finishing unpacking. La señora presented the girls to me: "Thees ees Shee-Loh [Shilo], Jaw-Neteh [Janette], ahn Mahr-goh Margo."

The girls greeted me with oversized smiles. "Welcome to Mexico," they said in unison. I thanked them, and Janette and Margo continued unpacking. Shilo had arrived two weeks earlier, with special permission from the Castillos, but Janette and Margo had arrived late yesterday.

La señora interrupted our frivolity as she removed the cigarette she had clenched in the corner of her mouth. "You will be sharing an upstairs room with one of the other roommates, Bow-bee Jeen," she said; I assumed that was Bobby Jean. She pointed toward a stairway across the living area. I acknowledged her orders with "Por supuesto" (Of course).

She excused herself, saying, "Con permiso," and nervously walked out of the room, her bony fingers reuniting her cigarette with her mouth.

"Well, so here we are! What do you think?" exclaimed Janette, whom I would soon learn was the extrovert of our group. She had an olive complexion, dark curly hair, and brown eyes. She was tall and built like a girl who could play football and win. She was of Italian descent, from New Jersey. Shilo, obviously much more reserved, was of average height with a trim figure and was as fair as a human could be without being an albino. Her hair was bleached platinum blonde, and it fell to her shoulders in a flip (the current giant bouffant hairstyle that was shaped like a balloon with an upward, relaxed half curl at the bottom). It was parted on the side, and fell halfway across her right eye, giving a hint of sexy to her pale blue eyes, which were rimmed with heavy black mascara. I had caught her Texas accent when I first walked in and was eager to learn about her life as well.

In response to Janette's query, I quickly responded, "Well, speaking for myself, I came here under the pretense"—I grinned—"of studying Spanish."

We all giggled.

"Of *course* you did," Margo said. Margo was a petite blonde with blue eyes, obviously the product of the upper crust. She was from San Francisco, I would learn. At first glance, I pictured her life (up until this point) as being like the daughter on the television program of *Father Knows Best* or *The Donna Reed Show*. She was the stereotypical all-American girl of the era. She wore a navy-blue skirt (not as short as a miniskirt, which would have been too risqué for her); a well-pressed, white blouse with a Peter Pan collar; and a red scarf tied neatly around her neck, setting off her prim-and-proper look.

She was a young Doris Day, and I wondered if she was going to start singing "Pillow Talk." Actually, she was quite shy, and I soon realized that she smiled more than she talked.

The four of us started sharing stores of "things that happened before we came to Mexico." We each touched on the highlights of our lives— where we were born, where we were from, what high school or college we attended, and whether we had any boyfriend commitments (none of us did, as it turned out, which was perfect).

I excused myself after we had covered the essentials, as I was eager to check out my room on the third floor. The maid had already carried my luggage up, which was a relief. La señora had advised me that Bobby Jean wasn't back yet, so I was hoping for some rest before dinner.

When I entered my new room, I realized immediately that it originally had been the maid's quarters. There was room for one twin bed, truthfully, but they had squeezed in two twin beds, with about six inches between them. A dresser was to the left of the door, and the bathroom door could be reached only by climbing over the corner of the nearest bed on the left.

My luggage was on the right-side bed, but I couldn't imagine where I was going to put the contents, let alone the suitcases, once emptied.

About that moment, a petite young woman, about five feet tall, with short, curly black hair walked slowly to the door of the little bedroom and stopped—there was nowhere to go with me in the room. She smiled a Mona Lisa smile, and her deep-blue eyes twinkled with a dainty glint of mischief. Coyly, she said, with a honey-laden Southern drawl "Hi, I'm Bobby Jean."

As she spoke, I was reminded of my uncle, who said to me many times in his Oklahoma drawl, "Why-ah, yer no bigger they-an uh min-nit" (referring to my five-foot frame). Bobby Jean's face showed some maturity, but her diminutive form and the penny loafers she was wearing made her look youthful.

"Hi, I'm Collette. It's really good to meet you," I responded.

She shyly stepped up to her bed and removed her shoes. Lying down on the bed, she said, "There's not much room in here, is there?" Now she smiled. "Where are you from? I'm from Arkansas. I've been staying here for the two months." I was so glad she was interested in getting to know me.

I sat at the end of my bed and propped my pillow behind my back as she continued to tell me more about herself. I was starting to enjoy her Arkansas drawl. The other girls had met her before my arrival. She told me she had graduated from ASU—Arkansas State University—a year ago and then had started working on her master's in cultural anthropology at UNAM last semester.

She told me the highlights of her life. She had been living in another home for students, not too far from the Castillos, during the previous semester. She'd had to leave that house to make room for an incoming student. She had luckily seen the Castillos' room-for-rent ad in the college housing office and rented it immediately upon seeing it. She was now in her final semester of study before receiving her master's degree.

As she narrated selected chapters of her life, her words projected a movie on the wall of my brain. She was obviously from a family of old money. That inheritance was most likely from tobacco (since she mentioned her father had grown up on a tobacco farm in Kentucky). Moving to Arkansas when he was twenty, her father parlayed his inheritance into a thriving construction business by the time Bobby Jean was born. I saw a father with a big cowboy hat and a diamond signet ring on his right hand that shouted, "I may not be educated, but by God, I can match any man's money, and I didn't need a college degree to get to where I am!" Soon I learned that Bobby Jean had traveled to Spain and countless other countries during her college years and was still sitting in Daddy's generous lap of luxury, dreaming her way around the world.

She was open and amiable, with a sweet temperament, and obvious familiarity with world travel. I began to unpack while she (surprisingly) lit a cigarette outside the door. I was glad she was a smoker because I was also. It was the '60s, after all, and we were oblivious to the health hazards. In fact, almost everyone smoked.

I unpacked what I could and then stored my luggage under my bed. After some twisting and turning in the tight space, I organized my toiletries in our little bathroom. At last, I was settled in.

I joined Bobby Jean outside the room on our rooftop patio and lit a cigarette. We sat on the chairs that the Castillos had set out for us. The sun was strong and bright, lightening the sky to a pale blue. Bobby Jean and I began one of the longest conversations of my life. As it turned out, we were incredibly similar. We were both young women who had earned high marks throughout our school years. We both had enough money (from our daddies) to enjoy our lives quite liberally. We both had ties to southern states. We both were 5-foot-2, with dark hair and bluish eyes. We were both looking forward to meeting eligible young men. We were both intellectuals and would-be poets. Dreamy-eyed, we had a romantic view of Mexico and were eager to travel wherever our hearts led us.

As the hours wound on, I realized that I had met one of the best friends I could ever hope for. We talked with such a comfort level, with such a thirst for new horizons. Bobby Jean divulged that she had been married two years earlier to the man she thought was the love of her life. Within the first year, however, they were divorced. The so-called love of her life turned out to be a playboy who got involved in an affair two months after they were married. Bobby Jean was the unlucky discoverer of that relationship. She filed for divorce one week later, and she was now a single woman, hoping for a more mature, enduring love with the right man. If that love resulted from her meeting a handsome guy during her stay in Mexico, that would be wonderful, she exclaimed.

As we brought the lengthy discussion of our lives to a close, Bobby Jean asked if I was ready to go downstairs to have *la cena* (dinner). I didn't hesitate to say yes, as I was starving. It was now 6:00 p.m. (4:00 California time).

11

MARIA'S KITCHEN

Bobby Jean and I descended the narrow stairs from our room and dropped by the dormer on the second floor to pick up the other girls for dinner and meet the cook, Maria. It turned out that everyone was in hunger mode, so we all followed Bobby Jean across the large sitting area and down the flight of stairs to the first floor. As we walked through the elegant living room area and approached the kitchen door, we saw Maria standing in front of the stove. She was overseeing some steaming green beans. Her dark-brown skin set off the bleached-white apron she wore over a bright orange cotton dress. Her blue-black braids, tightly pulled behind her ears, fell all the way to her waist, broadcasting her native descent.

The aroma of onions and garlic filled the kitchen, beckoning us to sit down at the rectangular table set in the alcove to Maria's right. My eyes began to sting, as I realized that Maria was also frying chiles on a flat, circular piece of metal with no handles. I would later come to know this type of pan as a *comal*. The acid from the peppers was leaching out, forming a heavy cloud of caustic steam that was held hostage inside the kitchen. A couple of us startied coughing incessantly but realized we would have to endure the discomfort if we were going to eat.

Bobby Jean began to explain the eating schedule at the house. The meal schedule for us was one hour prior to the family's schedule. This way, Maria could accommodate the family's specific meal requests after serving more common meals to us. *El desayuno* (breakfast) for us was to start at 7:00 a.m. and end at 8:00. *La comida* was to begin at 2:00 p.m. and end at 3:00. *La cena* (a late, light dinner) was to begin at 6:00 p.m. and end at 7:00. Bobby Jean couldn't stress enough that this schedule was *absolute*. She emphatically explained that either you ate on *Maria's schedule*, or you starved. Bobby Jean further clarified that Maria was dedicated to the family she worked for, *not we* American strangers. Her last words on the subject were, "If you miss a meal, go to bed, and try to fight the hunger pangs!"

We were all seated, but Maria had not so much as glanced our way. She was obviously not enchanted with playing cook to American girls who were chatting all the time, giggling, and speaking a foreign language. I felt humbled, thinking of what her life must be like. But before I became sentimental, she began slapping plates of food down on the table with no gesture of kindness. She uttered a couple of questions in Spanish, as if she were talking to people with whom she had no history and with whom she anticipated no future: "Que quieren comer? Bistec o pollo?" (What do you want to eat? Beef or chicken?) She didn't mention what would be served with it. The only acceptable answers were either *bistec* or *pollo*. I asked, in Spanish, for a medium-rare bistec. I was immediately met with Maria's piercing, punishing black eyes.

"Que?" (What?)

I knew I was being chastised, and I quickly learned that the way the steak is cooked is not my business. In Maria's kitchen, a razor-thin piece of flank steak is laid directly on top of one of the stove burners, seared for one minute, and then flipped with her fingers to the other side for one more minute. Then, she abruptly flops it onto your plate, and voilà (or, I *should* say, *olé*), it is unceremoniously placed in front of you.

I immediately thought, *Surely more sophisticated people in Mexico don't throw it right on top of the stove burners, do they? They must sear it in a small pan with a little oil. But then, we're in Maria's kitchen. And I am in Mexico!*

Quietly, with fear more than reverence, we began eating the food she had prepared: *huevos fritos* (fried eggs), hot corn tortillas (straight from the hot comal and then quickly placed in a round plastic container made for tortillas, which was lined with a generous cloth to cover them with, and *frijoles refritos* (mashed, pinto beans fried in lard).

I would learn a few days later that Maria bought her beef two blocks away at a butcher's shop. Bobby Jean took me to see it on our way to school one day. It looked like a mini-airplane hangar. Inside was a counter at the front, and at the back, whole legs, shoulders, and torsos of cows hung on hooks suspended from the ceiling. The butchers cut what you wanted to order from these huge cow sections. The bistecs were then brought home in a tidy paper wrap and, as I would witness a few days later, Maria hung them up with wooden clothespins on the clothesline in the backyard! *Is this a primitive way to age the beef?* I wondered. The flies were obviously happy, as they buzzed all over what would soon become our dinner. From that day forward, if given a choice, I asked for pollo.

With all in agreement, we left Maria's "hospitality" by uttering a quasi-sincere *gracias*. With our stomachs full—or queasy, as the case may have been—the five of us adjourned from her "courtroom," duly judged, and walked casually across to the stairs that led to our respective bedrooms. We all needed some rest from Maria, and I needed some time to finish digesting the cuisine. At least I would be very close to a bathroom if any reaction occurred!

12

SETTLING IN AND BRUSHING UP

Bobby Jean had some reading to do in preparation for her upcoming class. I was tired from my very long day and told her I'd like to do some reading myself.

The lamp on the tiny table between our beds gave off a surprising amount of light. I was thankful that what the room lacked in space, it made up for in practicality. If we didn't have a desk, at least we had our beds and a lamp!

I decided to brush up on my Spanish and opened the workbook I had brought from Mr. Valadez's class in high school. It presented the basics of Spanish in categories by verb tense and had a comprehensive section on nouns, dividing them by their feminine or masculine precursors. I had heavily relied on this book during my Spanish literature class at CWU. I thanked Mr. Valadez many times for choosing such a worthwhile book.

After about an hour of review, I felt a sense of familiarity with the Spanish language again. Thank God there was one *easy* characteristic I could always rely on: the vowels in Spanish always sounded the same, with very few exceptions. The letter *A* is always "ah"; *E* is always "eh";

I and *Y* are always "ee"; *O* is a short "oh"; and *U* is always "ooh." I felt confident that I could manage basic conversations with just about anyone now (except a judge, a doctor, or a rocket scientist).

Filling my head with grammatical rules and memorizing lists of words had finally made me drowsy. I lay my head on my pillow and decided to take a little siesta. My heart rate was a bit fast, I noticed, an effect I always felt when in high altitudes. I closed my eyes and tried to concentrate on slowing it down. As I relaxed, I entered that peaceful place between wakefulness and sleep and felt my heart settle into a slower pace. I silently thanked God for how content I felt.

"I'm calling it a day," I whispered to Bobby Jean.

"I am too," she said with a sigh.

In no time, we were both fast asleep.

13

SOCCER AND
CHOCOLATE

The next morning, la señora introduced her son, Gerardo, to us as we were leaving our just-tolerable breakfast in Maria's kitchen. Gerardo was in his soccer uniform, with "Universidad Nacional Autonoma de Mexico" inscribed on his jersey. Clearly, he attended the same school as we did; we had no idea when we moved into our rooms. He revealed his beautiful, broad smile as he warmly greeted all of us with "Hola! Que pasa?" (Hello! What's happening?) He was of light complexion but tan from his outdoor sports activities and muscular. He was the best-looking guy I had seen since my last visit to the Southern California beaches. A thick shock of unruly light-brown bangs floated over his eyebrows like a sparkling movie marquee that read *Handsome, Now Playing!* His coffee-and-cream eyes were the size of a camel's, with a look that said, *I am gentle, kind, and trustworthy.* His sinewy legs shouted, *I'm strong and powerful on the field!* We would soon see these attributes put into action.

Gerardo shyly announced that some friends were coming to take him and Shilo to his soccer game that night. (An unwelcome realization hit me—they were already dating!) Only two weeks had gone by, and she had landed a jock. He said there would be room for two more, if any of us would like to come along. I was out of my mind with excitement. Bobby Jean and I were the first to throw our hands up. Gerardo acknowledged our gesture with a big smile and told us his friends would arrive at six o'clock to pick us up. He added that he was sure we would enjoy the event.

A few moments later, la señora came to our quarters to give us "obedience training" and all kinds of warnings about what to do if we got lost, with instructions to stay close to our chaperones that night (her son and his friends). Inside our heads, we were saying, *Yeah, yeah, we've heard all this before*, but we forced well-posed faces that we hoped exhibited looks of interest. The most serious thing on our agenda was to plan our wardrobe, wash and dry our hair, chatter about what Gerardo's friends might be like, paint our nails, chatter some more, and wait for six o'clock.

At 5:45 p.m., we descended the stairs and sat down in the first-floor reception room, awaiting Gerardo and Shilo (the latter was still primping in the dorm room). Soon, Gerardo appeared, wearing his official game uniform very proudly. We had just greeted each other when the doorbell rang. Simultaneously, Shilo appeared, dressed in a pale-blue jacket and matching miniskirt, set off by cowboy boots.

La señora opened the door and greeted Oscar and Loco (the latter an obvious nickname. I was sure there was some history there). La señora introduced us, and we shook their hands as a formal response. They responded politely with, *"Mucho gusto."* Their amiable grins divulged their desire to have fun, which was also reflected in their animated eyes. Gerardo was driving to the stadium alone, as he would need to warm up prior to the game. As he waved adios to us, we followed Oscar and Loco out to Oscar's beautiful red convertible and piled into the back seat.

The game would be played at the National University's Olympic stadium, near a town called San Angel. It was about twenty minutes away, our chaperones told us. Oscar started the car, and off we went. I was going to a soccer game in Mexico City! It was so exciting to think that I was joining thousands of other Mexican citizens at a big cultural event.

I stared out every window in the car—it was lightly raining, so Oscar had to put the top up. I took in every scene, from the people walking along the street to the street vendors. The vendors carried all types of goods, from *dulces* (candy) to *juguetes* (toys) and offered them to us right at our windows at almost every traffic signal where we stopped. We were having so much fun just trying to communicate with each other in our respective languages.

Shortly after we arrived at the stadium, Oscar quickly took care of the tasks of parking and ticket-taking, and before we knew it, we were escorted up the stairs to our seats.

Our seats were at the very front of the second level; they appeared to be pricey reserved seats. Our escorts brought blankets for our comfort, and after passing them to us, they asked what we would like to drink. They suggested *cerveza* (beer), and we agreed. Their pleased expressions let us know that they had the same thing in mind. They asked if we would like *cacahuates* (peanuts). We chimed in with, "Sí, gracias!"

The lights on the field were intense, and the soccer players of each team were cheered with bravos by every single person in the stadium, or so it seemed. With the crowd whistling, standing, shouting, and clapping, the soccer players began volleying the ball back and forth to warm up. I had only played soccer in high school physical education classes, just between girls. I had never seen a soccer game of this caliber between men. I knew it was going to be exciting, if the crowd's attitude was any indication.

When the game began, I soon realized it took a Herculean effort to follow the ball. It was being flung from ground to sky, foot to head, head to head, shoulder to legs, like a ping-ong ball captured inside a huge glass bubble. I couldn't understand how it was contained on the field. The control that the players had over the ball was unfathomable. I lost sight of it many times, and a second later, I'd see the ball shooting up in the air like a shooting star across the night sky. The only way I knew that the ball hadn't gone into outer space was the sudden jerk of one of the players' heads, meaning the ball had descended and was met with a powerful pop from his head. He had knocked the ball back across the field to a teammate. Enough headway was made in one direction, finally, and the powerful kick by our friend Gerardo pounded it into the goalie's net, scoring for his grateful team (but we selfishly thought it was for us). We were so impressed because we not only lived with this obviously terrific soccer player, but he had invited us to the game.

The end of the game finally came. We had enjoyed the entire event, including the beer, peanuts, and camaraderie. To top it all off, Gerardo's team had won. We gathered up our things and began the descent to the entrance of the stadium, along with thousands of others. Gerardo was to meet us at the entrance after the game. We knew this would take some time, but we also knew it would take us some time to wade through the dense crowd. Not more than ten minutes after we arrived at the entrance, Gerardo magically appeared, dressed in a crisp white shirt and dress pants, ready for spending some after-game time with Shilo. He took her hand, and they committed to meeting up with us at the Zócalo (the enormous city center) to hear the *mariachis*.

Oscar and Loco led Bobby Jean and me to the car, and in a half hour, we were parking near the Zócalo. All along the main boulevard were groups of three to five mariachi groups singing Mexico's all-time favorite *canciones* (songs) to those who were gathered around them. The groups consisted of at least one trumpet player, one guitarist, a violinist, at least one vocalist, and sometimes a harpist. The combination of these instruments and the Spanish language, so descriptive of sensual feelings, moved my heart and mind into a zone of fantasy. Oscar and Loco handed us shots of tequila. The night air was comfortably cool. The black, starry sky, interposed with the colorful costumes of the mariachis, made for a vision I would never forget. The music, the people, the food, and the activity in the plaza was overwhelming. Gerardo and Shilo walked up to join in the crazy singing, and we all danced in a circle, arm in arm, laughing and managing to keep our tequila in hand. It was the height of pleasure seeking!

We sang along with the mariachis until we were hoarse. Gerardo suggested that we stop at a large, open-front restaurant named La Churrería El Moro (the Moorish Churro Maker—we Americans would call a churro a funnel cake). It was across the street. It was a perfect idea, since we knew we needed to pull ourselves together before heading for home (our curfew was midnight). El Moro turned out to be one of the jewels of Mexico City, where we sipped the richest hot chocolate I had ever savored. Our escorts told us that this was a favorite hangout for all the people of the city and for tourists as well. The list of different chocolates—from Mexican, to French, to Belgium—was exhaustive. The churros tasted like warm glazed donuts, just minutes out of the sizzling fryer. "Que rico!" shouted Loco, expressing how delicious the churros were. He had sung nonstop with the mariachis before we entered and was in need of some sustenance.

We joyously chatted for a while and then finally called it a night and walked back to Oscar's car. We climbed aboard to enjoy the warm ride home after a night of extreme excitement. The streets were fairly vacant, except for a small group here and there who seemed to also be calling it a night and walking home. Shortly, we arrived in front of our Mexican home, and Bobby Jean and I slowly pried ourselves out of the car. We thanked our hosts and bid them a good night.

When we stepped inside the gate, we noticed that Shilo and Gerardo were in an embrace on the front steps. We politely walked past them, and Bobby Jean quietly fit the key in the front door. As she nudged it open, there stood la señora. Shilo was still in Gerardo's arms, and la señora, a cigarette squeezed tightly between her bony fingers, puffed nervously on what was most likely her fiftieth cigarette of the day. Her face showed her disapproval; her glare could have stopped an army. It was five minutes past midnight.

We scuttled up to our room, leaving Shilo behind to meet her fate. We had, collectively, screamed, sung, danced, drank, and partied all that we could that night. Without further thought about Shilo, I fell under the spell of sweet dreams in short order.

14

ENCHANTING CUERNAVACA AND XOCHIMILCO

The next morning, after breakfast, la señora called another meeting with all of us in the dormer. She announced (as she sucked on her cigarette) that in two days, at eleven in the morning, another group of family friends was coming to take us to Cuernavaca, a little town forty-five minutes south of Mexico City).

We would be going to the family vacation home of one of the young men, whose name was Pato, where we would have lunch. We would walk around the little town, and then they would take us to a place called Xochimilco, the famous floating gardens of Mexico. The new chaperones, la señora explained, were named Tito, Alberto I and Alberto II, Pugi, and Jorge. She confirmed that between their two cars, all eleven of us could be accommodated. I pictured two very packed cars.

This was a big surprise to all of us. We realized that la señora had planned a great beginning for all of us in Mexico. I started to see her in a different light. She was a traditional Mexican woman, endeavoring to have her own business. Since it was not very acceptable for women to work outside the home in Mexico (they seemed to be about a decade behind women's progress in the US), she had brought an equitable business *to* her home. I thought she was doing a fantastic job—although her attitude could definitely use some work.

On Sunday our new hosts arrived right on the hour. La señora introduced each of them to us. They each responded with, "Nice to meet you," spoken in well-practiced English, as well as any foreigner could speak.

Each of our chaperones appeared to be well mannered and quite handsome. As they gently ushered us out the front door, we saw that Tito was driving a 1965 black Mustang and Alberto I was driving a 1964 blue Chevy Impala. La Señora was not surrounding us with ordinary young Mexican men. They were all obviously from well-to-do Mexican families and interested in meeting American girls. Their job was to take us touring. It was a sure way to keep us happy. I was catching on.

La señora bid us goodbye, beaming with confidence about her social arrangement for us. As with our first group of chaperones, our ride to our destination went by quickly. With such a big agenda, any ride with newly acquainted people is short.

The time flew by, but the beautiful drive didn't go unnoticed. I was amazed at the quality of the wide, nicely constructed highway that took us over a mountainous area that reminded me of California's Sierra Madre mountain range. When I mentioned this, Alberto told us that we were traversing over the mountains that were part of the Yoyolica volcano. That drew the attention of all of us.

"Is it an active volcano?" I asked with a bit of concern.

"Yes," answered Alberto.

"Well, I hope it won't choose today to blow its stack!" I tried to joke.

The tall pines were so appealing that we opened our windows to take in the clean, brisk air. We began descending the highway, and, just as la señora had told us, we arrived in Cuernavaca in just forty-five minutes. After our drivers found parking places, Pato led all of us to the center of the quaint little town, where a festive white gazebo was positioned. Tito told us that mariachis played here on weekends and for special gatherings.

"Visitors and village dwellers come out to dance or enjoy a cold *helado* [ice cream] when they hear the guitars, violins, and trumpets," he explained.

Since we had experienced the mariachis at the Zócalo several days prior, I felt smugly familiar with something in Mexico for the first time since arriving.

We walked along the sidewalks of the little town, looking in shop windows, enjoying the aroma of wonderful food, and even peering inside the doors of a beautiful church, where a mass was being held. Everywhere we looked, there was foliage and mature shade trees. Cuernavaca had a totally different feel to it than Mexico City (much as Palm Springs compares to Los Angeles). It had a tropical climate and was oriented to vacationers looking for a slow pace, nice restaurants, and gardens in which to relax.

As we walked back toward town from the church, Pato drew our attention to a very commanding building across from the pavilion where the gazebo was. He explained that it was the Palacio de Cortés, which was the residence of the conquistador after he moved to the town of Cuernavaca from Mexico City. Cortés decided to build his residence on top of this raised area, on the ruins of the Aztec lordship of Cuauhnahuac (*kwan*-uh-wock), to symbolize his dominance over the conquered territory.

"Since the days of Cortez, the palace has been used as a Catholic church, a prison, the Palace of the Mexican Republic, the seat of the Morelos state government, and, finally, it is now a museum," Pato explained. We unfortunately didn't have time to experience the museum but walking around its grounds and staring at its arched windows on the second story balcony was sufficient for now. A mural depicting the pre-Hispanic world was painted on the northern section of the building, with scenes inspired by Mesoamerican cultures. At the center, another mural, labeled "From the Conquest to 1930," represented events from the Spanish conquest, colonial times, independence, and modern Mexico, up to the Mexican Revolution. The southern section represented "Mexico today and tomorrow," depicting twentieth century conflicts as well as social exploitation of the peasants and the low-income working class.

Pato said the museum also hosted a collection of objects of historical and artistic value, including prehistoric artifacts found in the region and an incredible mural painted by the world-renown artist Diego Rivera, whose paintings and murals depicted peasants in colorful, larger-than-life scenes. Alberto encouraged us to visit the Diego Rivera art museum, as well as Frida Kahlo's home museum in Coyoacán, a small colonial town just south of Mexico City. It was very apparent that our chaperones had studied the history and geography of their state and surrounding areas of Mexico City! I came to respect this effort (and secretly thought that they were probably given a stipend by la señora and had most likely done chaperoning for her before).

"Both Diego Rivera and Frida Kahlo, his wife of many years, were very accomplished artists," he explained. "And their turbulent relationship and political views made for a very interesting life!"

I thought about the cultural anthropology course I had enrolled in for the semester and was eager to pick my professor's brain about which resources I might use to delve into the intimate details of the lives of these artists.

It was now two thirty, close enough to call it time for la comida. We had enjoyed ourselves in this wonderful setting, and it was obvious that we were a well-matched group. Tito and Alberto I led us back to our cars, and shortly we were on our way to Pato's parents' vacation home. As we weaved our way through the narrow streets of Cuernavaca, each block presented a vista of colorful facades of houses and small businesses. There was no demarcation between the businesses and the homes, except the color of the walls and the unsophisticated signs painted by the proprietors over their aluminum, garage-style doors. The bright pink, lime green, and purple fronts were adorned with bougainvillea, guava, Jacaranda, and palm trees that lined the sidewalks. All this was a strong reminder that there was no monotony in the architectural features in Mexico.

In little time we arrived at Pato's family's second home, and with a slight honk of the horn, Tito roused the caretaker. The huge wrought-iron gate slowly opened to us. As we drove in, our eyes grew wide-opened with shock. Before us was a huge concrete driveway, leading to a beautiful two-story white house with a red-tiled roof. And, unlike anything I had yet seen in Mexico, a green lawn reached out to us, looking more like California than Mexico. We parked and eagerly got out of our cars.

Pato led us around the back of the house to a huge blue-tiled pool, surrounded by more bougainvillea, guavas, and palm trees. The sun was so bright that the water in the pool glistened like glass. He welcomed us inside the huge living room, which opened onto the pool area. Immediately we were offered tequila, Coke, and beer by one of the neatly dressed house servants. Traditional Mexican music started playing on the stereo, and we were coaxed over to the dining room table that had been set up for us to the left of the living room. The dining room also opened out onto the pool area. We had the advantage of being out of the hot sun but with all the ambiance of sitting by the pool.

The table was set with brightly colored plates of blue, yellow, and white designs that were evocative of Mexican folk art. Pato explained that it was the *Talavera* design, which originated in Spain. A floral arrangement in the middle of the table showed off more of the incredible variety of tropical plants that are plentiful in Cuernavaca: bird-of-paradise; yellow, red, and pink hibiscus; purple, pink, and white calla lilies; and fuchsia.

The servers brought out beautiful platters of *antojitos* (appetizers): *aceitunas con sardinas* (olives stuffed with sardines), *poblano chiles con queso* (chili peppers stuffed with melted cheese), and *chicharrones con salsa* (crispy fried pork rinds with red chili sauce). We were having a fantastic time, munching and sipping and laughing and talking.

Our hosts were true gentlemen. They made sure we were always comfortable, that we were having a good time, and that they had answered any questions we had about Mexico (and we had so many). They obviously had a solid upbringing and were of good intentions. Next in importance to that trait, they knew how to have a good time. They all had known each other since grammar school or middle school days, which was amazing to us Americans.

I mentioned that American families typically move to at least two different towns over the course of their lives.

"That isn't the case in Mexico," Tito responded. "In general, Mexican children remain at their family's home until they are married. Even when they marry, they often remain in their parents' home, helping them with a modest monthly contribution and relying on them to help with child-rearing. The typical Mexican middle-income family has at least one maid, who further assists the family, whether they have children or not. Their clothes are laundered and pressed; their food bought, prepared, and served; and the house is cleaned by the maids."

"The typical American woman does all that," I complained, "and also works outside the home!"

It was now 4:30, time for us to leave for Xochimilco. There was plenty of daylight left, and we needed to take advantage of it. We had just finished eating a delicious meal, during which our hosts explained what each dish was and how it was prepared. We had *enchiladas suizas*, covered with *salsa verde* (green chile sauce), *frijoles enteros* (whole pinto beans, not mashed), and *arroz* (white rice). The meal was followed by an absolutely scrumptious dessert called flan, which looked like a piece of caramel custard pie, but the top was broiled for a moment to caramelize the brown sugar mixture, adding a nice crunchy texture. We couldn't stop uttering, "Mmm," to the delight of our hosts. (I think that was a new sound for them.) With the flan, we were served a steaming cup of hot Mexican coffee called *café de la olla*—coffee grounds cooked in a large pot of boiling water with a crude brown sugar called *piloncillo, canela* (cinnamon), and *vainilla* (vanilla bean). After a period of time, the mixture was left to rest while the grounds settled to the bottom. At that point, the coffee was ladled into small traditional clay cups that were placed in front of us. It was a deliciously flavorful drink.

After a little more chatting, we were on our way. The caffeine would keep us fortified for hours. We thanked our wonderful hosts and servers many times over for such a fantastic lunch. They went beyond standard protocol, and I hoped they understood we were very grateful guests.

Alberto I had explained that Xochimilco was about seventeen miles, or twenty minutes, northeast of Cuernavaca. That was fine with us, as our contentment was so complete, our stomachs so happy, and our hosts so amiable that we would have enjoyed a five-hour trip just as much.

Approaching the area of Lake Xochimilco, the country scenery we had been enjoying en route to Cuernavaca became more urban. Since it was not far from Mexico City, the enormous population had sprawled throughout the surrounding valleys, right up the sides of the mountains. Alberto I told us that Lake Xochimilco had special agricultural significance in the history of Mexico City. It was one of three lakes in the area that surrounded the capital city of Tenochtitlan, which was established by the Aztecs in the 1300s—it would become Mexico City more than four hundred years later.

As I later researched Tenochtitlán, I learned that it was established in 1325 in the middle of one of the other lakes, Lake Texcoco. The inhabitants of Xochimilco utilized a method of farming they called *chinampa* in their native language, Nahuatl, which meant "mud farming." They dredged up silt from the bottom of the lake and around the shore of the lake, and placed it on large, floating mats made of straw, forming plots of land. They then planted willow trees, the roots of which grew deep into the water, anchoring the mats. Once anchored, the mats became plots of land where corn, beans, fruit, and flowers were grown, thus the name *floating gardens.* Since there were so many inhabitants, and since water was difficult to distribute to planted fields, this made it simple.

Of course, what the surrounding area would have looked like over six hundred years ago was impossible to imagine now, with cars and homes and businesses crowding the bustling streets.

As we drove through the entrance to the Floating Gardens, though, it was possible to imagine an ancient world. As I gazed at the huge lake, it conjured up an image of the great city of Tenochtitlan that I had read about in one of the brochures that UNAM had sent to me. The lake was surrounded by huge willow trees, with long, thin, draping branches that appeared to be bowing reverently to the lake. They provided shade to the circumference, where many families were picnicking. I mused that the scene would have been much the same in the 1300s.

My attention was immediately drawn to the colorful boats floating on the lake. There were at least fifty of them. Alberto I explained that each was proudly handcrafted by its owner. Every color of the rainbow was represented by these shallow-bottomed wooden boats called *trajineras* (trah-hee-*nare*-aws). Each had an arched canopy made of plastic, wood, or metal. Some were close to the shore, so I could see that they were filled with partying groups. A few mariachis had managed to cram themselves onto many of the boats to add to the fun. I could hear the mariachis' trumpets, with their high-pitched, powerful notes causing everyone in close proximity to brace themselves. The whole lake was one big floating fiesta!

As we circled a section of the lake, I soon realized that each colorful boat had a tall sign at the front. Some had first names of women, like Renata or Anita, painted on them. One was simply named Xochimilco. Others had large frames mounted above the canopies, draped with stunningly colorful cloth banners. The names on the banners were outlined in bright contrasting threads, obviously made by local artisans. The boats were like bright flowers adorning the lake.

Alberto II (who rarely spoke) told us that each boat was owned by an individual who had to meet certain criteria (safety, most importantly), and each had to be certified and registered in order to sell boat rides. They all proudly steered their unmotorized boats around the lake, pushing their long poles into the deep mud with their muscular arms, seeming to enjoy the ride every bit as much as their occupants.

After parking, we walked down the dirt path to the lake and gathered at the dock. There were more mariachi groups standing around, wanting to be hired to entertain the guests who were approaching the boats. Pato immediately chose a group of mariachis and asked that we girls pick which boat we wanted to board. We chose one that was named *La Rosa* (the Rose). The owner pulled his boat over to the dock and tied it up with a rope, and we boarded from the back end. The mariachis boarded last. There was a long, narrow table in the center that ran three-quarters of the length of the boat, with benches along both sides. At the back was room for the mariachis to stand. At the front, the boatman slowly pushed us away from the dock and began to nudge us along, out into the interior of the lake.

Of course, our chaperones had taken care of the catering on the boat, buying various antojitos from vendors near the dock. They, of course, had not forgotten to bring along the tequila they had opened during our comida in Cuernavaca! We were learning that Mexico knew how to enjoy itself, to which the laughter and camaraderie on the lake was a testament. The partying began, and before too long, everyone on our boat was learning the words to various traditional songs, like "Cuando Caliente el Sol" (literally translated as "When the Sun Is Hot").

With lyrics, loosely translated, such as, "I feel your body pulsing next to mine," and "It's your face, your throbbing body, your kisses, we are teaching each other," these songs would never be heard in the US! But the Spanish language—and Mexican songs, in particular—are all about being sensual. It is a natural part of their culture, not a source of shame. We *gringas* (American girls) all felt very accepting of the sensual lyrics, and as we sang our hearts out, we felt more and more a part of their culture.

As the sun began to droop into the V-shaped dip between two distant mountains, we all agreed it was time to head back to the city. We couldn't have enjoyed ourselves more, buts even our youthful bodies had their limits!

Driving home, we thanked our chauffeurs and, more important, our friends many times over for their abiding companionship. We'd had the time of our lives—*again*!

15

GIRLS' DAY OUT

The next morning, Bobby Jean and I were greeted with the incessant, guttural barking of dogs from a nearby roof. Arh! Arh! Arh! A three-second pause; then Arh! Arh! Arh! Another three seconds; then Arh! Arh! Arh! I eventually gave up on sleeping in.

Bobby Jean awoke moments later. "Mor-nin'." She managed to project her soft voice from her sleepy head.

I came to life as I heard her comforting voice. "Morning. Did you sleep as well as I did?"

"I think so" She softly sighed as she turned to face me. Upon seeing each other, we started to laugh. Our '60s-era "big hair" and thick black eyeliner were a scary sight in the morning. The black smudges of makeup and the ratted, shapeless hair was a liability of the times—we had been too tired to wash our faces last night.

Bobby Jean and I propped ourselves up to officially acknowledge the beginning of a new day.

"You know what? I need to get out of this house and out into the city—just us girls, like we would in the States. I want to walk, conquer the shops, and eat lunch with the Mexicans. Would you be willing to go with us?" I asked.

"Sure!" Bobby Jean paused and then gave a resolute nod. She responded, "You're in for a real shock! I need to go with you so you don't get lost! You're going to need help with directions to understand the layout of this town. Let's go downstairs and see if the girls want to join us."

I jumped at the prospect. "That would be great! I'm dying to find my way around and see what it's like outside of this neighborhood."

We lugged our bodies out of our comfy beds, wrapped up in our heavy robes, slipped on our *pantuflas* (slippers), and crept cautiously downstairs. The door to the girls' dormer was shut, but we quietly opened it and found our partners in crime lying in their beds, talking lazily, trying to wake up as we had.

"Who wants to go shopping today?" I asked, startling them.

After a bit of rousing, it was a unanimous vote. Bobby Jean and I left to get ready in our room, where we maneuvered around the lack of space, hot water, and electrical outlets for our hair dryers.

In one hour flat, Bobby Jean and I were ready. We descended the stairs to the dormer, knowing we would probably have to wait for someone to finalize her primping. Within twenty minutes, all of us—except Shilo, who had a date with Gerardo—were trekking to the front door.

"¡Espera! Déjame hablar con ustedes!" It was la señora, asking us to wait, as she needed to talk with us. Looking well rehearsed, she stood with obvious intent to pound some commandments into our heads before we could get out the door. Blowing smoke out her nostrils like a baby bull, she sternly gave us a warning: She spoke quickly but sternly in Spanish, saying "All of you need to be careful. Here, it isn't like it is in the United States. You all need to tell me where you're going and when you'll return. I want you to guard your personal things, keep your purses close to you, and don't talk with anyone except the clerks inside the shops and restaurants."

We all had learned how to satisfy la señora. We gave her our complete attention, without questioning anything she told us. We adjusted our faces so that we looked naïve and interested in what she had to say. She seemed appeased, after we each responded with, "We will."

As we walked out the front door and down the walk to the gate, I felt like I was breathing deeper than I had in months. Freedom at last!

Bobby Jean directed us to turn right as we passed through the gate. Down the sidewalk we began our walk to the downtown area of Roma. If it weren't for the aromas and sounds around us, I would have thought I was in an upscale Los Angeles neighborhood. But this was not what I had seen from the freeway when leaving the Mexico airport. The houses along the freeway were the color of raw concrete, with nothing but a sidewalk to separate them from traffic. These homes had well-maintained stucco façades, with elegant wrought-iron fences and gates. Some had small, manicured front lawns behind their gates; others revealed concrete or brick patios enhanced with large, colorfully painted pots and succulents, along with other flowering plants. Seeing this neighborhood reinforced my thought that I was with the cream of the crop. The nicely appointed properties might have been familiar to me, but the aromas and sounds were completely outside of my experience. Bells clanged, horns honked, whistles blew, and various street vendors shouted out in Spanish. The side streets were teeming with riders on bicycles, with baskets attached to the front or back of their bikes. The vendors carried freshly made tortillas, fresh eggs, chiles, chicharrones, fruit, and who knew what else.

On a corner, just a block from the main street, stood a huge metal tank about four feet tall and three feet wide. It was sitting on a platform with short, sturdy metal legs, placed in front of a *tienda* (shop). As we approached, we could see a flame burning underneath the giant cooker. A short, dark-skinned woman, with long, tidy black braids and a well-ironed white cotton dress and red apron, stood beside the pot. She had a portable table next to her and a chair. As steam was forced out of the valve at the top of her huge covered pot, a shrill whistle blurted out to all within a two-block area. After each whistle, she yelled, "Tamales!" The blend of sweet and earthy aromas filled our nostrils. I was familiar with tamales, having enjoyed them many times at my Mexican friends' homes in California. I loved the steaming masa packages that concealed a delicious variety of sauces mixed with fillings, including one or more meats, cheese, fruit, and chile sauce. (Masa is a cooked dough made with corn flour.) Passersby stopped and asked for their favorite types of tamales. The little woman worked quickly, placing her tamales in a clear plastic bag, tying it, and exchanging her hot specialties for pesos. I soon learned that because tamales were so inexpensive in Mexico and so fortifying, they were a staple of the Mexican people. They often ate fruit-filled tamales for breakfast and the meat- and vegetable-filled tamales for dinner. As we continued our walk to the bus stop, it was a struggle not to be seduced by each vendor's delicacies. Their shouting was melodious, not annoying. It added such a quaint ambiance to the business-lined streets. *What a personal touch*, I kept thinking.

As we approached the main boulevard, El Paseo de La Reforma (the Boulevard of the Reformation), I recalled the brochure that I had received from UNAM with my acceptance letter. It contained a map of Mexico City, with highlights of some of its most renown venues—the Castle of Fine Arts, the National Palace, the Angel, the Museum of Natural History, Chapultepec Park, and the Castle. I remembered the labels on the map that showed the monuments and buildings along the boulevard with special architectural features. I also remembered that it was originally named the Emperor's Boulevard by Mexico's Emperor Ferdinand Maximilian in the nineteenth century to honor key episodes in Mexico's history.

At the end of the street, we paused for a moment to examine a fruit stand. The young vendor was a fast-moving guy, entertaining all who passed by with the flashing of his knife, like a samurai, as he cut all kinds of fruit into shapes that resembled various flowers. He had just finished cutting a piece of papaya into the shape of a tulip and had inserted a thin popsicle-type stick into the bottom of the flower. He followed up with a squeeze of lime and a sprinkle of chili powder over the "petals."

A professional-looking man in a black suit and white shirt with a crisp black tie asked, "Cuanto?" (How much?)

The vendor answered, "Cinquenta centavos, por favor" (Fifty cents, please.)

The man handed the vendor the change, took the tulip-on-a-stick, and walked off, enjoying his breakfast on the way to his office—the pinnacle of fast food.

As the vendor started cutting a *sandía* (watermelon), we had to divert our attention, as we had been warned in the information from our school (and again by la señora) not to eat *any* foods sold on the streets (as the vendors might not wash the fruit thoroughly). We complained to ourselves but persevered as we crossed the street and focused on our more important goal—shopping!

The first storefront display that we approached wooed us inside. The mannequins were dressed in high-class autumn business suits and sported red lipstick and nail polish. Their skin was a few tones darker than ours, and each had a well-placed beauty mark near her mouth or cheek bone. Their brows were arched as if to say, "I am very sophisticated! Don't touch me!" Their eyes were large, brown, and almond-shaped. *How funny,* I thought, *that the mannequins in a foreign country are designed to look like the general clientele.* The interior of the shop echoed the attitude of the display window. We didn't know then, but we were in the "Beverly Hills" section of Mexico City, which explained the price of the clothes.

We were greeted with "Buenos días!" by the tall, beautiful sales clerk. We smiled and answered with the same greeting, hoping we sounded seasoned. We approached the clothing racks, hoping we appeared classy enough to be buying something in the store. I spotted a silky, light-blue, spaghetti-strap dress that would be really great for the dance that was just two weeks away. The dance was planned by the university. Two days ago, la señora had nonchalantly handed us the flier with a smirk on her face.

I fell in love with the dress. I tried it on, and I had to have it! I anxiously stepped out from the curtained alcove and asked my partners in crime, "What do you think?"

They said, in unison "Get it!"

"It's really cute, and you'll probably need it again sometime anyway."

I looked at the price tag and thought, *Hmm, that's not too steep. That would be fifty US dollars.* Since my father had given me two hundred dollars in cash before I left home for "emergencies," I felt that this certainly fit in that category.

I reluctantly slipped the dress off and put my capris and short-sleeved top back on. I got out my wallet and confidently strutted over to the clerk. I pulled out five hundred pesos and handed it to her.

She smiled and graciously took my money. Knowing I was a gringa fresh out of the US, she said, "El precio es cinco mil pesos, señorita." (The price is five thousand pesos, miss.)

"Five *thousand* pesos?" I responded in Spanish, with a confused look on my face.

"Sí, señorita," she courteously replied.

I looked at the price tag she held in front of me and quickly realized that meant it would be ... what? Five *hundred* dollars! I stumbled along with my Spanish, asking if indeed that was five hundred US dollars.

"Sí, señorita, sí," she said, somewhat amused.

"Well," I said, "that's a little more than I thought it was."

Her frustration was starting to show. I was more than embarrassed, as I had made the stupid mistake of overlooking one digit. The peso was ten to one at the time, which made it easy to calculate prices. If something was ten pesos, it was one US dollar. Clearly, five thousand pesos would be five hundred dollars. I gave an *eek* look with my eyes and a smirk tinged with fear. "I need to think it over. Can I come back a little later?" I mumbled in Spanish.

Thankfully, she understood my attempt at an explanation! We walked out of there (all of us red-faced) and didn't look back. We managed to hold our giggles until we were out of sight, but my giggle only camouflaged a bruised ego. I hoped the clerk didn't hold her breath for my return.

Two doors down, we happened upon a storefront that intrigued us immediately. The well-painted sign on the window read *Estética* in large letters. Bobby Jean explained that an esthetician practiced there, or, as we said in the States, a qualified beautician. Also on the sign, in smaller letters, the application of fake lashes was offered. In the States at the time fake lashes were sold with a built-in adhesive on them. With one swift press, they stuck on until they were peeled off later—at least, that was what the package said. Unfortunately, they lifted up at the edges as the day wore on, and the adhesive border was thick and theatrical-looking.

It was an embarrassment, to say the least, to check myself in the mirror during (or after) a date and see that half of the adhesive on one eye had curled up, as if the lashes were trying to fly away.

But here, in this obscure shop in Mexico City, they were applying one eyelash at a time. They were supposedly permanent—at least for a few months, the clerk told us. We just *had* to have them! They looked more natural than the Twiggy-style lashes and wouldn't take nearly the work, we rationalized. Bobby Jean, Janette, and I made appointments for the next week so that we could all go together (strength in numbers was our theory), and we hoped we'd still have them for the dance. Such an extravagant idea was *not* appealing to conservative Margo.

We moved on to the next shop. The display window stated loudly that it was a well-kept, high-end jewelry store—a *joyería*. There was no hesitation in our decision to step inside. As we entered, our eyes led us to the cases that displayed earrings and necklaces. Glittering gold beckoned the visitors of the shop to gawk at every case, as the bright light bulbs glared down on them, making the little shop about ten degrees warmer than it was outside. This shop didn't bother to offer silver. Silver jewelry was a very inexpensive commodity in Mexico, as it was produced in large quantities in Taxco, a traditional, colonial town about two hours away. We concluded that although gold was not cheap, we could afford a pair of earrings, since they would last forever and remain a memory of our stay in Mexico.

Our first observation was that the earrings were all for pierced ears. Only one of us, Bobby Jean, had pierced ears. She had already succumbed to that temptation during her first semester at UNAM. This wasn't a fashion obligation in the States in the 1960s. We had grown up with mothers who wore clip-on earrings, and the pressure to move into pierced earrings hadn't quite hit us yet. As any young woman knew, however, that could be taken care of.

Janette and I, with our adventurous spirits, leaped beyond the practical and settled on the idea that we needed to progress (in a fashionable way). The shop didn't offer piercing, but we figured we would address that problem later. We decided to buy a very specific type of small, hoop earrings. They were eighteen-carat gold, guaranteed not to irritate our tender American ears. The part that threaded through the earlobe was curved and had a sharp point on it so that it could pierce through your ear and then be latched in one fell swoop. Janette and I bought identical pairs and decided that we would ask one of la señora's daughters where to get our ears pierced (which could be done by a doctor, the clerk had told us). Margo, of course, declined to participate.

Bobby Jean lost interest in the jewelry shop—she had bought plenty of jewelry over the summer—and said she would meet us at the next shop. As we giggled our way out of the jeweler's door, excited about our daring purchase, Janette and I began to look for Bobby Jean in the next shops. Before we got very far, we saw her waving her arms at us from a few doorways down, motioning us to come inside. We hurried our steps and filed into the rustic, bright-white alcove where she stood. As we bunched up inside the little archway, our senses were overcome by a warm blanket of rich aromas. Bobby Jean led the group down the narrow stone path to a wide, colorful entrance with La Fonda (the inn) inscribed in artfully painted blue and red letters.

As we sauntered with anticipation through the entrance, we couldn't overlook the red velvet couch and matching Mexican-style chairs that beckoned for us to rest our weary feet. We had entered a comfy oasis. Three of us collapsed on the couch, and Margo took a seat at one of the high-back adjoining chairs. The headwaiter approached us, saying, "Buenas tardes," or "Good afternoon." He clutched four very large menus in his arm. They were heavy black paper, with a hot pink ribbon tied at the top in a bow that seemed to say, "Open me; tasty treasures inside!" We had embedded ourselves in the couch and struggled to lift our bodies from its cushy hospitality, but our empty stomachs were sufficient incentive to rise to the occasion, so we followed the warm smile of our host to a table that was ready for us.

We were each given a menu, which we received as if a gift box had been presented to us. We eagerly opened to the first page and knew we had been blessed. The Spanish words that danced across the pages were in handwritten calligraphy, so enticing that we began to salivate, even though we only understood a few words listed in the descriptions. Our server arrived and asked us what we would like to drink. We all ordered a Tab, (the precursor to Diet Coke) which we rationalized would magically make our meal low-calorie. I asked the waiter if he would please explain the menu items to us. He understood my clumsy attempt at Spanish, and began, item by item, describing the ingredients of each one and how each was prepared. We were like Pavlov's dogs, sitting around a huge dog bone, waiting for the bell.

I chose the *chile en nogada*. Our server had described it as a large Poblano chili pepper stuffed with a mixture of ground pork, nuts, cinnamon, and raisins, fried in a light egg batter and topped with a sweet almond white sauce, garnished with pomegranate seeds. The combination of those ingredients made my mouth water. Janette chose *relleno de flor de calabaza* (a squash blossom stuffed with cheese; then coated with flour and fried). It turned out that Janette and I were the more daring spirits in our group. Bobby Jean ordered a "safer" dish: an *enchilada verde con queso y frijoles*—a corn tortilla stuffed with a special white cheese, covered with a mild green chili sauce, and then baked, with pinto beans on the side. She had experienced enough bad cooking coming from Maria's kitchen and wanted something reliable! Margo also leaned toward the tried-and-true and chose a meatball soup called *sopa de albondigas*. How could she go wrong with that?

As we eagerly awaited our authentic Mexican dishes, we reminisced about our adventures with our incredible hosts over the past week. We couldn't get over how polite they were, how respectful they were, and how handsome they were! What a serendipity we were experiencing. We could have chosen to go to school in a different country, we could have stayed in our hometowns, but here we were in Mexico City, like sponges soaking up the culture that surrounded us. We had chosen to be here, and we were more than happy with our decision. As young women, we were certainly a unique group. Most young women from the US would not even consider going to school in Mexico! Maybe Italy, France, Germany, or England, but Mexico? That wasn't considered very classy. What could they learn from a country that had no economic power, that didn't have a viable military force, that couldn't point to many conquests?

Little did the naysayers know that the Mayan and Aztecan roots that were laid down here and then blended with Spanish roots made for one of the richest cultures in the world. As for conquests, had they missed the fact that the Mexicans had defeated the Spaniards,—the same Spaniards that had given the United States a major run for its money?

Soon, our dishes were served to us. Janette was the first to react. Hesitantly, she put her fork into one of the squash blossoms, cut off a piece, and slowly nudged it into her mouth. We studied her eyes as she began massaging the morsel in her mouth. "Hmm," she said, followed by "Wow," followed by a garbled, "Wonderful!" (She was still chewing.) Once she swallowed, she said that at first, the feel of a flower in her mouth was strange. But then the flavor of the flower came through, and then, as she lingered over the taste and texture together, her palate rejoiced in the sensual pleasure of it.

Fortunately, each of us was dazzled by the fresh spices, chiles, and sauces on our plates. I devoured mine, one bite at a time, with ecstasy. The bite of the al dente chile pepper with the soft, warm cheese awakened my taste buds and shouted at my throat, "Here we come!" On the trip over the back of my tongue, the nut sauce calmed the whole swarthy adventure, and said, "Now, a sweet treat to savor!" We left La Fonda knowing that we would be back. We were *muy satisfechas* (very satisfied, the more discretionary Spanish term for "full") from our authentic Mexican lunches.

On the walk toward home, we boasted that we had conquered the neighborhood. We began talking about other venues we were ready to visit, as if we were seasoned travelers now, although three of us had no idea what lurked outside our safe Beverly Hills cloister. We threw out names of all the well-known places as if we were the world travelers we had only dreamed to be—Oaxaca, Taxco, Yucatán, San Miguel de Allende, Acapulco.

At ages ranging from nineteen to twenty-three, our hearts were very spirited and eager for adventure. We knew this was the time in our lives to explore. We intuitively knew that this era would not last very long, so we felt we had to seize the day.

As we approached la Señora's house, we hoped we could enter without being questioned. Fortunately, la señora's daughter Ariana opened the front door to our ringing (we weren't given keys for security reasons). Her kind, beautiful face was welcoming. In fact, la señora's entire family warranted framing. Each of the five shared the same warm, flawless skin, and their eyes ranged from brown to green, azure and blue. Ariana was blessed with the bluest eyes. She was quiet but always smiling. She seemed to be interested in our daily antics but knew that social boundaries couldn't be crossed. I often paused when I saw her walking, as she had a pronounced limp. At times, she wore a leg brace at home. We were too embarrassed to ask what had happened, but that story would probably reveal itself through the relationship that was growing between Shilo and Gerardo.

16

THE HACIENDA

After our incredible walking trip in downtown Roma that night, Janette and I made an appointment to have our ears pierced the next morning. We had asked Ariana if she could tell us how to get in touch with a doctor who would do the procedure—those earrings were screaming to get out of their boxes. Instead, she recommended the family's neighbor, Andrea, two doors down from us. Ariana said that Andrea had been providing this service for her friends and family for the last twenty years. With our enthusiastic gracias, Ariana phoned Andrea, and she agreed to come over the next morning to do the deed. With that settled, we were able to relax for the night. Each of us enjoyed some down time, doing miscellaneous things, like pedicures, manicures, trimming bangs, and eyebrow plucking. Of course, our appearance was our first priority.

At breakfast the next morning, la señora entered Maria's kitchen with a pinched, nervous look on her face, but that was nothing new. She told us that Oscar had phoned her late last night and asked if he, Tito, Pato, and Loco could take all of us to see another friend's *ranchito* (a small ranch) about two hours north of the city, just north of a town called Queretero. The family of their friend, Jorge, had built the ranchito as a weekend getaway. Jorge had offered to host a comida for us there. Afterward, we would go further north to visit San Miguel de

Allende, located about an hour away. He told la señora that he would make reservations for all of us to stay at the Instituto de Bellas Artes (Institute of Fine Arts) for the evening in San Miguel. He assured la señora that he and the guys would stay at a different place nearby. "San Miguel," explained la señora (in Spanish, of course), "is an old colonial town in the state of Guanahuato that has become an American artist's town in recent years. The Institute of Fine Arts is both a bed-and-breakfast and a teaching school. After breakfast and some sightseeing the next day, they will bring you home."

"What about our ear piercing this morning?" I blurted out. I couldn't trade one experience for the other; I wanted them both. "Can you guys wait just an hour?" I asked. "Andrea is coming in twenty minutes to pierce our ears."

Janette and I received only glares from our roommates.

"That's okay with me," offered Bobby Jean.

"I can wait, but just make it happen in an hour," Shilo said.

With sincere surprise, Janette and I looked at Shilo, thinking maybe she and Gerardo had broken up. Why would she agree to go anywhere without him?

Then she said, "Gerardo is going out of town for a soccer game today, so I would really like to go."

We were obviously glad, as she was really a kindred spirit. And as long as she was catered to, she was easygoing. We looked at her and Bobby Jean with grateful grins, and Margo shortly threw in her approval of our ear-piercing appointment. (I knew they would all use the extra time to primp anyway.)

Maria's breakfasts had become quiet affairs, as we were always sleepy, and with her attitude permeating the room, we just ate as fast as we could and got out. We were like cattle that came to the trough. We ate whatever was put in front of us out of necessity and then left. And now, once again, we were all too excited to care. We were bound for another adventure. (Well, Janette and I were bound for two adventures.) We scrambled to our rooms, got our earrings, and went to the sitting area upstairs for our procedure. Andrea arrived right on time (9:00); we heard the doorbell from our chairs, awaiting the surgery like obedient patients.

Andrea was led upstairs by la señora, who appeared worried—she probably was concerned about anything catastrophic happening to two of her charges. Andrea had a plastic bag with her. She reached into the bag and pulled out an aerosol can and a hard case that looked like a glasses case, a cotton towel, and gloves. *Hmm*, I thought, *this is getting a bit complicated.*

Andrea broke the tense silence with a smile. "This is a very quick procedure," she said comfortingly. "Don't let all this stuff scare you. All I'm going to do is place a small dot on your earlobes with my pen, and then I'll freeze your earlobe with this gas—it's just Freon. You won't feel anything but the freezing. When I'm done, you can admire yourselves in the mirror."

"Okay," I said, "that sounds simple."

"Who wants to go first?" she asked.

Neither of us jumped at the opportunity. Instead, our eyes shifted side to side at each other.

Andrea asked, "How about you, Collette?"

Eek! I thought. "Okay," I said, squirming, "I'm ready." I reluctantly sat down in the chair Andrea had positioned next to her.

She immediately wrapped a towel around my shoulders and began drawing dots on my ears. My first thought was wondering if the towel was to catch all the blood that would shortly pour from my earlobe. Andrea sprayed the Freon on my left earlobe, and I felt a freezing sensation, just like she explained. It hurt like the time I was up in the mountains in California on a toboggan with my friends. I had no hat, and the freezing wind made my ears ache. After a short pause, Andrea asked if my ear was numb (she was pinching it to test it).

"I assume," I said—the aching had stopped just then.

Andrea proceeded to push the pointed flange of the earring into my earlobe, but I didn't anticipate the amplified, grisly, crunching sound it made upon entry, followed by a disgusting squishing sound as Andrea forced the prong through the other side of my ear! My inner ear had become a stereo speaker, and my head was the amplifier. "Ugh! That's horrible!" I said.

"Don't move," Andrea ordered gently. "I'm almost done!" She sopped up the drop of blood that had oozed out of my ear. I only knew this because Janette's eyes were popping out, and she exclaimed "Yuck! I didn't know it would *bleed*!"

I heard Andrea clasp the point of the flange into the other end of the hollow hoop; the pressure of her shaking hands on the side of my head adding to my anxiety. She dabbed my ear with a cotton ball saturated with peroxide and announced that it looked beautiful. I felt relief just knowing that half of my discomfort was over. Andrea placed a large mirror in front of me, which subdued my trauma a bit as I admired the gold earring perfectly hanging from my earlobe. I'd done it! (Well, *she* did it.) The trendy look inspired me to get through the next half of the surgery.

In thirty minutes, the procedure was repeated on Janette, until we were both more interested in gawking at our new selves in the mirror than in what pain we might endure later. Andrea was pleased, and la señora gave her an approving nod. We thanked Andrea profusely for our transformation and bid them goodbye. Andrea had given Janette and me a small bottle of peroxide, which she said we needed to dab on our ears, as well as moving the earrings back and forth a few times a day. We assured her that we would be diligent, since she warned about infection if her instructions were not followed.

Within an hour, following our well-rehearsed routine for showers, hair, and makeup, we were ready to go on our weekend adventure. Just like clockwork, Oscar, Tito, and Loco came to the door at ten o'clock. We had our sunscreen, lipstick, bottles of water (that la señora had filled, using glass soda bottles she had saved), two changes of clothes, and all our toiletries packed and ready. We greeted them with hugs, as we were now close friends, and it was acceptable. I piled into Oscar's convertible (I trusted his driving most) with Bobby Jean and Janette. Shilo and Margo climbed into the back seat of Tito's 1964 blue Chevy Impala, with Loco riding shotgun. La señora sent us off, saying, "Drive carefully. Be home by ten o'clock Sunday." She chewed her bottom lip and then puffed on her cigarette.

In half an hour, we were leaving the Districto Federal (Federal District, aka Mexico City—the equivalent of our Washington, DC) behind.

Within a half hour, the scenery took on an "old Mexico" postcard appearance—enormous open space, dotted with the figures of boys and girls on donkeys, their mothers walking behind in colorful clothing. They were traveling from one *pueblo* (village) to another, along a dirt path that skirted the highway's shoulder. A few minutes later, we saw groups of goats stumbling along rocky slopes that dropped away from the shoulder, followed close behind by their attentive shepherds. The landscape looked like an enormous brown-suede quilt, appliquéd with bright-green polka-dot cacti. Here and there, a cactus showed off its recently sprouted bright pink or yellow flowers. These were the prickly pear cacti that were so famous in the California deserts.

It was going to be a day full of wonder and anticipation, as we girls talked constantly about what we were about to experience. Oscar had divulged that we would be having la comida at the hacienda, and afterward, we would be treated to a private, "nonviolent" bullfight.

"A bullfight?" I exclaimed. "You're kidding! How could there be a fight without violence?"

All of us were silent, hoping Oscar would provide more consoling information. He and Pato just smiled cunningly, and Oscar said, "You'll see."

We were happy to wait. I secretly wondered if there was a macabre side to Oscar and his friends.

In another hour, after spending most of the time talking back and forth with Oscar and Pato, we became silent as Oscar took his foot off the gas pedal abruptly, and we turned onto a dirt road that obviously had only one destination. In the distance, the only structure in sight was a one-story, sprawling white building with a red-tiled roof. It was surrounded by low stucco walls, topped with black wrought-iron fencing. Huge trees sprouted up within and outside of the walls. As Tito and Loco (close behind us) drove at a slow pace to keep the dust down, I silently hoped that I had judged these guys accurately. *Or are they taking us to a remote place to have their way with us?* I wondered. *This is going to be an overnight trip, after all!* I knew there was no phone, since there were no wires in sight. *Oh God, have we been duped? And what about their surprising us with the bullfight subject only after we were well on our way?*

My worry took a back seat as the building that looked like the size of my thumbnail from the highway grew into what appeared to be one great quadrangular hacienda, just as promised. To the right of it, some distance away, was a white stucco circular structure. It had to be the bullring, but I tried to ignore the subject for now.

As we approached the hacienda, Oscar brought the car to a gentle stop to the right of the enormous wrought-iron gate at the center of the building. He opened his door and hoisted his tall, lanky body out of the car. Pato got out from his side and pulled his seat back so that we could get out. Tito and Loco had pulled up next to us and ushered Shilo and Margo out of the car with their usual gentlemanly comportment. I noticed the mischievous smile on Loco's face as they walked toward us, which heightened my suspicion about what was in store for us.

We walked back to the gate and peered through it. The low walls of the hacienda were white and covered with a chunky texture. The bright sun bouncing off the walls was almost blinding. Someone approached us from the right side of the enclosure, shouting, "Espera, espera por favor!" (Wait, wait, please!) The greeter unlocked the gate, and immediately gave Oscar a masculine hug; then he welcomed us with "Bienvenidos!"

Oscar then introduced each of us to Jorge, who turned out to be Oscar's cousin (and obviously a member of the wealthy family that owned the hacienda).

Jorge led us across the beautiful, wide green lawn area. We all followed him through an archway to the massive wooden door that would finally reveal the interior of the home. But instead, this door led to a beautiful, private garden area with a generous clay-tile patio as the centerpiece. It was such a different configuration but one that I would come to know as the typical hacienda style. Jorge motioned for us to come sit with him on the patio. An enormous, rustic wooden table was elaborately set with colorful plates, rustic blue glasses, and amazing floral arrangements. I quickly estimated that it could seat about fifty people. Giant banana, palm, ficus, and fruit trees surrounded the dining area. A fig tree struggled to keep its bounty from toppling onto the ground. Altogether, the trees formed a giant living curtain around the patio. Tito walked over to one of the trees and picked three pieces of fruit to add to our table arrangement. He called them *guayabas*, which were small yellow fruit. He handed one to me, and I was happy to oblige him. The fruit had a sweet citrus taste. "Muy rica," I exclaimed.

A dark, well-groomed young man wearing a white guayabera asked each of us what we would like to drink. He offered *aguita de limon* (water with a splash of lemon and sugar), tequila, or cerveza *a tiempo* (at room temperature). Since ice, or *hielo*, is not always available in Mexico, Mexicans have acquired a taste for drinking things at room temperature. *Galletas* (crackers), *aceitunas* (green olives), and *queso* (cheese) were laid out on the table. Fresh leaves from the surrounding trees and samples of ripe figs, avocados, and some unfamiliar fruit were placed down the middle.

Oscar stood up and exhibited a suspicious look of mischief. Exuding dramatic intrigue, he announced that his cousin was going to take us to the hacienda's bull pen, where we would get a chance to see some bullfighting. The warm ambiance seemed to vanish. Then, in unison, we shouted, "What?" The notion that we would witness a gory bullfight was ludicrous. Where had their gentlemanly manner gone? The countenance of our hosts had changed to a feigned appearance of nobility and pride (as if there was some challenge in their culture that we Americans would find greatly impressive). They put on somber faces and led us out the front door to the driveway. About two hundred yards away was that white circular wall that we had noticed upon our arrival.

"Now for the real fun!" Pato exclaimed. "We are going to show you the prize bull!"

"Which one of you is going to fight the bull?" I asked. "Who is the *real* macho man?"

Instead of an answer, each of our hosts looked at us with a grin and a coy look.

Outside the ring was a small grandstand. Pato led us over to it, and as we sat down, he said he was going to go get the bull. We were getting excited now. We felt secure behind the tall wall of the bullring, and our view from the top of the grandstand allowed us to view the show from a safe distance. (We could always close our eyes if things got ugly.)

17

A LITTLE BULL

We surmised that the heavy metal gate across the ring was where the bull would appear. Anticipating its debut, we giggled and taunted a yet-to-be-seen bull, full of bravado and confidence. Slowly, a man appeared at the gate. He was bronzed from years in the high-desert sun. Seeming to push with all his strength, he opened one side of the gate and then walked back to the other side and opened it. Another man appeared, leading a horse from the adjacent barn and walking him into the ring. The man mounted the horse and began coaxing him from a relaxed walk to a slow gait. They proceeded around the ring, as if sizing it up for action.

There was a still, quiet pause. Then, without any pomp or circumstance, a young bull came walking through the opened gates, out into the ring. He seemed to be looking for some grass to eat rather than someone to fight.

Shilo surprised us by insisting someone take a photo of her with the bull. With the bull's seemingly naive behavior, she assumed he was more like a puppy than a young bull. I figured she just wanted a trophy picture to take home.

"Well," Oscar said with a quizzical smile, "let me talk to the trainer and see what he thinks."

Oscar came back after talking to the trainer and said that the trainer had agreed. The trainer had worked with some of the most famous bullfighters in Mexico, teaching them the ropes until they were capable of entering the arena with mature bulls. He told Oscar that he had some costumes in the building that were used for dress rehearsals for his students. The latest bullfighter he had trained was now the owner of the previous bull the rancho had housed. This training of the bull and the fighter had been the income-producer for the hacienda, as well as a fun spectator sport for the family's visitors.

Shilo walked with Oscar to the gate of the bullring, where the trainer was waiting to escort her to the room where she could change into one of many costumes. Within fifteen minutes, she appeared at the gate, which the trainer had eased open in order to escort her to a platform to the right. The gateman accompanied them after closing the gate behind them. The bull was on the other side of the arena, still sniffing for grass. He was oblivious and disinterested in the human activity.

Shilo had donned a bright-green bullfighting costume with gold lapels and tight pants. The sun reflected off of the sheen of the satin fabric. She had a huge smile on her face, and it was evident that this was a highlight of her life. With her blonde hair and fair skin, it was easy to imagine that she was a young, world-renown bullfighter from Spain. Calmly, the trainer walked over to the bull and led it slowly over to the platform. Still trying to graze in the powdery dirt, the bull allowed himself to be pulled wherever the trainer wanted him to go. The gatekeeper stood with Shilo until the trainer stepped up on the platform, between Shilo and the bull on the lower ground. Moving slowly to the front of the platform, the gatekeeper took Shilo's camera and snapped several pictures. The trainer then led the bull back to the other side of the arena, and the gatekeeper escorted Shilo out of the gate.

I now was convinced that I had to have a picture with the bull as well. I walked over to the gate where Oscar was applauding Shilo for her bravery. "Hey, I'm next!" I announced with a huge smile.

"Are you sure?" Oscar asked.

"Are you kidding? I'm sure!"

He told me to walk back into the building with Shilo, who would show me the dressing area.

Soon I appeared at the gate, just as Shilo had, wearing a bright-orange costume, similar to the one Shilo had worn. She, however, hadn't noticed the cap or red scarf that hung among the various costumes. I wanted to wear the full regalia of a bullfighter, so I proudly tied the red scarf around my neck and donned the cap at just the perfect angle, as I had seen toreadors on television.

Once again, the gatekeeper opened the gate, took my arm, and escorted me over to the platform for my photo opportunity. Now that I was positioned, the trainer walked over to the bull to go through the same steps he had so confidently taken with Shilo.

But the calm routine quickly changed. The bull, for whatever reason, stared at me and began scraping his hooves into the powdery dust in the arena. I heard him snort as he moved his big head from side to side. The trainer hadn't reached him yet, and the bull came to life like a light bulb had gone off in his head (or more like an electric prod had been shoved into his rump). He lunged forward in a mini-stampede and then rushed toward the platform where I stood, frozen. The gatekeeper and the trainer yelled Spanish expletives at him, but nothing had any effect.

The next thing I knew, the bull had screeched to a halt about eight feet away from me. His nostrils were dripping like rubber hoses and breathing like a giant steam engine. He seemed to have no intention except to quell his curiosity, but that didn't comfort me.

"Get out of there!" yelled Bobby Jean.

"Run!" screamed Shilo.

But I couldn't run. I couldn't move. Instead, I started talking to the bull like I'd talked to my teddy bear when I was ten. "You're such a sweetheart. You wouldn't hurt anybody, would you?"

The bull started scratching the ground again with his front hooves. Evidently, he didn't like hearing a woman's voice. The problem was he wasn't looking at the trainer now—just at me! He lunged a few feet toward me, breathing and snorting deeper and faster. I slowly backed up to compensate for the distance he had gained on me. He took two more steps. I backed up four steps. Now I was off the platform and standing on the arena floor. He took four steps. I backed up eight steps. Now I walked as quickly as I could toward the gate, trying not to appear to be running.

All the while the trainer was trying to come alongside the bull, demanding good behavior. But the bull lunged at me—and then stopped dead in his tracks again! He was slobbering something fierce. I feared moving again, as I expected that he could overcome me in a few seconds if I tried to run. Everyone was yelling a different directive at me. Loco, hanging over the wall to my right, was waving his shirt, trying to distract the bull. But the bull showed no interest in Loco.

The bull scratched at the dirt again, this time with both hooves, which gave me no alternative but to make a run for the gate. I didn't look back, knowing I couldn't afford a split second of pause. My legs were spinning like wheels. I held my breath in sheer terror and pleaded with my grimacing face, "Open the gate!"

Thankfully, Pato and Oscar responded in time. I skidded and fell to the dirt, my body barely inside the gate. In a flash, Oscar pulled me to the side of the gate, and the gatekeeper slammed and latched it. The bull's hooves slid part of the way under the gate, causing it to bang its head on the unyielding gate and career onto its side. Holy cow! (Pardon the pun.) He was finally robbed of his target. The girls, whose giggling had turned to screams, ran over to the gate to help me, but I managed to stand up and found my balance. "Okay!" I said as I paced like a would-be matador. "Yo soy la conquistadora!" (I am the conqueror!) Laughing was all I heard from the "crowd" I thought *I'll show them!*

Like a peacock, I strutted to the dressing room. As I took off the jacket and pants, I thought about the red scarf that was still around my neck; the hat had flown off, of course. "What a well-chosen target!" I said to myself. I had unwittingly put on the very color to which bulls are attracted! After yelling "Stupid," I recovered and told myself I had been very brave. I might not have a photo to show for it, but inside my soul, I stored a great satisfaction!

Half of the group had gone to the waiting cars by the time I came out of the dressing room. Oscar was waiting for me, and as I walked up to him, he took my hand and apologized for the horrifying incident. "I would have never guessed that a baby bull would give you such a terrible time! I have never seen that before, unless people threaten the bull. You didn't do anything to excite him; he was just crazy!"

"No, Oscar, he wanted my scarf," I said. "I don't think anyone thought about the color I chose; we were just going to take photos."

I saw some relief in Oscar's eyes, as he forgave himself for the unforeseen event.

It was getting dark, with the sun setting in the hot pink distance. Pato had the servant bring our suitcases out, and once all was packed, we found our places inside the safe cars. We said our goodbyes and thank-yous to Pato for a second or third time. Oscar started the car. Pato yelled, "Toro!" as Oscar started down the driveway. All that this matador could think of was sleep in San Miguel de Allende at the art institute. It was purportedly a nice, safe retreat, popular with Americans, that we would find more than comfortable.

18

QUAINT SAN MIGUEL DE ALLENDE

The sky was turning a deep blue as we made our way down the dirt road and out to the highway. As rich as our experience had been that day, our talk immediately shifted to our destination: San Miguel de Allende, the "artist's town," as it had been referred to for many years.

I leaned my head against the window in the back seat. The stars were putting on an amazing show against the now black drape of sky. It felt mystical, as if it held more wonders and surprises for us. I looked up at the crescent moon, imagining it was God's thumbnail pressing against the sheer veil of heaven.

The mood inside the car was reverent. Our adventurous spirits had been abundantly fed by the events of the day. Now, just the sweet bliss of reflecting was ours to savor. Soon, the only person who was still awake in the car was Oscar, who was driving, and me. I tried to stay awake to keep him company, but he told me he was fine and that the drive was just one more hour, so I gave in to my exhausted mind and body and fell into a deep sleep.

The next thing I heard was Pato's gentle voice. "Despierten. Estamos aquí!" he whispered. Shyly, he hovered over us from the front seat, trying to wake the sleeping beauties in the back seat. "Despierten, despierten!"

Oscar brought the car to a slow stop, parking in front of the dimly lit art institute. Janette nudged me on my right, sluggishly uttering, "We're here; we're here," as she dug her elbow into my stomach.

"Okay, okay," I groaned. "Wake up, Bobby Jean. "We're in San Miguel."

"Okay," she mumbled.

Somehow we adjusted our minds and bodies and knew we had to break our cozy arrangement and get out of the car. Bobby Jean managed to open her door, allowing the brisk night air to permeate the interior of the car.

Slowly responding to the discomfort, we managed to untangle ourselves and emerge, one by one, bristling at the chill. Oscar patiently waited for all of us to stand up while he and Pato gathered our suitcases from the trunk. Finally, they led us to the entrance of the art institute.

At the front desk, a young man with a pleasant smile welcomed us. After checking us in, Oscar and Tito said their goodbyes, promising to meet us at nine the next morning in the lobby. The young man handed us our keys and led us down the hallway to our rooms. The first room had only one double bed, but Bobby Jean and I were used to being mashed together in our cramped dorm room. We thanked the young man for carting our bags from the lobby, and we managed to pull a few pesos out of our pockets to show our appreciation.

"You take that side," I said to Bobby Jean. "I'll take the side against the wall. Just don't kick me!"

Margo, Shilo, and Janette walked with the attendant to the next room, which had one double and one twin bed. Within a quarter hour, our rooms were quiet except for gentle snoring. The night was kind to us, providing us with safe, warm beds and the sleep we craved. Many dreams would drift above our heads that night. It was the perfect intermission.

Morning came. A misty light entered through the muslin curtains that draped the windows of our room. I reluctantly raised my eyelids just enough to confirm its source. I reached for my watch on the nightstand and managed to focus on its face. It was seven o'clock. I was glad to wake early, as I always enjoyed having time to myself in the morning. With a cup of hot, creamy coffee and a writing pad, I was in my glory.

This morning was no different. I tossed off the covers, quietly got up in my comfy flannel pajamas, stepped into my fuzzy slippers, and was almost ready for a writing session in San Miguel de Allende. Before I could write, however, I had to get that creamy coffee. I quietly opened the door and padded down the hall to the front desk.

"Buenos días, señorita," the young woman behind the front desk said cheerfully.

"Buenos días!" I reciprocated.

"Con que puedo servirle?" she said, asking how she might serve me.

When I asked where I might find a cup of coffee, she sweetly directed me to a table to the side of the desk with coffee, milk, and fruit, saying, "Acá, a la izquierda está una mesa con leche, café y fruta. Provecho!"

With a "muchas gracias" to her, I went to the table, and in no time, I was back in the room with my creamy coffee and fruit and comfortably seated at the desk under the window with my writing tablet. Bobby Jean was still sound asleep. I looked over the brochure that the housekeeping crew had positioned on the dresser. I learned that this quaint colonial town was established in 1542. Over the centuries, it served as a military outpost and was named for Ignacio Allende, a hero of Mexico's War of Independence. As time passed, it became simply a tiny village made up of humble peasants, with farming on a small scale, and it was left to languish. But after World War II, it took on a new importance. An old convent in the town, determined to take advantage of its cultural position, offered art courses and lodging for veterans from the United States to study pre-Columbian and colonial art within its restored walls. The historical site was transformed into a respectable art institute in 1960. It became a home away from home for thousands of visitors over several decades. It hosted artists from a multitude of foreign countries. Now, it was richly appointed with amenities of the highest standards. The sculptures, historical artifacts, and colorful, handmade textile hangings along its walls spoke of many world cultures that had commingled here and enriched the quaint town's history. The artwork had been donated to the center as a testimony to the international friendship that had been engendered there. While art whetted the spending appetites of the elites who vacationed in the town, the local cuisine whetted their developing taste for Mexican food. My stomach reminded me that I would soon be ready for breakfast at the local restaurant that Oscar had told us about, but my writing session was the morning's first activity, so my appetite would have to take a siesta for now.

As I began to write, my eyes were distracted by a flickering of color outside. An orange monarch butterfly was flitting around the edge of the window, seeming to celebrate the morning light. I wondered how many hundreds of miles it had flown down the butterfly corridor from Canada; I assumed it was the second generation on that journey. It would end its sojourn in Michoacán, in southern Mexico, where it would lay its eggs and start another generation.

As the butterfly continued to flutter from flower to flower, I finished jotting down the events of yesterday, one of the most amazing days of my life.

Bobby Jean remained in a deep sleep. I knew there was just enough time left for us to get ready for the day, so when I finished writing, I patted her shoulder. "Despierta! Despierta, Bobby Jean! We only have forty-five minutes before our escorts will be here."

They had committed us to a morning walking tour of San Miguel, followed by breakfast at their favorite spot.

"Oh-kay-uh!" Bobby Jean grumbled. "Give me a minute to wake up!"

"Okay, while you wake up, I'll go wake up Margo and the others."

"I'll be ready in time; don't worry!" she assured me.

After knocking on our neighbors' door several times, I heard them shout back at me with the same grumbling. I crept back to my room and stepped into the shower. Bobby Jean went to get a cup of coffee and then took her shower, and we left our room exactly forty-five minutes later. I called it synchronized showering.

We quickly walked to the lobby, where our partners in crime were waiting. Our chaperones arrived within five minutes; they had stayed at a separate hotel a couple of blocks away. "Buenos días!" we greeted each other. And we were off to savor the town.

The sun was already drenching the quiet village with its warm, golden rays. Like a stalk of corn reaching to the sky, I stopped for a moment to stretch my arms up. It was glorious! Oscar had told us there was a great café just a few blocks from the art center that we gringas needed to experience. I wondered what he meant by that, but the answer would have to wait awhile.

The town's streets were paved with rustic cobblestones and brick. It seemed that almost every street led up to a hill. The intrigue led us to discover its nooks and crannies and cultural richness. We walked along a narrow, rustic residential street. As in Cuernavaca, each cozy yet ample home front was differentiated only by a distinct color that defined where one home started and the next began. Most of these concrete façades had a symbol of welcome at their door. Custom-made, hand-painted tiles were hung with words such as *Bienvenidos* (Welcome), *Que Dios les Bendiga* (May God Bless You), and *Mi Casa es Su Casa* (My House Is Your House). The sunny colors of bleached terra cotta, turquoise, coral, maize, and sienna brown were strewn together like a patchwork quilt that was stretched to fit each block.

In the next block, we came upon a hole-in-the-wall *tortillería* (tortilla factory). It had just opened its iron gate that guarded it during the night. We loitered in the immediate area until the tortilla machine began to press and bake its special *maza* into Mexico's answer to bread— hot, thin, tender rounds of melt-in-your-mouth pleasure. The steamy aroma of freshly ground corn, kissed by a hot grill, was more than we could stand. The tortillas were sumptuous. With some calories to burn now, we walked up a steep block to a produce shop. Inside, a maid wearing a well-pressed white apron lugged a woven nylon bag, called a *bolsa*, that was almost as big as she was. It was full of fruits and multicolored vegetables that had been delivered that morning. She was short in stature, but she carried herself with confidence, and her serious, expressionless face said she could do it all. Eager to find the freshest and tastiest of the lot for the family she served, she had arrived the minute the iron curtain was opened. Her hair was blue-black and shiny. It was parted with precision down the middle of her head, revealing her well-scrubbed scalp. She had arranged it into two perfect braids that hung in front of her shoulders and all the way down to her waist.

I thought, *Whew! Washing, combing, and parting that hair just one time would cause me to chop it off.*

The next item on Oscar's agenda was the Cathedral of San Miguel. The narrow streets of the town radiated out from the *Jardín Principal* (Central Garden), beckoning visitors to discover what lay beyond. Oscar motioned us forward along one of the streets, and very soon the majestic spires of the gothic cathedral came into view; they dominated the skyline. We were enthralled with the rustic beauty of this centuries-old edifice. Inside, the solemnity was rescued by the beauty of the ceiling and the elegant altar. The lavish marble glistened, and the figures of Christ and his angels looked down on us with forgiving gestures from above, as we silently walked down the aisle like pilgrims on a mission. Full of wonder—and a modicum of guilt, perhaps—we made a turn at the altar and went outside, where the fresh morning air brought us back to our true desire—adventure!

We ambled up two more blocks of enchanting neighborhood homes and arrived at the café that Oscar had promised. Its entrance stood about thirty feet back from the street, with beautiful palms and tropical plants forming an arbor over the stone walkway that led to the entrance. Magnificent scents of sautéed onion and chiles hung in the air. Something wonderful was being prepared ... and we were ready to eat it.

The headwaiter welcomed us as we approached the opened doorway. "Bienvenidas!" rolled off his tongue with genuine delight. "Estamos a sus órdenes!" (We are at your service!)

We knew this was not an ordinary café.

He seated us in front of an open window at the back of the modest-sized interior. We had passed the immaculate, colorfully tiled kitchen as we entered the dining room. The attention to detail in the café was noticeable immediately: The tan tile flooring was inlaid with an attractive pattern of mosaic tiles, obviously a replica of some ancient cultural artifact. Loco explained that it was the Aztecan calendar. The headwaiter explained in Spanish (which Loco then translated for us) that the Aztecan calendar was created in the twelfth century. According to the Aztecs, the world was always in a delicate equilibrium due to a spiritual war between the gods. Without the calendar, the world would come to an end.

Loco, his eyes animated with a dramatic, sinister glare, told us that because of that calendar, hearts were ripped out of sacrificial men, virgins were dropped into one hundred pits that led to underground caves and rivers (*cenotes*), children were buried alive, and women were beaten!

"Well," I said, "the gods must have really been hungry!" I laughed a rather nervous laugh, and the others timidly followed. I brushed aside the horrific visions that had been conjured up in my mind and reeled myself back into the much-more-pleasant present. (Little did I know that I would read about the sun god *Tonatiuh*—and many others—in my anthropology class just a couple of weeks later. Loco was right!)

The dining room was a tropical delight. The chattering of parrots outside the open window drew our immediate interest. We stretched our necks to capture a glimpse of the choir. We were enchanted. Bright red-and-blue parrots, yellow-and-green macaws, and blue-and-green cockatiels sang and talked as if they were carrying on a political convention. We were practically sitting in an aviary (well shielded from any indiscretion that may have befallen us). What a paradise!

We read the menus, and Oscar explained all of the various offerings. One of the items intrigued me. I asked Oscar how to pronounce it. He indulged me with a phonetic version of *chilaquiles* (*chee*-lah-*kee*-les). The idea sounded great: toasted tortilla strips mixed together with scrambled eggs, then topped with a mild green salsa and sprinkled with *queso fresco* (a fresh, white grated cheese). I placed my order, along with the others, stumbling a bit over *chilaquiles,* and we began sipping our *aguitas* (aw-*wee*-tahs—flavored waters). In Mexico, the water has to be boiled to make it safe to drink, but the taste of boiled water is not very appetizing. Thus, Mexicans everywhere have learned how to make their water drinking a pleasant experience.

The cooled boiled water is poured into a pitcher. Whatever fruit on hand is then used fresh or cooked (depending on the type of fruit), then mashed, strained, and/or squeezed to render its delicious flavor. The clear liquid is then added to water with some *azúcar* (sugar). There were a variety of flavored waters, we learned. *Jamaica* (ha-*mike*-uh—the flower of the hibiscus plant), for example, is dried and boiled; then the liquid is strained from the boiled juice. Sugar is added, and the mixture is stirred well and then refrigerated. *Limones* (limes) are squeezed and the seeds are strained out; then the juice is sweetened with sugar. For *horchata*, white rice is boiled, and the milky liquid is reserved and then sweetened with sugar. Guava (a small yellow fruit) is seeded and mashed in a sieve, producing a juice. Bottled water can be added to thin the juice, but no sugar is needed.

Before we were able to laugh sufficiently about the happenings of the previous day, our platters arrived. They were brimming, bubbling, and exuding the fragrances that had lured us into the dining room when we first arrived. "Mmm" was all that I could utter.

"Wow!" blurted Margo.

"This is incredible!" Janette exclaimed, as her plate was set before her.

Bobby Jean was silent. Her lack of joining in with our exclamations drew our attention. She was staring down at her plate, motionless. As we looked at her plate, we understood her reaction. She had ordered something on her own, without asking for a description of the dish. What she was served was a black, thick "goo" that oozed across her plate ... with chewy chunks the size of large corn kernels under it. A side of white rice and diced green chiles were the only discernible menu items.

"Oh, that looks interesting," I said, hoping to sound optimistic.

Bobby Jean grimaced. "Looks like black lumpy gravy!"

Oscar rescued the moment. "That is *huitlacoche*, an Aztecan dish. It is a delicacy. It's made from corn that has—how do you say... rotted."

All of us, being gringas from our heads to our toes, wailed at the same time.

"*What?*"

"Yuk!"

"Why didn't you tell her what she was ordering?"

"Why would someone want to eat rotten corn?" Janette asked. "That's disgusting!"

Oscar bit his lip. He was such a gentleman. In his dependable way, he gestured to our waiter and asked him to exchange Oscar's plate for Bobby Jean's. It was done with much calm and class, and in a flash, Bobby Jean had a plate of scrambled eggs with chiles, warm tortillas, and frijoles (beans) on the side. Oscar thanked Bobby Jean several times for giving him the occasion to eat his "favorite" Mexican dish. Chivalry was not dead!

Our stomachs were full, and our minds were full of wonderful memories. We would cherish those memories for the rest of our lives; I was certain.

Oscar and Tito escorted us to their cars, and we reluctantly accepted that it was time to return home. The three-hour drive was a quiet one, as each of us had enjoyed every moment *a todo dar* (to the utmost), and the sweet feeling of joyful peace overcame us all. Some napping was sneaked in, and the next thing I knew, Oscar was coaxing us awake and escorting us to the door of la a señora's house.

With lazy hugs, we bid farewell to our hosts, thanking them, as always, for an extraordinary adventure. We quietly crept up to our rooms for much needed sleep.

19

CLASSES AND STRANGERS

The first day of classes began with a lot of chaos at the Castillo house, as we all tried to get ready at the same time. We gringas required hours to prepare for the day. Five showers, hair drying, application of makeup, dressing, enduring Maria's breakfast, and gathering our supplies for the day was not an easy accomplishment (with limited bathrooms and Maria's attitude). Finally, at eight o'clock, we scrambled down to the front door and came to a screeching halt as we spotted la señora blocking the door, with her arms crossed in front of her.

Gee, what a surprise, I thought with a sneer.

La señora had already talked to us about the dangers that might await us on the long bus trip to the university. She had drilled us about how to get to the school. First, we were to walk to La Reforma (where we'd had our shopping spree, two blocks away). Then we were to wait at the corner for a city bus that would have number twenty-three on it. Next, we were to find a place to sit down on the bus that appeared safe. We all looked at her quizzically.

She continued without acknowledging our confused stares. "It will be impossible to sit together. All types of people take the city buses," she warned. "There are beggars and thieves on the bus. "Just keep your purses and book bags close to you, and get off at the university stop. It will be obvious, as the bus always stops at the university, year-round. Be sure none of you miss this stop!"

The idea of being left alone on the bus and ending up in an unknown place was horrifying to us. Without further discussion and with frustrated grimaces on our faces, we fled out the door, fast-walking to La Reforma. The morning was cool, although we knew the afternoon would be around seventy-five degrees. It was so much like Southern California weather. I felt very much at home. The altitude, however, placed a burden on our lungs, and we panted for oxygen. We were reminded that the city was one mile high, forcing us to slow our pace. We were entertained along the way, thankfully, by the various vendors along the sidewalks and streets, shouting their special advertising slogans in the city of entrepreneurs.

We arrived at our bus stop right on time. Within five minutes, bus number twenty-three came rumbling along. La señora was right: it appeared to be full to the brim with a motley crew of every level of society. We climbed up the stairs and handed our centavos to the driver. I was the first to head down the narrow aisle. I walked toward the back, passing people with chickens on their laps and past some of the more desirable open seats, in consideration of my roommates. The last open seat available to me was, as luck would have it, next to an old man with a young pig on his lap in a wooden crate. I thought, *Well, at least the pig won't glare at me, or beg for money, or steal my wallet.* I was correct, except that once the bus started rolling, an old lady dressed in a dirty long dark skirt and blouse crept up from behind me in the aisle on her knees. Just as she came into my field of vision, she stopped her crawl, turned to me, and began begging, just as La Señora had warned.

"Por favor, unos pesos por mis hijos?" (Please, some money for my children?) She pleaded in the most dramatically rehearsed way, holding her hands out to me, as if praying, and saying something to the effect of "Please. I have no food. Please. I need money. Please. My children need clothes."

Remembering la a señora's words about beggars on the buses, I was puzzled. Had she been warning us against them, or was she telling us we would need to give the beggars a peso or two? I rummaged around in my purse, looking for my wallet. Then I remembered that I had asked Bobby Jean to put my wallet in her purse, which was bigger than mine. But she was sitting at the front of the bus.

I looked away from the woman, hoping she would move on, but she had zeroed in on *me*. I was an American woman, who, she likely assumed, had money. I decided to stand up for myself. "No tengo dinero." (I don't have any money.) I enunciated carefully as I looked her in the eye with sincerity but firmness. Surely she would be overwhelmed with embarrassment and let up. Wrong! This made her even more determined. I wasn't about to explain (nor could I have done so in Spanish very well) that I *didn't* have my money with me. Bobby Jean was at the front of the bus, and I had a stack of books on my lap.

Much to my dismay, she struggled to a standing position, looking very pathetic, and held on to the back of my seat. She started yelling hideous things at me so that the whole bus could hear. "Hija del Diablo!" (Child of the devil!) "Que bárbara mujer!" (What a lousy excuse for a woman—or something equivalent to that).

My face flushed. This was close to unbearable.

I wasn't about to give in to her and let her have her way. I put my purse over my shoulder, bundled my books into my arms, and got up as the bus swayed from side to side down the highway. I tried to hang on to the seat backs with one hand as I struggled up the aisle to where Bobby Jean was seated.

"Hey, move over as much as you can. I've got a beggar stalking me."

Bobby Jean quickly moved as much as she could, but it only allowed me about four inches of space to totter on the edge of the seat. Fortunately, the old woman must have decided that maneuvering fifteen feet farther was not worth it, and she ended the whole ordeal with seemingly the loudest voice a woman her age could conjure up: "Eres una puta Americana! Vaya al diablo!" (You are a [expletive] American! Go to hell!)

She's a tough little thing, I comforted myself. *She's survived all these years before I came along. She'll make it another day.*

My introduction to my classes that day was interesting: ethics, cultural anthropology, and "Five Hundred Years of Mexican History." I was intrigued by the American teachers. I figured they must be having a great time in Mexico, while they were obviously serious about academics. I, on the other hand, was a novice and not quite sure I could pull off the same balancing act as they did. There was a formidable conflict of interest in my cultural adventure—studying seemed so counter-intuitive to the omnipresence of the partying opportunities around me. I half-heartedly promised myself I would go through the rigors of school, studying at night, and attending classes during the day. But the partying and playing tourist were *not* going to be missed.

The first week went by quickly, with long bus trips, all-day classes on Monday and Wednesday, and trying to get organized. I managed to get enough sleep in between the chaos. We all had good experiences, except Janette, who fell off the last step of the bus on Friday on the Reforma and skinned her knees quite badly. Fortunately, she was with Shilo when it happened, and with no broken bones, they made it home. She lay in bed the rest of the day, knowing the Get Acquainted dance would begin at seven the next night. Shilo let us know that she was going *without* Gerardo. She said it was the "right thing to do." We all wondered what was up. Was she cooling her heels or just wanting to be a part of our group as much as possible? I hoped for the latter.

To my complete surprise, a good-looking guy in my Mexican history class asked me to go to the dance with him. He had been living in the city all summer with a host family in a Jewish neighborhood and had the use of their car. He was also Jewish.

I thought, *How odd—a Jewish neighborhood in Mexico*, but I would later learn of the large population of Jews in Mexico, the result of a large immigration from the 1930s and early '40s, during the Hitler years in Europe. I felt smug when I told my roommates that I had a date, since no one else did.

Saturday morning finally came. All of my roommates (not to mention myself) were eager to pull out the treasures from our girls'-day-out shopping spree two weeks ago to wear to the dance that night. We had done some extra shopping the prior week for makeup and other essentials. I had bought an inexpensive Mexican cologne that was a bit heavy, but didn't Mexico warrant something provocative? We spent about three hours getting ready—hair dryers buzzing, nails being polished, nylons being checked for runs.

I had told la señora on Friday that I had a date who was taking me to the dance. I knew the rules and wasn't about to break any. We were to request permission to leave the house at all times, and we were to notify la señora with whom we would be leaving. My date, Michael, arrived right on time at seven o'clock. When the doorbell rang, I hurried down to meet him, but la señora beat me to it. She answered the door immediately and abruptly said, "Michael?"

"Yes," he replied.

She immediately asked for his address and phone number and grabbed a pencil and a piece of paper from a table near the door. She wrote furiously as Michael obediently gave his information to her. But it wasn't over with that. She then told both of us to follow her upstairs while she called his host family and inquired about his attendance at the university. Michael had turned red when she first questioned him. But la señora dismissed his chagrin, her hands on her bony hips, elbows jutting out at her sides, as she glared at him with self-appointed authority.

To drive her point home, she made the phone call a public event. The girls were all sitting in the area upstairs outside the dormer. They were giggling, which didn't help my already horrified state. I wondered what Michael was thinking as he reached the top of the stairs and saw this audience. How humiliating!

Finally, after what seemed an eternity, la señora said, "Gracias, muy bien," and hung up the phone. She obviously had satisfied her suspicious mind that this was indeed Michael's host family, as she then gave the person my name and her phone number and address.

I was actually glad, though embarrassed, since she was the only person in Mexico City who was responsible for my safety. Establishing the legitimacy of any callers was a good thing, I decided, and I appreciated it.

We were "released on our own recognizance" and went gladly down the stairs and out the door. Michael, a gentleman, opened the car door for me, and off we went. The rest of the girls waited for the taxi that la señora had called from her prescribed taxi company.

The house where the party was being hosted was a half mile away. As we approached the address, we saw a white Greek-revival style façade, with imposing columns and a portico. It appeared to be a small replica of the White House. I imagined it probably was owned by a prominent law firm or other corporate entity and used to host upscale parties and political events related to American cultural, educational, and business affairs. UNAM was a well-respected institution, and the use of this building was certainly in line with that respect.

We were greeted at the door by ushers who took our invitation (as proof that we were, in fact, invited) and gestured us to a room to our left where we could sign in. Just inside the room was a long table with several people sitting behind it. They were some of the professors at the university. We smiled as they introduced themselves. One of them was my Mexican history teacher, Ms. Alvarez. She and I had a short but congenial conversation, and I found out that she was married to a Mexican citizen she had met when she attended UNAM. She was originally from Wisconsin. *Wow,* I thought, *She's a long way from home.* She said that she had lived in Mexico for two years and was loving it; I was envious. She warned that Mexican history would take a lot of memorization, since there had been something like fifty leaders in as many years.

I thought, *Well, I'll try to fit that into my social schedule.*

She stamped our right hands with the date—"Sep 12, 1966"—and ushered us on.

Michael led me into the huge ballroom area with a wooden floor and speakers, set up for dancing. A small crowd was at the bar across the floor. A friend of his caught up with us in the line, and in a few minutes, my roommates walked up to us. As we waited for our drinks, we looked around the room to check out the opportunities. Michael was a nice guy, but from my perspective, we fit more in the classification of friends than special interest.

As I panned the enormous space, I saw an array of blondes, brunettes, and even a redhead making small talk in little groups. The expensive suits and dresses of the crowd mimicked a scene I imagined taking place in Newport Beach. It was incongruous, but I reminded myself that Mexico City was modern and cosmopolitan.

Michael handed me my drink with a big smile and said he'd ordered me a large margarita. The drink was new to me, so I asked what it was made of.

He quickly gave me the ingredients: "Tequila, a liqueur called Cointreau, and lime juice."

It was full of ice, and I took a sip. "Wow! That's delicious! It tastes like limeade."

Of course, it wasn't limeade, and I learned very soon that it was a potent intoxicant. Michael couldn't believe I'd never had one. "Well," I said, "I haven't really had that much experience with tequila. In the States, most people drink beer or wine I think."

Before we had a chance to get into conversation, the music started. *Am I in Orange County, California?* I thought—the song, "You'll Be Gone," was by Elvis. It had a Spanish sound, though, one I had never heard. I was stunned. For some reason, I had expected Mexican music in Mexican restaurants and clubs.

A dark, handsome Mexican guy in a pale-blue dress shirt and black dress pants walked up to me and asked me to dance. His voice was melodiously deep, like a sophisticated radio announcer. His milk chocolate–colored face set off his symmetrical, handsome white smile that was as wide as a Cheshire cat's. He was about five foot eight—just right for me—with a perfect body, obviously very fit.

"Uh, well, uh … I'm with someone," I stammered.

He panned the room from right to left and flirtatiously responded with a grin, "I don't see anyone."

"Oh, well, uh … okay," I stammered again. (Michael had left me standing there; what was a girl to do?)

"My name is Carlos," he said in perfect English, as he bowed slightly.

"Uh, I'm Collette."

With a glimmer in his deep-brown eyes, he offered his left arm, bent at the elbow. In a very pathetic attempt, my better judgment did not win. My hand encircled his arm without hesitation. He led me gently but firmly out to the dance floor.

We began dancing to the slow rhythm of the music. My knees felt weak, but I was at the same time fortified by adrenaline; my heart was beating rapidly. It was a brief encounter, as the music stopped within just a few minutes. I started to pull away from Carlos, but he gently stopped me, just a few inches from his body, as a new song resonated from the speakers. I was so drawn to him. The cool air from the ceiling fans lifted the edges of my silky dress against my legs, helping to cool my electrified body. The song was a fast-paced rock-and-roll song called "Do You Believe in Magic?" by the Lovin' Spoonful. I thought, *I do now!*

He displayed his magnetic smile again, and we began to pick up the beat of the music in a synchronized back and forth. He lifted his right arm like a bridge, and I floated under it to complete a turn. I came back to face him as our hands came together again. This was definitely magic! His confidence felt so warm and secure. My heart and mind felt they were right where they were destined to be. We danced as if we had been trained together. He was, hands down, the best dancer I'd ever danced with.

The records kept playing, one after another—fast songs, slow songs, sad songs, happy songs. It was like being back in California, dancing at the community dance hall near my high school, or at the Rendezvous dance pavilion in Newport Beach. All the familiarity brought me such a comfortable feeling. Carlos and I walked over to the bar for a break. He ordered a drink for each of us, and we found an unoccupied corner of the reception room. We sat down, both glad to rest awhile. I welcomed the chance to talk more intimately, but the lights began to blink, signaling that the party was coming to a close.

Where is Michael, my date? I thought. I hadn't seen him since I'd met Carlos. I thought I'd better go find him and at least get a ride back home. I was sure he would be mad as hell, but I still hoped for common decency.

Carlos walked with me. We found Michael. He was clearly drunk, near a corner of the room that was filled with girls.

I told Carlos, "I need to find a ride. He's definitely not capable of driving me, and I need to get back to the house before midnight."

Carlos immediately comforted me. "Don't worry. I will take you home. Let me introduce you to my friend, Felipe. I came to the party with him. He is a perfect gentleman, as I am," he added, with a grin that mimicked the style of an honorable caballero.

I thought, "His sincere smile, his obviously educated mind, his well-pressed look, his skill in dancing—this is no different than the US." I trusted my new acquaintance with all the faith that I would put in any young man in my own hometown. *Step out, young woman! You're free, remember? Fly!*

Carlos introduced me to Felipe. They each removed their licenses from their wallets to show me that they were legitimately who they said they were. They offered to call la señora to request that they be able to drive me home.

"Oh, no! You can't do that! She would never allow such an arrangement! I trust you to take me; it's okay."

They showered me with kindnesses. "We will take special care with you. You will arrive safely at your home in Roma. Don't worry; we live nearby and know the area where you're living."

Fortunately, my instinct was sound, and I was driven home in Felipe's car, a nice late-model Chevrolet, nicely kept. We arrived in five minutes. Carlos helped me out of the car and walked me up to the black wrought-iron gate at the Castillos' house. He accompanied me through the gate and up the walk to the front door. He stopped before the door and, reaching around my waist, kissed me tenderly on my cheek. I was lit from inside like a light bulb, tingling in every pore of my body. A feeling of elation gripped me as I fought the urge to embrace him. Fearing that la señora would open the door at any moment, I whispered, "I'd better get inside."

"Did I do something wrong?" he asked.

"Uh, no," I responded. "I just have to be inside by midnight."

"Well," he said, "I just had the best night of my life, and I hope you did too."

"Oh, yes! Yes, it was wonderful!" I said as I leaned toward the side of the doorway and pressed the bell. "I am so glad I met you, and I am really thankful that you drove me home. The whole night was great!"

"Well," he said, "can I call you in the morning?"

"Of course!" I eagerly said and gave him my phone number. As he stepped back, la señora abruptly opened the door, stepped out on to the top step where I was standing, and stared first at Carlos and then right at me. Her disapproving face grimaced under the glow of the overhead light fixture. As she saw Carlos, she realized that he was *not Michael*. "Who is this!" she demanded.

"Uh, this is Carlos," I said. "He brought me home from the dance."

"Come inside!" she ordered with uncontrolled anger. As I stepped into the house, la señora, without a word, slammed the door on Carlos. Her action was more than stern. I fast-paced it up to my room, hearing her heels stomping on the stairs right behind me. I made it to my room, where Bobby Jean was already in bed. La señora didn't show any regard for our privacy as she jumped inside the door and started raving in Spanish at me. I was able to figure out enough of her words to know that she was livid. "You will be put on probation from leaving this house except for classes if you ever come home with a stranger again! Your contract gives me the right to cancel your residency if you disobey the rules. You are not to go out with any strangers. I must meet and approve of anyone that you leave with or return with at all times. I am more than disappointed with you. If this happens again, I will call your parents!" I was smart enough to be silent. I knew that telling her that my date was too drunk to drive would just add to her case against me. Whether it was true or a quickly contrived alibi, she would have found it a lack of good judgment on my part. I resolved, in the face of the obvious threat, never to leave the house (or return to the house) with *anyone* la señora didn't know, from that point forward.

20

A STRANGER NO MORE

Carlos called the next morning, just as he said he would. La señora's oldest daughter, Cuca, took his call. It was a nice change to be told, *with a smile*, that the phone was for me. It was thrilling to hear his voice.

"Do you have plans for the day?" he asked. "If not, I would like to take you to Chapultepec Park to visit the Museo Nacional de Antropología de Mexico [the National Anthropology Museum of Mexico] and have lunch on the park grounds."

"I've heard how incredible the park is," I said. Bobby Jean had showed me the brochures she'd brought home. With my keen interest in Mexican culture, I had decided the museum was a big must-see priority for me. "Of course! I'd love to go."

He wanted to come for me at eleven, but I knew it would be like pouring salt into an open wound if I asked la señora for permission to go with him. Wisely, I told him I would have to meet him there. I decided to ask Bobby Jean if she would go with me—she was going to visit her brother that morning, who was a sophomore at UNAM and rented a room not far from the park. Carlos was taken aback, but I explained, and he agreed that it wasn't worth la a señora's wrath. As luck would have it, Bobby Jean was happy to accommodate me.

I was in my glory! I picked through all of my clothes for the perfect outfit. I settled on a straight black skirt and a pale-blue top with a scooped neck. I took extra time with my hair, making sure every hair was in place before spraying it to keep its round, puffy shape and the flip on the ends. My makeup was painstakingly applied, and the final result was a young woman of confidence, eager to experience Mexico with a perfect Mexican date.

Bobby Jean and I told la señora that we were both going to the museum, and she called for a taxi for us. She was fine with this idea, since she trusted Bobby Jean implicitly (if not me).

On the ride to Chapultepec, Bobby Jean asked all kinds of questions about Carlos. I realized that she was a bit jealous and was hoping that he had a friend for *her*. I told her I would pry a bit during our date and come back with the name of at least one eligible prospect for her.

When we arrived at the curb in front of the museum, I saw Carlos waiting on the steps at the entrance. My heart almost jumped out of my mouth. It took several seconds for me to regain my composure—he was more handsome than the night before. He was wearing a crisp, long-sleeved white shirt with a button-down collar and jeans. I admired his skin even more in the sunlight. His hands and forearms were muscular and spoke of a guy who was dedicated to honing a strong physique. *He looks proud as a peacock*, I mused, *and if he were a peacock, he would surely shake his feathers right now.* He smiled at me with that same warm smile from the night before, strong evidence that the day held great promise. He gave Bobby Jean a formal handshake, saying, "Nice to see you again." As she left with a goodbye smile, he took my hand. "I'm so glad to see you. This is going to be a great day!" He led me to the cave-like entrance to the museum. We walked by a huge stone image of the face of an Aztecan god, and Carlos opened the door for me. He bought our tickets, and I felt so taken care of as he again took my hand and guided me into the main hall that led to the exhibits.

As we began our tour of the museum, I felt that Carlos had *invented* Mexico. He seemed to know the history of every artifact, adding his opinion about why history evolved the way it had in Mexico. He was my personal tour guide, and I wouldn't have wanted anyone else in the world. I felt a part of the culture just by virtue of his closeness to me, as if he was validating that I belonged there. He seemed to feel an intimate pleasure in observing my surprise and delight at each exhibit we viewed. He demonstrated a true love of his country.

We finally emerged from the museum two hours later. The daylight was startling at first, but our eyes quickly became accustomed to the fact that the day was still young. We continued our grand tour of Chapultepec Park. It was much larger than I had expected. Carlos explained that the name Chapultepec was derived from the Nahuatl word for Grasshopper Hill.

"You'll probably be learning about this in your Mexican history class," he said, "because the park also contains the Chapultepec Palace, which was home to Ferdinand and Carlota Maximilian, the emperor and empress of Mexico from Habsburg, Germany, from 1864 to 1867."

About three blocks away was an amusement park. Carlos insisted we give it a try. Shortly, we were riding the Ferris wheel and were elevated to an uncomfortable height for me. But I got used to the altitude each time we crested the highest point as I took in the incredible vistas of the park and the surrounding city. Carlos pointed out the neighborhood where he lived, trying to identify his house among the buildings. "I will take you to my house one day soon," he assured me.

As our ride ended, Carlos suggested we try the whirling saucers mounted on an undulating platform. I was game, of course. We spun up and down and around like high school kids on a crazy weekend. I felt I was still spinning as I stood at the end of the ride and attempted to step down from the platform. Carlos noticed my struggle and offered his hand to steady me. I took it gladly, and we walked together off the ramp and out of the fun zone.

To settle our stomachs, Carlos suggested that we eat lunch at a *fonda* (a small, informal café) set up under a gigantic shade tree not far from us. Settling ourselves at a brightly painted table for two, a pretty young waitress came to take our order, asking, "Que van a querer?"

We both opted for a *torta* (sandwich) of *pabo y queso* (turkey and cheese) and a Coke. We found ourselves staring at each other as we ate, trying hard not to blush. The warm feelings we both experienced were becoming very strong, and I shuddered to think of where it would take us.

When our stomachs were satisfied, we got up and walked across the park to the zoo, an afterthought on Carlos's part but one that he insisted we act on. "I haven't been to the zoo since I was a child," he said. "I want to see what has changed." Hand in hand, we walked over to the entrance. Inside, we seemed to float amid the various species of animals. I was feeling more and more as if I was in paradise. Carlos broke my musing when he looked at his watch and announced that it was five o'clock.

We left the zoo grounds and headed to Lago Mayor (the Big Lake), which Carlos said was just a ten-minute walk away. On our route was a wide, long granite promenade lined with tall, imposing statues of famous people, posed proudly in their bronze clothing. Among them were singers and composers who had contributed to Mexico's rich musical history. Carlos was intimately familiar with each one. "My father has always loved music," he said, "and my entire family enjoys classical Mexican ballads, as well as American music of all genres."

As we approached the lake, we saw families strolling along the sidewalk that skirted the shore, as children preceded them on bicycles and tricycles. Dogs pulled on leashes, wanting to be released so they could dive into the lake to fetch what other dogs were chasing—their owners were casting sticks and balls out into the cool water. As we completed our walk around the perimeter of the lake, we made our way out to the boulevard that cut through the park.

Small traffic circles were accented with large, tall statues of angels, political figures, and beautiful fountains, reminding everyone that Mexico was a country where politics, the Catholic faith, and a reverence for beauty coexisted. After our all-day excursion, the only equivalent to Chapultepec Park that I could conjure up was the Smithsonian promenade in Washington, DC, Central Park in New York, and Griffith Park in Los Angeles, all rolled together!

But unlike most famous American parks, this park was not lavishly appointed with exotic plants and fountains, nor was it perfectly groomed. This lack of meticulous attention gave it more character and warmth, a broader sense of the Mexican culture. No one had attempted to groom it, to sterilize it, to control every blade of grass, as in the US. Rather, it was allowed to reflect the attitude of the Mexican people in general: live and let live. The warm brown faces that smiled at us as we walked by, the happy chatter of the Spanish language floating on the gentle breezes, and the brilliant orange sunset that was now performing for us all made ours the perfect day for a budding romance. The six hours we spent there were the true beginning of my love relationship with Mexico and my complete and utter entrance into life as a woman in love.

Walking back toward the area where Carlos had parked his car, I realized that all day Carlos had made it a point to walk on the outside of the sidewalk. If I happened to somehow switch places with him as we talked or made room for others walking toward us, he would gently maneuver me back to the inside, explaining that he was there to protect me from any offensive person or an out-of-control car. I had never experienced chivalry. The comforting feeling of being protected enchanted me. In California, we girls were on our own.

We arrived at his little Datsun—it was sporty, and it spoke of fun and good times. Carlos opened the door for me before he got in. He pressed an audio tape into the tape player, and as soon as he started the car, I was captivated by American rock and roll echoing out of the speakers, déjà vu from last night. He sang every word of every song with a beautiful, deep, resonating voice as we motored down the block and on to La Reforma, the longest boulevard in the city. As we darted around in traffic, Carlos reverted to listening to the radio. Once again, I was so surprised to hear an array of hit songs from the US. He explained that Mexicans were enamored with American music and theater. I believed it wholeheartedly now.

Carlos's knowledge of American music was very broad, from classical to rock and roll. "I went with my father and mother to American movies when I was growing up," he said, "and we have a collection of both classical and contemporary American music albums in our home. We watch American movies on television—with Spanish subtitles or voice-overs." He was obviously happy to be with a *gabacha* (another word for an American girl)—and I was ecstatic to be with a Mexican national.

From my seat in the car, I continually studied his magnetic persona. His jet-black wavy hair was cut very close to his handsomely shaped head and made a perfect horizontal line at just the right height across his forehead. His face was square, with a strong jawline. His eyes were the color of strong coffee ringed by curly black lashes that made them appear to be dancing. His nose was straight, the icon of an Aztecan heritage. His lips were generous, which softened his otherwise serious look. I continued to study him with acute interest. His hands were well manicured and exuded masculine capability, yet gentle intentions. His clothing was impeccable. I loved the fact that he wore black low-top Converse sneakers. He was not naïve about the icons of the American '60s!

Carlos shifted gears so smoothly and maneuvered through the little streets and big boulevards with a well-rehearsed mental map. He seemed to gravitate to action and people, as he spoke of his friends and the great times they continued to have since he was a little boy. His intelligence was impressive. He had life and people figured out. I was utterly lifted out of my previous world, completely overtaken in mind and body, just by looking at him. The feelings I had that day would never leave me. I could not have known the amplitude that this new relationship would acquire.

We ended the day with dinner at a nearby nightclub. It was on the same street as UNAM but much closer to the city. As we entered the building, its atmosphere was reminiscent of a Las Vegas casino. Unlike in the US, at age nineteen, I was one year beyond the legal drinking age in Mexico. I was a pseudo-adult.

The entrance opened into the lounge area, and there, in front of us, sat an Elvis impersonator, singing "Love Me Tender." Again, I was caught by surprise at the popularity of American music in Mexico. Carlos and I sat down to listen to this not-so-gifted vocalist. Carlos asked the entertainer if he could pay him to play an Elvis song on the guitar, but Carlos wanted to sing it. What followed was amazing. Carlos sang "I Can't Stop Falling in Love with You." He sounded just like Elvis, and a sizable group of people gathered around us. It was beyond flattering. Carlos kept pulling away from me on the dance floor, just enough to look into my eyes. He kept asking me, "What color are your eyes?" I was flattered, as he seemed to be enchanted that my eyes were not blue or green but somewhere in between. He told me that he had never dated a gringa before me, so I was evidently a novelty.

After dancing all night, it was time to call it a day. We had spent enough time together to know that this was not going to end with tonight. We were like hand in glove, as if we had been custom-made for each other. Nothing about him was distracting to me. I was attracted to everything I saw. It was beyond my expectation. I thought, *Two weeks into my adventure in Mexico, and I'm falling in love? Shouldn't this happen a little later?*

He drove me toward home, knowing it was very close to my curfew, which was midnight. We made it in time, but I had him stop a half block away. My plan was to tell la señora that I took a taxi home. Our time in the car saying goodbye pushed the clock ahead way too quickly, and before I knew it, it was 11:10! I pulled away from Carlos's loving embrace and opened my own door. As I closed it, I leaned into the car and thanked him for a fantastic day. He responded with, "Te llamo." (I'll call you.)

Carlos waited until I reached the front door of the house and knocked on the door. As he pulled away, la señora whisked open the door, obviously springing straight from her "curfew seat" next to the door, waiting to chastise me as soon as I arrived. Bobby Jean had come home at ten o'clock, so I was the only one still at large. She enunciated her words contemptuously, "Son las once y once!" (It is eleven minutes past eleven!) I tried to explain that the taxi took more time than I'd anticipated, but that I had left in plenty of time.

She wasn't in the mood for explanations, but she had to swallow it, since she obviously hadn't seen Carlos's car, and I couldn't control the *supposed* taxi's delay!

"Buenas noches!" she retorted. "No tardes otra vez!" (Don't be late again!)

I walked up the stairs, with la a señora's stomping heels right behind me, to the seating area. Fortunately, she turned toward her bedroom, and didn't follow me to my room.

As I started to ascend the stairs to my room, I could hear the girls chattering and giggling in the dormitory. Janette broke out in her usual husky laugh as I popped my head in the door, and their cover was blown. They had been making bets about me and Carlos.

"We were wondering if you were gonna come back tonight!"

I blanched at Bobby Jean's suggestion. "Why were you thinking that?" I asked, obviously offended.

"Well," Bobby Jean said, "we just knew you were in love with Carlos. We figured the two of you would have eloped!"

"Well, we might do that next week, but we didn't tonight!"

The faces that stared back at me were not catty, just impressed that I had volleyed back so quickly to Bobby Jean.

It was late, and we had all been burning the proverbial candle at both ends. Bobby Jean and I climbed up to our rooftop abode, too sleepy to talk but knowing that we would make up for it in the morning! The last thing I heard, after brushing my teeth and putting on my pajamas, was Bobby Jean asking, "So, what happened? Tell me everything!"

But my head had dropped onto my pillow like a heavy water balloon, conforming to the soft cotton stuffing. All I could say was, "Tell you in the morning. Good night." I was in a deep sleep within minutes.

21

BURGLARS AND MARIACHIS

The next morning, five o'clock, once again I was awakened by the howling dogs next door. Not only had I been out partying Friday and Saturday nights, but I had been out with Carlos for the entire day prior. I tossed and turned but could not get back to sleep. Bobby Jean, on the other hand, had her earplugs in and was snoring. I was glad, so I made sure not to wake my inquisitive roommate.

Speed-reading was never my strong suit, but I whisked through the chapters I needed to review for class that day. Then, quietly, I got into the shower and tried to memorize what pertinent facts I could. As soon as I got out of the shower, Bobby Jean was knocking on the bathroom door. "Way-ell. Are yuh gonna tale me the juicy details?"

"I'll tell you tonight. I'm so late!" I shouted back without opening the door.

I left in an uproar. I didn't have time for grumpy Maria. Instead, I decided to grab a quesadilla from a vendor I had seen last week on the way to the bus stop. Her comal had a good fire under it each day, nice and hot (to kill any germs that might be lurking). It looked clean, as did her hands (an important criterion). Carlos had told me that quesadillas (tortillas with cheese melted inside) were a safe bet when you were a hungry gringa out on the streets. I had confidence in his advice.

I hurried out of the house, walking at a fast pace to get to the street vendor's yummy melted treats. Luckily, she was there, and I gave my order. I exchanged three pesos for a quesadilla and an orange juice and went on my way. The bus stop was crowded, and I knew I was in for a challenge, trying to find a seat this morning. I stood there, having placed my notebook and books between my ankles, and began to tear at the quesadilla with my teeth. It was pure bliss. The cheese, from the state of Oaxaca, was like jack cheese but more flavorful. The tortilla had obviously just been baked, and together the two were the ultimate comfort food. I was soon fortified and sipped contentedly on the orange juice. *I definitely can get through the day now*, I thought.

Janette arrived with just a few minutes to spare, as the commuter busses whizzed past us with a roar that left no room in our ears for hearing each other's chitchat. In no time, number twenty-three stopped in front of us. Surprise—there was room on the bus! We walked up without any problem, gave our centavos to the driver, and moved to the midsection of the bus. Then Janette's questions began: "So, what do you think of Carlos? Are you going to date him exclusively now? What happened to Michael—did he ever call you back? Did you, you know, did you ... well, did you at least kiss Carlos?"

I was already perturbed by my lack of preparedness for class; now, my lack of preparation for the volley of questions that felt like shots flying over my head was even more perturbing. "Whoa, whoa! Slow down!" I said. "It was just a date!" (I diluted the truth from a boil down to a simmer.) "I really like him, and he's really fun to be with. I had a great time at Chapultepec Park, and we had a great night dancing. But we'll see. You never know." That seemed to satisfy her for the time being.

My class went well, as the instructor was ill and had sent a substitute. I wondered if my instructor had partied a little too much at the dance Saturday night. Then I thought better of her and assumed her illness was legitimate. The substitute was quite interesting, telling us about his travels throughout Mexico. Although an American, he had been raised by two missionaries in the state of Yucatan in the 1950s. His stories about the jungle life and the indigenous peoples there were fascinating. I was so relieved that he wouldn't be calling on any of us but just engaging us in interesting cultural diversity issues, such as the superstitions of the Mayans and their sacrificing of virgins in deep *cenotes,*

Between classes, I grabbed a sandwich and milk and sat outside the main building under an enormous shade tree on a spare bench. Michael happened to walk by just then and turned a quick 180. "Hey, uh, I'm so embarrassed about Saturday night," he said sheepishly. "I felt lousy all day yesterday. It's obvious you got home okay, but I owe you a big apology! I hope you can forgive me?" He sat down next to me, and I looked in his eyes, which were a bit hollow-looking even now.

"You know what, Michael?" I said dramatically. "Some things are just meant to be. I'm over it. Let's just leave it where it was, okay?"

He wasn't sure exactly what I meant, and that was how I wanted it. We never dated again.

By midweek, it was obvious that school was taking its toll on all of us at the Castillo household—it was beginning to cramp our time for socializing! Now glaring at us was our homework, which had become voluminous and demanding. We were either reading, writing essays, working on take-home exams, doing research, or studying for short exams. We collectively became a study hall.

That night, I fell asleep studying around eleven o'clock. At approximately 2:30 a.m., I was awakened by someone knocking on our door. The knocking was soft at first but then got really loud. I knew that Bobby Jean, with her earplugs, couldn't hear anything. I, on the other hand, was frozen with fear! Only someone of bad intent would be trying to get us to open our door at 2:30 in the morning! "Oh my God!" I exclaimed. I grabbed Bobby Jean's earplugs and shook her awake.

"What?" Bobby Jean said in a daze.

"Listen!" I whispered directly in her ear. "Someone's trying to get in our door!"

"Oh Jeez!" Bobby Jean whispered. "What can we do?"

I quickly pointed to the bathroom, motioning for us to get in there and lock the door. The knocking at the door was turning into banging now, as if someone trying to break the door down!

We could barely get our two bodies into the tiny bathroom. There was room on the pot, and room for one person to stand between it and the shower. We turned the light on, just because it was too scary in the dark.

"Shhh!" I warned her. "Be quiet!"

"But, what can we do, Collette? No one's gonna hear us anyway!"

"Oh God, Bobby Jean! I don't know!"

Just then, we heard someone screaming outside our door. "Wake up! Open the door!" It was Janette's husky voice, screaming as loud as she could.

"What?" I yelled back at her. I carefully stumbled to the door and unlocked it. As I opened it, I saw la señora and Janette staring at me. Beyond them, I could hear someone singing really loudly, as if they were on the street below. Suddenly, a trumpet bleated out its brassy shrill tones, and there was guitar strumming with a chorus of mariachis backing it up.

"What's going on?" I asked.

"Es Carlos, tu amigo!" la señora said, wearing the most contemptuous grimace yet. She went on to tell me that Carlos was serenading me and wanted to see me. "Que le diga que salga," she said, insisting I go and tell him to leave.

What I heard affected me very differently than what la señora felt. I heard a deep, melodious voice enveloping the neighborhood, accompanied by an amazing quartet of musicians. I heard my lover reaching out to me, and I wanted it to continue! This was Mexico! This was the Mexico I'd dreamed of. Why would I want it to stop?

I ran down to the second-floor window that faced the street, next to the stairs. My roommates in the dormer had opened it already; all of them were enjoying the serenade. They moved aside as I approached, and when Carlos saw me, he shouted, "Buenas noches! Esta canción es para ti!" (Good evening! This song is for you!)

The mariachis were grinning from ear to ear. The violinist jabbed at his strings, in short movements, starting the next arrangement. The guitarist joined in, and Carlos's strong voice brought the two together in a beautiful melody and lyrics, which I remember contained the words "Que bonitos ojos tienes"—"What beautiful eyes you have." He continued singing in his rich voice as the trumpet player hit crescendos that were timed to accent the end of each line of the lyrics.

I was entranced. I recognized the songs as "Malagueña." I was mentally translating as Carlos sang, becoming more and more mesmerized and excited with each word. *I am the object of his love! I am the woman of his dreams! I am being serenaded! This is not a dream! I am in love! "Fly, butterfly, fly!"*

At the end of the song, Carlos threw a kiss to me and thanked la señora for letting him sing to me. She winced at his graciousness, seemingly thinking the whole thing was nothing but a rude awakening. She uttered something in disgust beneath her breath that sounded like "Aye!"—a neutral expletive that can be loosely translated as "Oh crap!"

We all quietly stepped away from the window, but not until I had the last word for Carlos and the mariachis: "Gracias a todos!" (Thank you all!) With that, I threw a dramatic kiss at the air, as if to include everyone. Carlos and I stared at each other in wonder, and he said he would call me tomorrow.

In the evening, as all five of us were eating la cena at Maria's table, the phone rang. La señora came to the door and, with an irritated demeanor, told me it was Carlos on the phone. "No tardes, por favor," she added, telling me not to take too long. The girls gave me a look that read, "Oh brother! There they go again!"

Carlos's voice was so deep and tender. He asked me what I'd thought of last night.

"You mean this morning, don't you?" I said coyly.

He chuckled. "Well, yes, this morning, I suppose."

"It was a very exciting event for all of us and a very sweet thing to do. You have a very strong and beautiful voice to be able to be heard over the mariachi's instruments! Thank you again."

He was obviously pleased. He told me the real reason he called was to invite me to go with him to a beautiful park called Las Estacas, south of Cuernavaca, on Saturday. "We'll be joining a group my friends. Bring your bathing suit, a towel, and whatever you might need afterward for the evening. We'll be swimming at the lagoons or springs there. My friends and I will bring a cooler with beer and food."

"It sounds fabulous," I told him.

"I'll pick you up at eleven, Saturday morning."

After our phone conversation, I went back to the dormer, where eager ears were still waiting to hear something juicy. I fended them off with, "Nothing has happened to tell you about—I swear! Why don't you pick on Shilo? She certainly has a lot more to tell than I do!"

Shilo turned her head slightly, with a Mona Lisa smile. Somehow, she managed to keep her relationship with Gerardo quiet, and because she didn't react to questions, she had the smug privilege of not being questioned. I was annoyed not to have the same privilege.

22

LAGOONS, NEW COMPADRES, AND BOY SCOUTS

I stayed in Friday night, even though Oscar and friends had called for a night out on the town at Mariachi Square. It didn't interest me, especially having Carlos in the wings and Cuernavaca to look forward to the next day. I also had a truckload of homework to do and reading to catch up on. Somehow, I had to pull off decent grades, or I wouldn't be here next semester!

I woke up at 8:30 Saturday morning. I barely made it down to Maria's for breakfast, with only ten minutes to eat. Janette was the only one left at Maria's table. "Well, if it isn't the dating queen!" she teased.

"Oh, shut up! You're not doing too badly yourself! Weren't you out all night with Oscar and Tito?"

"Yeah, but Margo and Oscar are starting to be an item, and he's the only one I would have considered. They were snuggling and kissing instead of dancing to the mariachis last night. And Tito is too short! I tower over him, and we don't have much to talk about except drinking and dancing. So Bobby Jean and I just had fun dancing with the wind and sipping tequila."

Carlos would be arriving in a couple of hours. I had peeked out of our tiny bedroom window before coming down for breakfast, and it looked like a picture-postcard day. The sky was cerulean blue, with vapors of clouds that hinted at just enough moisture to make skin feel supple but not humid enough to make me feel like a steamed marshmallow. After two hours of my showering, drying and styling my hair, applying makeup, and choosing my wardrobe, I was ready for another magical day with Carlos. I grabbed my well-stocked tote bag and purse and ran down the stairs.

I was hoping that la señora wouldn't even notice I was leaving. My hope was honored this time—she was not waiting for me at the door. She must have had a bigger fire to deal with that morning. I opened the front door before Carlos had a chance to ring the bell. As soon as I saw him, my heart fluttered. He greeted me with his gorgeous smile, and I stepped down to meet his waiting arms. He held me and whispered, "I missed you last night."

"Me too." That was all I could get out of my quivering mouth.

The trip to Las Estacas took about an hour, but it seemed like fifteen minutes. Once we had descended the mountainous area south of Mexico City, Carlos drove along a series of two-lane country roads and pulled over as we approached a beautiful old stone wall with a time-worn fountain in front of it. It appeared to be the remains of a once-opulent hacienda. I looked closer and saw the expansive arched entrance to the right. As we got out of the car, I saw Carlos' friends walking toward us. They obviously were eager to meet their compadre's gringa girlfriend. They seemed fun-loving, handsome, and warm.

"Hola, compadres!" Carlos said. Each shook Carlos's hand informally. Carlos gestured toward me, saying "Les presento a Collette." Literally translated, this was "I present to you Collette," but informally, it was "I'd like you to meet Collette." Carlos then introduced his friends to me: "Collette, te presento a Antonio, Rafael y a Jaime y Jaime." There were two Jaimes. One was relatively short in stature and had a marked limp. He wore a special shoe to add height to his right side. The other Jaime was the tallest of the group. He was referred to as "Tall Jaime."

Each of the guys took a turn gesturing with a slight, dramatized bow, followed with "Mucho gusto" ("It's a pleasure to meet you"), said with pronounced respect. They sat down around the rock fountain and looked toward Carlos with approving expressions. I felt that I was accepted immediately as their friend, and I hoped we would remain as such.

The compadres spread out some blankets, food, and the old standby, cold cerveza. Antonio set up his speakers. Carlos had brought his large portable radio, set to his favorite rock-and-roll station. They hooked it up to the speakers, and we were surrounded by the '60s music we loved. With the cold beer, salsa, and chicharrones to go with it, we were in business. I soon started chatting in Spanish like one of the boys. When Rafael asked me how I liked e *Gabachalandia*, however, I asked Carlos to translate for me. Carlos and the others started laughing, and he explained that Rafael was joking, asking me how I liked "the United States of Gabachas"—or "American girls." Rafael was referring to the fact that Mexican men teased each other about going to "Gabachalandia" as if it were Disneyland. I finally answered, "Well, for an American girl like me, *Macho-landia* is much better!" We all giggled at my reference to *macho*. My tongue-in-cheek response was taken in the spirit I had intended.

After a wonderful picnic lunch and dancing on the lawn, we drove a little further down the road to a lagoon with a sandy beach to swim and enjoy the sunshine. "Las Estacas is located in Tlaltizapán," Carlos explained. "We're in a valley in the Sierra Montenegro Mountains that encompasses over a thousand of hectares." (A hectare is about two and a half times as large as an acre.)

Carlos was a natural tour guide. His mind seemed to have grabbed the history of every place in Mexico. I thought he could have earned a living as a professional guide, just drumming up business with tourists at the venues of his choice.

"The water there is like crystal, and there is a great variety of plants and animals. There are trees there that are hundreds of years old,"

Carlos added. He located an idyllic spot and pulled the car to the curb. Little *palapas* (huts) were set up around the lagoon. Carlos pointed out a building where we could use the restrooms and change our clothes. With its deep-green lawns and shady spots under trees, Las Estacas seemed like heaven on earth.

Carlos walked me to the dressing room so I could change into my bathing suit, then he and his friends changed in the men's room nearby. Out we came with our beach towels, bathing suits donned and ready for a fun-filled afternoon. Antonio had brought a football. They tossed it back and forth and insisted I pass the ball a few times to them. Rafael was tall and lanky, and his straight black hair was brushed to the side in schoolboy fashion. He was easy going and obviously idolized Carlos—they called each other compadre, an endearing term among Mexican men that signifies a lifetime friend or someone with whom you've built a trusting relationship. Rafael was, I would learn, Carlos's closest compadre. He knew *everything* about Carlos.

One by one, we entered the beautiful cool water. It was so calming yet invigorating. Antonio decided to put our lawn chairs into the shallow water. I thought it was a brilliant move, as it would keep us cool while allowing us to enjoy the sun. As we sat down, Antonio brought our cervezas to complete the hedonism. We laughed and took turns swimming, floating, and even dancing in the shallow water. It was magnificent.

Antonio was a jovial sort; his happy spirit oozed out of him. Although surely an honest and sincere person, it was obvious that he had a bent toward fun. The shorter Jaime was a tender soul, certainly honed by his disability. He was quiet and just wanted to belong. He smiled and played his guitar as if he wanted to be in the background yet be an integral part of the group. Something told me his silence belied secret knowledge about each compadre in the group, given his role as an observer. But I could tell that he would not be the one to divulge even one detail. After a few comments were made between them, I knew they all had experienced more things together than they had apart. They had created fun when there wasn't any fun otherwise available to them during their formative years.

Carlos reminded Antonio about an incident that took place when they were about seventeen. Antonio had come home at about six in the morning after partying all night with the compadres. Just as he approached the front door of his parents' house, his father opened it; he was leaving for work. Antonio was stupefied—not to mention still inebriated—as his father asked him why he was coming home so late. Antonio quickly retrieved his wit and said, "Oh, I got home at midnight. I just left an hour ago to exercise at the park. I'm just coming back to shower and get ready for school. We have a football game today so I want to be ready for it."

His father looked him straight in his eyes and asked, "Why are you wearing your nice clothes to exercise?"

Antonio realized the obvious and said, "Well, I didn't have any clean gym gear." Out of the corner of his eyes, he saw his father smirk and continue out the door. His father's comment was all that was necessary. Without further words, an unspoken order was laid down that this would not happen again. From then on, Antonio said he *never* stayed out past midnight until he lived under his own roof. And he never went to the park to exercise at six in the morning, nor had he ever before.

I thought about the closeness of these young men. Their neighborhood was such a small community that it allowed them to play together and create their own fun from an early age. In the US, on the other hand, small communities were not common. Those vanished with modern tract houses and shopping centers. Americans, in general, no longer had a corner store or a barber or beauty shop they could walk to. People didn't really congregate on the streets; they sat in their private backyards. They lived in bedroom communities and drove to a shopping center, where they typically did not see their neighbors. What a great contrast existed between the little neighborhoods that were the fabric of Mexico City and the towns that I was accustomed to back home.

23

MEETING LA FAMILIA

The next weekend, Carlos was coming to get me for a special dinner that his mother was going to prepare. He explained that she had personally invited me to their home and that she loved to cook. I was a bit nervous about it, thinking that this was a sign that we were definitely a couple. Did I want this? Was I limiting myself? Should I consider slowing down this relationship by declining? But the moment these thoughts came to my mind, they were countered with very strong emotions. *Why would I do that? I love my time with Carlos. I need to pursue it and see where it leads.*

At six o'clock, Carlos was at la a señora's door. She answered with her typical disapproval (I had the *pleasure* of watching this scene, as I had arrived in the little sala before her). I had told her about my plans and had received her nod to go. As soon as she opened the door and gave her crumpled-up look to Carlos, I squeezed out.

"See you later!" I said with my back to her as we walked to his car. It was so gratifying to let her know that she had limited power over me now. All I owed her was proper notice and my return by eleven o'clock.

"Boy, she's really an unhappy woman," Carlos commented as he started the car. "Does her husband pay attention to her?"

"I don't think so. He's always up in his office, taking care of his business," I said sourly.

"I don't blame him! Who would want to spend time with a grump?" Carlos reached over to me and smiled, holding my face. "You're so precious. I love being with you. You are *nothing* like her!" He kissed me gently. For the first time, I'd heard the word love. I could feel my head and neck tingle.

Carlos's home was just ten minutes away. As we drove past Chapultepec Park, I felt a rush of warmth just recalling our first date. And now, I knew I was taking an epic step as we entered the little *colonia* (neighborhood) where he lived. Would this also be the entry into an enduring relationship? The neighborhood was a blend of lower- and middle-income homes, with some private businesses thrown into the mix. Some houses were very modest and plain, with no adornment on the windows, and were in need of painting. Others were neatly painted in bright colors and had ornate wrought-iron work over the windows. Several of the homes were fronted by a wrought-iron wall and gate that created a patio that could double as a secure parking place. Some were ornately and lovingly appointed with potted plants, tables, and chairs to complete the ambiance of the prized outdoor living spaces.

I was enchanted when we pulled up in front of Carlos's home. It was a subtle rose color. It was one of the few houses with an attached garage. The garage doors, as well as the front door and large living room window, were arched and graced with ornate black wrought iron. On the second story, three windows jutted out, which I assumed were bedrooms.

I knew that inside would be very special people. I came to this conclusion from my observations of Carlos's behavior and knowledge, his sophisticated manners and grasp of Mexican history, and his admiration for his own culture. I knew that Carlos was not a mirror image of his parents, though, as he was a 1960s argonaut, just like me: We had different views than our parents, as all young people do. I wouldn't have wanted him to be a reflection of his parents, except in his morals, family traditions, and intelligence! I knew that his antics with his friends and their adventures were their own inventions, and I wanted and expected that.

As we got out of the car, I noticed an alcove at the very top of the roofline over the front door. Inside it, a female spiritual figure gazed out to the sky. She seemed to whisper to me that I was about to be blessed. I somehow felt a strong tie to Carlos's parents, sight unseen. It was as if I was about to meet my new family.

Carlos opened the door with his key and called out to his mom— "Mami! Mami! Dónde estás? Quiero presentarle a Collette?"—asking where she was and saying he wanted to introduce me to her. His voice held obvious joy and anticipation.

"Un momento, hijo. Estoy arriba," his mother responded with a sweet lilt in her voice, saying she was upstairs.

As she descended the spiral *marmol* (marble) staircase, I became inexplicably aware of a very pleasant soul approaching me. I heard the gentle sound of her footsteps coming down the stairs. And now, the person I had been anticipating appeared, wearing a flowing navy-blue and white dress. Theresa offered a kind "Bienvenidos! Mucho gusto!" as she took the last step and extended her arms for a hug from her son. Her smile announced her spirit before she spoke.

Oh my gosh, she glows with kindness and purpose, I thought. *She is all about her family!*

Carlos responded with. "Te presento a Collette," to which Theresa gave a nod and a welcoming smile as she extended her right hand to me. Her left hand settled on top of my hand, and we hesitated a moment, our hands together in an acknowledged trust. We saw each other's souls, it seemed, and our eyes reflected an instant comfort with one another.

Theresa said, "Nuestra casa es su casa!" (Our house is your house!)

I replied in my much-improving Spanish, "It is an honor to meet you. I have been looking forward to this day. Thank you for accepting me into your home."

Theresa graciously asked Carlos to show me the house "para que la conoce"—so that I could familiarize myself with it.

I thought, *Has Carlos spoken of me? How much has he said to his mother?* Without further ado, I followed Carlos up the stairs to the bedrooms. His sister's bedroom was at the top of the stairs. Her name was Andrea; she was at work. She was two years older than Carlos and was going to be married in January. The bedroom had beautiful wooden floors, and Andrea's bed was full of fancy pillows. Nothing was out of place, I noted. I surmised that she was very feminine and fastidious.

To our left, an open tiled corridor allowed a view over the spiral staircase we had just climbed. The other two bedroom doors were down the hall on the right. In his parents' bedroom, I noted the rustic wooden crucifix over the head of the bed. The room was very traditional and modestly furnished, with wooden floors and a darkly stained headboard and dresser. I felt an eerie holiness in the room. The only ornate piece was the framed mirror over the dresser. The bedspread was a simple one, in gold cloth that appeared to be made of quilted nylon, inexpensive yet dressy, compared to the rest of the room.

The last bedroom down the hallway was where Carlos's brother and sister-in-law stayed with their new baby, Marisita. They were out—his brother working and his sister-in-law shopping with the baby—but I looked forward to meeting them as soon as possible. I was feeling like this was my home. *What is it that feels so visceral?* I asked myself. *Why am I so effortlessly, so naturally feeling bonded to Carlos's mother, to his home, and to his father, brother, and sister, whom I haven't even met yet? What is happening to me?*

Just as that thought coursed through my mind, Carlos directed me across the hall to another door, which he said was the boiler room. It was the room where the water heater was kept. He explained that the boiler was kept separate from the living quarters of the house as a precaution, so that any leaking gas would escape out the windows that opened onto the street.

"Well, why is there a bed in here?" I asked.

Carlos explained, "Well, it is just temporary while my brother and sister-in-law stay here. They are looking for another apartment, so I sleep here in the meantime."

"I hope you keep the windows open at all times!" I said.

"Would you weep if I died?" he asked coyly.

"Stop it!" I said with a feigned indifference.

Carlos led me back downstairs to the dining room at the foot of the stairs. His father had arrived and was sitting at the table, reading the newspaper. He was dressed in a perfectly fitted suit with a crisply ironed, snow-white dress shirt and tie. He was the accountant for a very successful law firm. Home for his lunch, he looked up with an analytical expression over the top of his glasses and caught my eyes.

Whoa, I thought, *this is a serious man.* He had a lighter complexion than Carlos. I remember Carlos telling me that his father was pure Spanish. I also knew that his father had been to the States in the early '30s in San Diego and loved American movies and the beauty of the coastal areas.

I endeavored to give a slight smile to Mr. Herrera, overcoming my tension.

"Hola, Papi!" Carlos almost shouted. "Te presento a Collette!"

His father stood up from his chair, no smile on his face, and robotically walked around the edge of the table to where we were standing. He stood very formally, square-shouldered, facing me. "Mucho gusto." He maintained his very formal demeanor as he extended his hand to me.

"I am very pleased to meet you," I said in my most perfect Spanish. "Your home is very pretty."

"Gracias," he said. "Pues, hemos luchado quince años construyendo esta casa. Toda es de nuestros sueños." (Well, we have struggled for fifteen years to construct this house. All of it is from our dreams).

I immediately thought, *What a beautiful perspective! Oh, if only everyone felt that way about their homes.*

"I am very impressed with your dreams," I replied, hoping he caught my sincerity.

He seemed to understand, as there was a glint in his eyes, and he gave me a gentle smile. He was obviously a very astute, disciplined man—one of honor and pride, which he wore with confidence.

"Vas a comer con nosotros?" (Will you have dinner with us?) he inquired.

"Yes, I would be delighted."

"Maybe you would like to see what I have been working on in recent weeks?" he asked as he returned to his seat. "I have the responsibility of writing for a section of the newspaper. Perhaps you will enjoy it. It is in Spanish, but you seem to have a good grasp of our language. Give it a try."

I was spellbound to think that he would consider me important enough to read his own work. As formal as his gestures were, I decided I could be confident that he'd accepted me. He passed the newspaper article to me, and I began working feverishly to read his column. It was a commentary about the poverty in Mexico—that much I was sure of. It spoke of ways that each citizen could help those who were impoverished, independent of any formal organization. It was about generosity in little impactful ways that could greatly improve their lot in life.

"I am very impressed," I told him as I finished the article. "Have you written for other publications? This is a beautiful idea!"

He calmly answered, "Yes, all of my life."

"Well," I added, "I have written poetry since I was thirteen. I have written about twenty-five poems and have them in a special book that I keep at home. It is obvious that you are a professional writer, and I am honored that you have allowed me to read your work."

He smiled more grandly now, as if at ease with me and genuinely touched by my openness. "Well, maybe one day I can read your poems, when you become famous," he said with slight humor.

I blushed deeply.

Theresa came into the dining room with plates in her hands—one for her husband, and one for me. "Provecho," she said as she placed each plate in front of us (telling us to "Enjoy!").

"Muy amable. Gracias!" I responded with pleasure, which meant "That's very kind of you. Thank you."

Carlos returned to the kitchen with her and helped her with the other two plates. Soon, we were four people together at the family's table. I felt so at home, as if I had always known this family. I remembered a line of my poetry that read, "Heaven radiates from the hearts and minds of those who offer sincere love."

The dish that Theresa had prepared, Carlos explained, was *tinga*, a mixture of shredded chicken, diced poblano chiles, onion, and tomatoes. For variety, she added raisins. She served a side dish of sautéed *nopales* (prickly pear cactus), peeled and cut up in lengths of about one by two inches. A special round wooden tortilla container was placed on the table. The tortillas were wrapped in a thin cotton cloth inside to maintain their piping-hot temperature. As Carlos offered a tortilla to me, the steam from the wonderfully hot, layered stack escaped in a dense billow.

"Mmm," I said. "Thank you. I love hot tortillas!"

Carlos's mother and father both smiled, seemingly pleased with their dinner guest.

24

VISITING SKELETONS

Carlos had invited me to a fiesta for El Día de Los Muertos (he Day of the Dead), hosted by his longtime friend's mother, just down the street from Carlos's house. Her name was Lupita. As we walked down to the fiesta, Carlos explained to me that the Day of the Dead in Mexico has been practiced for thousands of years, first by the Aztecs and then—in spite of the wishes of the Spaniards—by the Spanish-Indian (*Mestizo*) culture, which was spawned in the 1500s when Columbus took control of the Aztecan civilization.

Lupita greeted us at her door, and Carlos introduced us. She was a humble woman, both in demeanor and in appearance. She wore a gray shawl, black blouse, and gray skirt. Her gray hair blended with the ensemble, adding to the very somber atmosphere in the dimly lit living room.

I noticed a group of candles glowing in the corner to the left of the door, and Carlos informed me, "As part of the celebrations that are held each year, a large segment of the population sets up a shrine in their homes to their deceased family members and friends. The little shrines may be on a buffet in the dining room or little table in the living room, like this one. Many people believe that the dead come back to visit during the entire month of October and leave on November 2, after all the festivities have ended."

As we walked toward the shrine and studied its proudly displayed photographs of Lupita's late husband, Lupita offered us hot Mexican chocolate (pronounced "cho-ko-*lah*-tay") in mugs and motioned for us to have a seat near the shrine. Various neighbors and friends were sitting in chairs against the walls. Their faces were solemn, but they greeted our glances with tempered smiles.

Carlos continued to reveal his incredible grasp of the historical details of his country, whispering in English to me as I sipped the cinnamon-infused chocolate. "Over the centuries, both Mayan and Aztecan rituals related to the dead were merged with Catholic beliefs. They still live side by side. The Roman Catholic Church changed the original date of the Day of the Dead from October 28 to November 2 to coincide with All Saints' Day, a holy day appointed by the church to commemorate all martyrs of the church's history, and All Souls' Day, a day the church commemorates the dead. This way, the Catholic Church hoped to downplay the pagan Day of the Dead.

"The irony is that a large portion of the Mexican people downplay any relationship to All Saints' Day when they celebrate the Day of the Dead. The creation of shrines to commemorate the dead, the preparation of special foods for the dead, the street vendors selling marzipan *candies* in the shapes of skulls and skeletons. It is all about the ancient customs, not the Catholic Church. The favorite foods of the deceased are set on the shrine, and candles are lit to welcome them home. As November 2 approaches, the candies are eaten by the loved ones of the dead, as if to express a unity with the dead person by enjoying what the deceased loved in this life. Then, it is acknowledged that their memories live on in their loved ones' homes and in their hearts."

Carlos and I took time to talk with each of the visitors, and as we did we were blessed by the goodwill they expressed for Lupita's husband, as well as for Lupita. Afterward, we excused ourselves, embracing Lupita and a few visitors Carlos had known for many years. It was a surreal experience for me, as I'd sensed that I had been sitting among both the dead and the living. I mused over the fact that Americans are so uncomfortable with the idea of death.

As we walked back up to Carlos's house, I told him that my father's friend called himself a *permanent* real estate salesman—he sold burial plots. I tried to describe to Carlos the bizarre awkwardness when my parents made jokes about the "cemetery salesman" (as we called him privately) when he came to visit. One of the best jokes was, "Ray will never do anything to hurt you. He will be the last one to 'let you down.'" I giggled as I tried to explain the play on words to Carlos. Then I said, "In the States, it is a relief to joke about death. We are not comfortable with it, and so we call an ambulance when someone dies and have them take care of everything as fast as we can. Then, the almost-gruesome task of making funeral arrangements and choosing a coffin and a gravesite becomes a very disquieting experience. We would prefer to transition straight from someone's death to a covered grave, where we can decorate the gravestone with flowers and feel more settled."

"I think that the Mexicans adopted the Aztecan ritual so that death could be viewed just as a continuation of life, not the *end* of life. It's much easier to accept the death of a loved one if you're not really losing the person but are just beginning a different type of relationship with him or her."

Carlos agreed with a smile, as if to say *You get it.* "Then you can understand," he said, "why people all over Mexico often visit the cemetery where their loved ones are buried. It's not a sad thing; it's a celebration of their lives. The Day of the Dead is just one of the days the graves are visited; we also visit them on their birthdays—or their saint's day—and just about every other holiday that they enjoyed so that we participate in it together again. We scrub their headstones and shrines and then decorate their gravesites with flowers and candles. If the deceased was a child, we place toys on the gravesites; if they were adults, sometimes it's *tragos* (shot glasses) of tequila. We often sit on picnic blankets next to the gravesites and eat their favorite foods. So throughout the year, the dead are visited and kept alive, in a sense. We don't view them as living in an isolated grave but as living here on earth in a spiritual form; they are *among* us. We are very comfortable and, in a sense, at home with them."

My view of death was forever changed.

25

LAS POSADAS

Christmas decorations started appearing in the city in mid-November, not long after the Day of the Dead ended. Noticing this, I asked la señora why they started decorating so early. I was accustomed to celebrating Thanksgiving first. But then, I had to remember that the pilgrims didn't land in Mexico. La señora explained, as she puffed nervously on her cigarette, that the official beginning of the Christmas season was December 12, when Mexicans celebrated La Fiesta de Nuestra Señora de Guadalupe (the Feast of Our Lady of Guadalupe).

Ariana was standing next to la señora and gently entered the conversation. She related the tradition to me in English, which she had mastered as a result of her position at a well-known American company in the city. She gestured for me to sit down on one of the soft chairs in the sitting area, and she sat next to me. It was obvious that she wanted to give this sacred tradition the attention it deserved.

"The feast is celebrated as the commemoration of the appearance of the apparition of Mary in 1513 to a poor Indian boy, Juan Diego, in Puebla, a town about an hour east of Mexico City. A shrine and *basilica*, or church, dedicated to Our Lady are located there. On December 16, las posadas begin—nine days of religious observance based on the nine months that Mary carried Jesus in her womb, culminating on December

24. These celebrations are, in fact, a *novenario*, or reenactment, of the difficult journey that Mary and Joseph had to endure from Nazareth to Bethlehem in search of shelter for the imminent birth of Jesus; in Spanish, the word *posada* means lodging."

I was transported by Beatrice's soft voice as she gave her intimate account of this time-honored Mexican tradition.

"A party is held each night, beginning on December 16, in a neighborhood home. At dusk, families and friends walk together in groups, gathering outside the house of a host family, with children dressed as shepherds, angels, and sometimes Mary and Joseph. An angel leads the procession, followed by Mary and Joseph or by guests carrying their images. Lighted candles are carried by others behind the procession. The pilgrims sing a song as they approach door after door in their neighborhood, asking for shelter.

"The residents of the homes open their doors and sing a reply back to them, which tells them that there is no room in their home for them. Finally, the door of the host family is opened to the guests, and they are invited in. Hot *ponche*—punch—is offered to them, along with tamales. There are hundreds of authentic Mexican recipes for ponche. Every Mexican cook and kitchen has its favorite variation. But all of them have a several ingredients in common: an apple-like fruit called *tejocote*, and *piloncillo*, which is semi-processed sugar cane, much like brown sugar. The fruit and sugar are cooked with other fruits, such as oranges, prunes, pears, and raisins. It is like a liquid fruit salad, served hot.

"Often, a piñata in the shape of the North Star is hung in an outdoor area near the home, and children take turns hitting it with a stick until it breaks open, and its contents—several pounds of candy and coins—spill all over the ground. The frenzy that ensues is worth capturing on film, as the excitement of the children is high drama as they grab and hoard as much of the candy as their little hands and pockets will allow.

"The last posada is held on December 24. It is more solemn, as the birth of Christ is symbolically imminent. Many families host a dinner for this last night, offering a traditional meal of *bacalao* (dried cod that is rinsed and then cooked), *ramas* (a type of grass that is tender when cooked), and various sweet delicacies. It is followed by a midnight mass at the neighborhood's favorite Catholic church."

Trying to come out of the trance that Beatrice had put me in, I brought my eyes back into focus. "Thank you so much for taking the time to explain all this to me, Beatrice. I am so impressed with the traditions of this country, and I know that this is just one of so many. I am looking forward to experiencing what I can of this beautiful time of year in Mexico." I privately hoped that Carlos would invite me to join in a posada celebration next month with his family and friends, just so I could be a part of the real thing.

As December came upon us and finals approached, I felt short pangs of longing for my family and friends back in the States. But Carlos kept my social calendar busy, with endless ideas for adventure. He told me that Jose Luis, a former classmate of Carlos whom I had not yet met, had offered to host a posada at his parents' house. Of course I was immediately excited.

"I want to have a big posada"—the word was used in Spanish for a Christmas get-together with friends or family—"with *all* of my friends, so you can get to know them," he said. "It will be a perfect place for the party. I want you to get to know the girls that I know as well, since all you have met so far are the guys I hang around with. "You will love them! Most of them I have known since kindergarten. They are nice people, and I know you are going to have a great time with them."

Carlos then recited the details of how he was arranging the posada. Everyone was bringing something, from chicharrones (fried pork rinds) to tinga (finely shredded chicken in a spicy red sauce). Carlos also would make sure there was plenty of tequila, as that was *not* to be left out. He was bringing his record player, and a friend had some speakers that would enhance the sound to equal a nightclub, he assured me with glowing pride.

Music and people were Carlos's favorite things. He loved being surrounded with the synergy of them. I was cut from the same cloth, loving that same rejuvenating feeling, which seemed vital to my being.

I was busy almost every hour of every weekend now, studying for final exams, spending only limited time with Bobby Jean (no time for shopping, gossiping, or dreaming about out futures), and putting up with the everyday house rules. I tolerated the immediate necessities of studying for the end goal: Carlos's farewell posada for me. It was coming up in two weeks, and I was already planning what I would wear (an important part of my agenda). I needed to produce a new outfit from my wardrobe that looked new, like a combination I hadn't come up with yet.

I would be leaving Mexico the day after the posada. It was impossible to absorb. I felt like I had been here for only a few weeks. Worse, I felt that I *belonged* here.

The posada was set for seven o'clock on Saturday night, four days before Christmas. Carlos picked me up at six so I could help him set up a beverage bar and buffet table at Javier's. Within a half hour of arriving, Carlos and I had set up a perfect configuration for drinks and appetizers. A table for *guisados* (casseroles) was positioned across the patio. Javier brought ice from the corner grocery store and set plenty of beer and bottles of tequila in it. "Listos!" Javier shouted, saying he was ready.

The first arrivals were Alex and Benjamin. They were students at the polytechnic college Carlos had attended. After introductions, Javier led them over to the beverage bar. Within a half hour, twenty more guests had arrived and were ceremoniously introduced to me. I felt like the star of the show but made sure to show as much graciousness to the guests as they were showing to me. Carlos nudged me from one conversation to another, taking delight in my becoming an integral part of his social circle.

The whole patio was teeming with laughter, dancing, and camaraderie. Before I knew it, hours had passed, and I had enjoyed myself tremendously. I could not have been more at home than I was with these great personalities and kind-hearted peers. We were on each other's wave lengths, intellectually and morally. I became part of them almost instantaneously as we spoke so openly about our mutual interests and shared keen insight into the issues between our countries. It was as if Mexico and the United States had come to a United Nations conference with genuinely good intentions. Only open-minded youth could have achieved this.

When the last guests departed that night, I succumbed to tears. I felt so enlightened by the good will I was graced with that night. I was left believing that, were it not for the political machinery that had long controlled the relations between Mexico and the US, the youth of each country could have done a much better job.

26

THE END OF AN
AMAZING SEMESTER

The morning reared its ugly head. The semester was over. The posadas were over, and the inevitable was coming—I would be leaving Mexico for the Christmas holiday that afternoon and would be leaving school in Mexico for good! There was no going back. My grades were not impressive.

"Too much partying and not enough studying," my father said to me on the phone when I'd called to beg for another semester in Mexico. He expected more of me, especially with the concessions he had made financially. He had been proud of my 3.67 grade point average during my first year of college. For my semester in Mexico, it was 2.5. "I think you need to come home," he had said. He knew I wasn't serious about studying, and he didn't feel like paying for my "good times."

Realizing I would have to finish my college career in the US, my first thought was, *Does this mean that my life's dream is over too?*

I had learned so much about values from the Mexican people. Although some things were similar about our cultures, the Mexican culture had many additional alluring qualities. I couldn't imagine that life in the States would ever satisfy me again. The US life seemed so sterile. So easy. Too convenient. Mexico was *none* of those things … and I loved it for that. People had to struggle with daily life to simply live because nothing was easy to do. The traffic and high-density population, the frail economy, the lack of an efficient government, the lack of the convenience of a mail system, and many more inconveniences ensured constant struggle. But somehow the struggle was stimulating. It fed an innate drive to conquer, and at the end of each task, whether it was just trying to get to a familiar place by taxi or bus (a huge segment of the population did not have a car) or working hard to feed your family, it was a distinct, identifiable satiation in the Mexican's soul. The common struggle seemed to solidify them in their celebration of life.

What was fortunate was the issue of housing. Unlike the US, the majority of high school graduates simply stayed in the home they had shared with their parents from birth. If their attempts to move out on their own became difficult, they moved back in with their parents. This was completely acceptable. In the US, there was a sense of urgency in the middle and upper classes for their teenagers to either go away to college (because the parents could afford it) or to get a job and an apartment and move out on their own.

I bit my lip as I got into the cab. Bobby Jean agreed to accompany me on my ride to Carlos's house. My heart was beating as if I had run a mile. I was miserable, teary-eyed, and dreading my destination. I had just said goodbye to the two remaining American girls in the house— Shilo and Margo were staying through Christmas, as their parents were coming to visit. We were on our way to Carlos's house now to say goodbye. Bobby Jean was the lucky, postgraduate student who was leaving just for the Christmas holidays. She would be returning and staying for another semester.

The cab driver stopped at Carlos's address in a matter of minutes. Bobby Jean and I got out of the car, and I knocked on the door. Theresa answered with a big smile on her face, as usual. She asked us to sit down and make ourselves comfortable. Carlos had gone down to the corner market to get a few things, she explained. We felt so at home in this precious house that Carlos's father had built, "one door and window at a time," as Carlos had told me.

Theresa offered us hot tea. As she walked toward the kitchen, I studied the colorful tile flooring. It was such an interesting pattern, reminiscent of an Italian design. Stylized circles with pinched points at each quarter of the circle orbited the floor like buxom stars. They were pale aqua and outlined in a darker stroke of the same color. The dining room, which was open to the *sala* (living room), had the same tile pattern but in a rose color. From where I sat, I could see the pale-green spiral staircase. As I looked up at the ceiling, my eyes traced the rococo scrollwork that graced all of the edges of the ceilings in the house. All this, taken into perspective, was a delight of color and charm to the eyes. Again, I recalled that this was the dream house of a loving couple.

The door opened. Carlos entered, looking across the room at me, as if to say, *How can you leave?* His eyes burned right through me. We had talked on the phone the night before. He had wanted to be with me separately, not have me come to his home to say goodbye with Bobby Jean. But I was too emotional, too worried about my inability to stick to my decision if I were alone with him. It was overwhelming. I needed to think clearly and still have enough will to leave for the airport. He had come home for lunch for his two-hour break. He was not happy about the prospect of my leaving; it was evident.

"Y que vas hacer, Collette?" He'd asked me what I was going to do.

"Well," I responded, "I'm here to say goodbye."

"Ven! Ven!" (Come! Come!) He gestured for me to come to him. I got up slowly, and he took my hand as I approached. He was sad, tense, and frustrated. He led me up the stairs to the hallway above, where we could be out of range of anyone's hearing. He turned to face me.

"What are you going to do?"

My mouth quivering, I replied, "I'm going home; you know this. We talked about it last night."

"Sí," he said, not looking up at my eyes.

He felt powerless, which he did not like. I felt sad, lost, and worried, which I did not like. It was impossible to find any comfort in this situation. He held me close. He kissed my forehead. He kissed my cheek. He told me he loved me. I told him the same. It was a magnetism that was too strong for either one of us. It was the sense that if we were separated, all the electricity that ran through us would be lost, and we would shut down, never to come back to life. He looked down at the floor and then looked up at me and muttered, "I cannot bear this."

I gazed at his face, the face I loved, the face that warmed me, the face that personified Mexico to me. "Come visit me! We'll work it out," I said excitedly. "You can stay with my mother. Please do everything you can to make it happen!"

His eyes showed some relief. "I will!"

We reluctantly walked downstairs. Each step bruised my heart. This whole counter-intuitive action of leaving someone you love more than anything else in the world led to panic. Panic led to numbness as I said goodbye to his mother and then to Bobby Jean. Carlos opted not to eat his lunch, saying his stomach was upset. We would eat at the airport, and then he would go back to work.

Bobby Jean and Theresa escorted us to his little white Datsun as we promised we would see each other soon. While Carlos loaded my luggage in his car, the cab that he had called for Bobby Jean arrived. Bobby Jean and I both knew it would be difficult to get together again, but we vowed we would try. Theresa and I embraced gently. I told her I would write to her and that, somehow, I would return to visit. I thanked her for the tea and the previous times that she had welcomed me into her home. I asked that she give a special adios to Señor Herrera. I'd hoped that he would come home before we left so that I could see him before leaving Mexico, but his schedule that day didn't allow time. Theresa promised to tell him goodbye and would give him a warm hug from me.

Bobby Jean held her arms out to me. We hugged each other so hard that it was obvious how tense and upset we both were.

"I *will* come to visit you," Bobby Jean murmured to me. "There's no way this is good-bye."

I bit my lip and got in the car. I turned my head as we drove off, waving to two people for whom I cared tremendously. I hoped they would remain a part of my life. I tried to stare down every street as we drove to the airport, afraid that I would forget some detail about the Mexico that I had come to love. Oh, how could I leave this life, these people? I knew I had become accustomed to something profoundly foreign to my country of origin. I knew that I would never be the same again.

Carlos and I didn't talk on the way to the airport. We looked at each other at each stoplight, me crying and him with a grimace on his face. He kept shaking his head, as if asking why this had to happen.

We finally arrived at the airport, and Carlos hailed a skycap to carry my luggage. When we reached my gate, neither of us could hold back— we embraced and wept as one. It was so bittersweet. Knowing we were in public view, we slowly allowed the invisible bond that kept us together to loosen its grip. Quietly struggling, we slowly moved apart. I looked at Carlos one last time and then turned my head by sheer necessity and walked through the doors of the gate, my head down, tears streaming, and pain totally absorbing me.

I couldn't keep myself from looking back. I knew he was standing there, poised to see me all the way to the airplane's door. I ambled along like an injured animal, looking desperately for a place to die. My legs felt the weight of remorse as I dragged them up the stairs to the entrance of the plane. I came to seat 21A (next to the window, which Carlos had arranged for me). I fell into the seat and turned my head toward the window for privacy. As we pulled out of the gate and began to taxi, it was excruciating to watch the black asphalt pass under the wing. It evoked a sense of the darkness I would experience without Carlos. Soon, I would be out of touch with the one I loved, who was staying in the world I loved.

The plane jettisoned down the runway and took off. I kept my eyes focused out the window, not wanting to deal with anyone. I hoped that no one else was sitting in my three-seat row. I slowly turned my head, and my peripheral vision caught the shadow of a large man. His profile completely filled my would-be view of the other side of the plane. His head just cleared the bottom of the overhead luggage compartment, and his knees looked like he had squeezed them into the inadequate space in front of him. His size seemed to miniaturize the cabin. I felt like a little child in comparison. As I stuffed my tote bag under the seat in front of me, I resumed my position in my confining chair, keeping my face turned toward the window to hide my distress.

But my neighbor spoke to me anyway, requiring me to turn my attention to him. He extended a gargantuan hand across the seat that divided us and gently shook my hand. "Mucho gusto. Me llamo Señor Rodolfo de Gutiérrez."

I responded numbly, "Mucho gusto. Mi nombre es Collette."

He smiled and asked me what had brought me to Mexico. I kept my response short, saying I had just completed a semester at UNAM. He tilted his large head back and nodded. "Ah, sí, yo conozco a la Universidad. Soy profesor de la Universidad. Es una escuela muy bien conocida y excelente." (Oh, yes, I am familiar with the university. I am a professor at UNAM. It is well known and excellent.)

My mood had been usurped. I actually felt relief at his insistence on talking to me. I inquired about his area of teaching, and he was obviously proud to let me know that he was a history teacher. When our meal was served, he poured the wine he had ordered into a glass for me and offered *salud*! (Cheers!) As we sipped the wine, I became more comfortable and was grateful that such a gentleman (and a scholar) was there to involve my attention. We pondered the fact that Mexico had survived a very tumultuous political history. I thought about how tumultuous my own leaving had been.

Our conversation tapered off as our trays were retrieved by the flight attendants. I nudged my seat back and gradually fell into a deep sleep. One hour before the flight landed, my eyes struggled to open, and I found myself in a huddled position next to the window. I was physically refreshed but emotionally still reeling. A trip to the bathroom was in order. As I washed my hands, I dampened a paper towel and dabbed my face, my neck, and the inside of my forearms. The water felt cool and stimulating against my still-sleepy body, coaxing my conscious to wake up and face my return to the US. I knew it would be an endurance test.

After an easy landing, I thanked Mr. Gutiérrez again for the nice conversation, the wine, and the company. He wished me well, and I mimicked a smile. I gathered my tote bag and purse and began my walk down the aisle.

As I approached the gate, I saw my father waiting for me. He was peering at the ever-oozing line as it crawled through the gate and into the airport terminal. He seemed to be concerned whether I was part of that line. As our eyes met, tears filled his eyes, and mine reciprocated. As I reached my precious father with open arms, we hugged with all the life in us and simultaneously sighed with relief that I was home safely after four months.

27

BACK IN THE USA

Our trip from LAX to my father's home in Yorba Linda was sweet. For that hour I absorbed the warmth of his presence, knowing I would be taken care of, no matter what might happen. We talked about the high points of my adventure, and he caught me up on the family happenings. When we arrived home, I found that my stepmother, Barbara, had prepared a sumptuous dinner—a savory roast, mashed potatoes, gravy, green beans … oh, it was such a welcome treat! This was something I couldn't have found in Mexico. We stayed up late as I presented them with little gifts I had bought for them during my travels. I shared most of my experiences with them but didn't mention Carlos. Finally, exhausted from such an emotional day, I gladly went to bed in my familiar bedroom. Lights out, I thought about how glad I was to be home, at least for now.

I spent the next week making phone calls to old friends and meeting up with a few of them. I answered letters from two guys who were still in Vietnam and were to come home soon. So much had happened while I was in Mexico. Although a few friends had come home from the war, two friends had been killed, and one severely wounded. I was faced with the reality of American life again. War was part and parcel of our culture.

I had decided while in Mexico that I wanted a break from school. I planned on looking for a job as soon as possible and then registering in the fall at the local state university. I knew that this decision meant I would have to support myself, but I knew I wouldn't be content to live at home again. I had experienced too much independence in my first two years of college, and there was no going back.

Fortunately, after my first visit to the employment agency, I landed an entry-level accounting job at a nearby aerospace company. A week later, I ran into an old high school friend at a local restaurant; she was my waitress. We chatted in between her serving duties and learned that we were both looking for an apartment. The following weekend, we found one and moved in a week later. Life was at least more palatable now. I was loving the independence, and my father was relieved from having to fully support me.

I sent my address to Carlos, telling him about the recent changes and details about my job and my apartment. Thankfully, I began to receive letters from him a couple of times a week. Within a few weeks, he had written a virtual journal about the happenings of each day of his life since I left. He elaborated on his feelings for me and how much he missed me. To my surprise, he posed various ideas for resolving the problem of our living apart.

After two months of my being back in the US, both Carlos and I were miserable without each other. I called him, and we talked about taking a vacation together. Since I had only been working for one month at that point, I had no vacation time so going to Mexico wasn't in the cards for me. I told him he could come and stay with my mother at her place, which was near my apartment. I wouldn't be with him during the day, I regretted, but we could be together every evening and on the weekend. The very thought of his coming made me tingle from head to toe.

Carlos told me he had saved enough money for the flight, and I offered to help pay for our entertainment and the few meals we would have to buy while he was here. The rest of the time, my mother would, I knew, enjoy cooking for us whenever possible. We agreed that I would talk to my mother and father to be sure their calendars were clear to meet Carlos and take some time to get to know him. Having told each other "I love you" throughout the conversation, we hung up with hope in our hearts. I felt like I was floating on a cloud! For the first time since I'd left Mexico, I believed there was a way for us to find a balance together. Just what that would look like had to remain a mystery for the time being.

When I talked with each of my parents, they happily marked their calendars for Carlos's visit in mid-May. I phoned him the next day, and we finalized the date for his flight to Los Angeles. All I would need after that was a letter with the details of his flight. That letter arrived five days later. Now I had reality looking me in the face, not a dream. I was infused with eagerness for the future. I felt a sense of promise surrounding my life and reveled in the fact that I would be with Carlos in just two weeks!

I talked to my boss and explained the relevance of the friend who was coming to visit from Mexico. I told him that I hadn't known when I was hired that this would be happening but that I would greatly appreciate taking a sick day in order to accommodate the arrival at the airport.

I learned that my boss was a genuinely kind person when he smiled and said, "No problem. Have a great time. I think you're very fortunate to have gone to school in Mexico, and I'm sure the friendships you made there will be lasting ones."

I was amazed. Smiling back at him, I said a very sincere thank-you.

28

A SPECIAL VISITOR

Finally! The morning of Carlos's flight arrived. My mother and sister went with me to the airport, as I had asked. I thought it would be a treat for Carlos to be greeted by all of us. What a fun list of activities I had in store for him to make his first US visit a memorable one. I could only imagine how he would see *my* world, now that I knew *his* world.

We arrived a half hour before his flight was to land and got to the international gate in plenty of time. I was as giddy as a schoolgirl, and my mom and sister were almost as excited as I was. In the '60s, you didn't get on an airplane or pick up anyone at the airport wearing casual clothes. You dressed up! It was a special event, and your attire reflected that. My mother wore a pretty navy dress she had made (she was a wonderful seamstress), with a small red-white-and-blue scarf tied neatly around her neck in the shape of a necklace. My sister wore an emerald-green knit dress and gold earrings. Her hair, a lighter red than my mother's, was long and beautiful. She was slender with beautiful facial features. Together, they were two women with whom I was proud to be standing.

I saw Carlos walking toward us from about fifty feet away. He looked so sharp in his black suit, white button-down dress shirt, and that dark skin that just shouted *guapo* (handsome). I couldn't help but scream, "There he is!"

My sister caught sight of him waving at me. "Wow! He's a looker!"

By then, Carlos was approaching us and smiling from ear to ear. *Oh God, I'm going to grab him!* I screamed within my brain. My arms flung outward, and he was in my arms immediately. Wearing high heels enabled me to press my face against his cheek, a feeling I hadn't had for what seemed like a year.

I broke away, and with joyful tears, I introduced him to my mother and sister. He reached out his hand to shake my mother's first, smiling, and saying in his perfect English, "It is very nice to meet you." Both my mother and sister greeted him with a respectful hug and welcoming words.

"Let's get your luggage," I said, "and then we can go have a nice lunch, and you can get acquainted with my family."

Carlos spotted his bag as soon as we arrived at the conveyor, and soon we were driving down Sepulveda Boulevard in the heart of West Los Angeles. Carlos looked around, taking in the scenery, and said, "This doesn't look much different than Mexico City."

"Just wait," I said. "You'll notice differences when we get out of the city. Los Angeles isn't a good example of Southern California. It's a big city, like Mexico City, but as we drive farther away, you'll see the little communities that are more relaxed and organized."

My mother chose an Italian restaurant for us near her home. We were famished and glad that the service was not only friendly but prompt.

"Well, this is a different meal than I usually have in Mexico," teased Carlos. "Now I am having an American-Italian experience."

It was so fun just being together, the four of us, as we talked about various things and laughed several times about family stories. Carlos seemed right at home, and I felt the same way.

Arriving at my mother's, we parked alongside my little white Volkswagen bug in her driveway. Her home wasn't large, but it was comfy, and she had a nice corner lot with grass and a little patio. She showed Carlos her home, and then showed him the closet in the second bedroom where he could hang his clothes and set his things on the nightstand. He was delighted with her hospitality and couldn't have appeared more at ease.

My mother offered us all lemonade she had made, and we moved out to the patio for a little break.

"I would like to offer a toast to my sister and Carlos," my sister proudly said, holding her lemonade high in the air. Smiling, we lifted our glasses. "I have never seen my sister so happy," she said to Carlos. "I hope the two of you find a way to realize your dream of spending your lives together. We want to be a part of that life."

It was a joy to hear, and it made me feel one step closer to that dream. We talked and enjoyed each other's company for a few hours, recounting all that Carlos and I had done together in Mexico, interspersed with news from my sister about all the recent goings-on with her own family, including my two nephews and niece. I helped my mother set up Carlos's room and then I relented to the late hour, and my sister and I said our goodbyes to Carlos and my mom. I drove off to my nearby apartment for some much-needed sleep.

My alarm clock woke me the next morning at eight o'clock. I hadn't gone to bed until midnight, and I wanted to be sure I was up to show Carlos around the towns where I grew up. That would involve three different areas of Los Angeles and Orange County, so I knew I had to be alert for another long day.

I called my mother at nine o'clock, as I was almost ready to leave. She told me she had already fixed him pancakes with eggs. "He said they were 'muy rico!'" She laughed at herself giving Spanish another try.

"Tell Carlos I'll be over in about a half hour. And thank you for being so kind and generous to him."

"It's no trouble," she insisted. "I'm enjoying his company. He's entertaining!"

When I arrived at my mother's, Carlos was reading the newspaper and drinking a cup of coffee at the kitchen table. He was dressed and ready for the day. He rose, and I stepped over to kiss him. "Your mother gave me permission to call her Mom," he said. "That's fine with me,"

I said. "Ha! That's okay for now, maybe it will be permanent in the future."

Carlos gave my mother a wink.

We left for our tour of my hometowns. I drove him first to the little town where I was born. I found my way to the little neighborhood where my childhood home still stood.

"It's very little and modest," he said. "For some reason, I thought your family would have had bigger property and a bigger house."

"Well, my father started with nothing, probably just like your father when he first moved to Mexico City from Vera Cruz. As with your father, mine slowly earned his way to a better living. I lived in a very small house—just like the one you described to me when I asked you what your first house was like. We have lived a very similar lifestyle, just in different countries. The next town I will show you is nicer, and the home is nicer too. Just like your house in Mexico now—much bigger than the little one you lived in before your father built it. We have our fathers to thank for the nice homes we've lived in and, of course, our mothers for the wonderful meals and loving care."

We arrived in La Mirada about twenty minutes later, where my family had moved when I was seven. I pointed out the Spanish names of all the streets, including the name of my elementary school Escalona. I pulled up in front of the home my father had bought for us on La Barca Drive.

"See, Carlos? Remember I said that I grew up around Spanish names and buildings and people? This is just one example. All the streets are Spanish names."

"It is amazing," he agreed. "The cultural connections here in the States are a surprise for me. It is very nice. This kind of neighborhood is what I expected to see. I guess my previous vision of the United States was from movies shot in Hollywood, so I am learning what the *real* US looks like now."

"No, you didn't hurt my feelings. I'm glad you didn't think we are rich because we are not. We are middle-class people, like your family."

I decided to stop by the new fast-food attraction on our way back to my mother's place. It was all the rage—McDonald's. Carlos had his first American-branded hamburger, and we had a great time talking about the possibility of a McDonald's coming to Mexico, although we thought such a prospect a pipe dream at the time.

That night, we drove out to my father's home. We were to go out to dinner with him and Barbara. Carlos and my father hit it off immediately. My father, as embarrassing as it was, held his hand next to Carlos's hand, and said, "You could be my son!" My father was the same height as Carlos, with black hair and the same skin tone. Coming from French blood, my father tanned quickly and was the color of a cup of coffee with just a spoon of cream.

Thankfully, Carlos loved his joke and responded with, "Mucho gusto, compadre!"—a nod to both respect and familiarity.

Our ride to and from dinner was full of music coming from Dad's tape deck—"The Lonely Bull" by Herb Alpert and the Tijuana Brass, and the entire album of Sergio Mendes and Brazil '66, which included "The Girl from Ipanema," "Mas Que Nada," and "The Look of Love." It was his way to show Carlos that he too had an admiration for Latin music. Our dinner was full of camaraderie and laughs. It was a perfect way to end Carlos's visit with my family.

The next morning, Carlos and I took off for a whirlwind tour of Universal Studios and Busch Gardens in the Los Angeles area. It was ambitious, but we were young and needed the time spent together, just the two of us. I was proud to be a host to Carlos, as he had been to me in Mexico. In my little Volkswagen bug, he and I were content just to play the radio, singing and reminiscing about our times in Mexico.

"Now, if only we had mariachis!" I said with a chuckle.

"Aye, Collette, dónde vas a encontrar mariachis aquí" (Oh, Collette, where are you going to find mariachis here?)

"Well, you may not believe it, but on weekends there are mariachis in the downtown area of the town where I went to high school. We will go there tonight. You'll see!" Carlos was stunned, but I reminded him, "I told you that I have been around the Mexican culture most of my life!" I didn't tell him that my sister and her husband were going to meet us there at seven o'clock.

Universal Studios was an all-day event. We barely had time to swing by Busch Gardens, but we did it all. By the time we arrived in my school town, we were starving. That was the perfect situation, as we were going to have dinner at seven, and it was now six thirty. I drove past my high school, telling Carlos a few quick tales about my cheerleading days and high school shenanigans with friends, both Caucasian and Hispanic. A full history of those incredible years would take far more time than we had.

I turned toward the downtown area that had been settled more than fifty years earlier. As we approached the street where the restaurant was located, I told Carlos about the large number of Mexican people that had come to work in the packinghouse, located across from the restaurant. A railroad ran on the other side of the packinghouse, which served to distribute the plentiful loads of avocados, oranges, and lemons that were grown for miles around. Mexican immigrants to California were plentiful and welcomed in those days. They were hardworking and eager to fill labor opportunities that many Americans found unappealing. It wasn't long before they began to establish their own businesses, mostly in the service and restaurant industries.

We parked and walked across to the 421 Club. The Hispanic owner of the restaurant had lived in the town all her life. Her father had come to California as a bracero many years prior and had managed to successfully provide for his family by working in the construction business. Her restaurant was famous for miles around and was always a special pleasure on a weekend night. We were seated, and by the time our drinks came, my sister and brother-in-law walked up to our table with big smiles.

"Hola, Carlos," my sister said, clearly proud of her Spanish greeting. "This is my husband, Ron."

Carlos arose, so surprised that he almost fell over himself as he reached for Ron's hand. "I am very proud to meet you!" he said with perfect pronunciation and a big smile.

It was apparent that we were in for a night full of good food and frivolity. More drinks were ordered, in between lots of talking and laughing, and we eventually ordered dinner. Carlos loved the menu and said he felt like he was at home! The only exception he mentioned was the burrito, which wasn't on Mexico City menus.

At eight o'clock the mariachis arrived, their trumpets bleating loudly and startling the whole establishment. I knew it would be very special when they strolled by our table to allow us to request a song or two. Carlos was excited to hear the familiar Mexican songs. Now, it was an authentic display of his culture in the very town where I went to school. My past and present love of the Mexican culture had come together in one place. Carlos later told me that he finally understood that I had lived among Mexicans.

As the mariachis roamed around the room, Carlos hurried to finish his dinner. I knew he had something up his sleeve. He held his hand up and snapped his fingers, gesturing to the mariachis, motioning for them to come to our table. He requested that they sing "Que Bonitos Ojos Tienes" (What Beautiful Eyes You Have). That was the song he had serenaded me with in Mexico at la señora's house! By the second stanza, Carlos was standing and singing with the mariachis. By now, the entire restaurant was watching us, and at the end of the song, everyone stood up and gave rousing applause. We were stunned. Carlos took a bow. I could not have felt more pride and contentment.

We talked and laughed until eleven o'clock, when we finally called it a night. With hugs and promises to visit them soon, my sister and brother-in-law walked us to our car.

"I want to talk to you about our future," I said to Carlos as we situated ourselves in my car. "I think it's time for us to have some private time and to figure out what we both want."

Carlos agreed immediately, as evidenced by his wink and smile.

"I'm inviting you to my apartment," I added. It was just ten minutes away.

"I could not be happier with your decision, Collette," he said with a twinkle in his eyes.

As we got out of the car, I pointed up to my cozy new place. "It's up there, above that garage. See the light on?"

Carlos closed his door and looked up. "That's really nice, Collette. I'm really happy for you." We climbed the outside stairs, and I opened the door to reveal my quaint digs. Carlos was impressed and was quick to tell me that I had a great eye for color and comfort.

"Make yourself at home," I said. "Why don't you sit down on the couch, and I'll get us some iced tea?" I scrambled to the kitchen, getting the tea out of the fridge. "Do you take sugar?" I asked.

"No, you will be enough," Carlos said.

"Very funny!" I was blushing from his remark.

When I gave him his tea, he set it down. I sat next to him, taking a sip from my tea. "Now," he said, "we are here, alone, with just our tea." He turned to me, put his arms around me, and began kissing me tenderly. "Collette, I'm in love with you. It's impossible for us to keep this feeling tied up inside. It isn't natural."

I was overtaken with emotion. The couch was a proper place for us, but my bed was shouting at us. The forces were against us. I had to admit to myself that this was exactly what I wanted to happen. I had kept us isolated from a physical relationship for as long as I could. My heart wasn't capable of that task any longer. In all our escapades in Mexico, we were never truly alone. There was always family in the house, and everywhere we went, there were either friends surrounding us or the general public. But here we were, in my apartment, and my roommate was out of town.

"Collette, I must make love to you." It was a short sentence, but it packed a lot of emotional charge.

All I could say was, "Are you sure?" Which meant *absolutely yes.*

Carlos led me to my bed. "I have protection with me, Collette. Come; it will be fine." He met my fears with confidence and comfort.

I can best describe what followed as mysterious and transforming. Never before had I allowed such unfettered emotion to take over. Softly spoken words, his gentle touch and so many months of repressed desire culminated in an unforgettable interlude. I laid my head on his chest afterward and was lost to the world until morning.

Within an hour of sunrise, I awoke to my alarm clock and went directly to the kitchen to make coffee for us. We had just an hour before we had to leave for the airport. Carlos heard me shuffling around and got up five minutes later. After a long embrace, we managed to gulp down our cup of coffee. We dressed hurriedly and then headed to the airport. We were silent as we made our way north on the freeway.

Tension held us both captive. As we arrived at the airport, the tension only heightened. I pulled into a parking spot, turned the car off, and laid my head against the steering wheel—my hands had been wrapped so tightly around the wheel that they felt permanently affixed.

I turned my face toward Carlos and shattered the silence. "This is the most difficult thing I've ever done. I thought that leaving Mexico was the hardest, but this day is like delivering our relationship to the wolves! Everything is even more uncertain than it was before. Why did we even have to meet?" My tears were dripping down my face like a fountain.

Carlos offered an empowering Spanish word. "Venceremos, Collette!" (We will persevere! We will conquer this!) I reluctantly pulled my hands from the wheel and leaned over to him. Embracing him was the only thing I could manage. No words were left in my heart.

After an impossible attempt to console each other, we separated slowly and got out of the car. Walking to the terminal, Carlos held his suitcase in one hand and took my hand with the other. He allowed the imposing sadness to take hold of him. Of course, it enabled me to do the same. We dropped what we were carrying and just held each other outside the doors to the terminal.

"I will not live without you, Collette, no matter what the future brings upon us. Venceremos, Collette!"

He picked up his suitcase and pressed forward into the terminal, leading me as he had on the dance floor when we first met. But this time, the clinical feel of the surroundings was more reminiscent of going into the doctor's office for a painful injection.

Orders were shouted by a porter. "This way, please!"

Didn't he know we needed more time to hang on to what was about to be taken away? But he persisted, and the distraction enabled Carlos and me to give up our hand holding so his bag could be checked. Carlos, feigning a courageous demeanor, hastened toward the gate.

As the distance grew between us, my breathing became shallow. Could I survive without him? One last turn, and he waved goodbye. I put my head down to hide the tears that had started to build again and walked as fast as I could to my car. There, I wept until I couldn't any longer.

29

COLLEGE
COMMUNICATIONS 101

My classes at California State University would begin in mid-August.
I had registered for school in June. Having just turned twenty, I felt
like my life was stuck on a suspension bridge, and I didn't have the
experience to choose which side of the chasm I should venture toward.
Did I want to pull up my lifelong roots and move to Mexico, following
my heart? Or did I want Carlos to move here? Could I be so courageous
as to push my reluctant self aside and get my degree without a man
interrupting my goal? I asked myself why I felt so weak. Why couldn't
I shake my sense of belonging to Carlos and Mexico? I was so lonely for
him and distressed. The only thing that moved me now was necessity.
My father had paid for my tuition and room and board for the semester.
I was committed now, by obligation, if not from within my heart. I
knew I needed to follow through to be fair to him.

I wrote to Carlos, arguing that when the time came, I would rather
move to Mexico than have him move here. If I moved to Mexico, I
reasoned, I would have the best of everything—him *and* the country I
adored. Yet at the same time, I was troubled by the idea of moving to
Mexico permanently. I wondered if I would be, in effect, forsaking my

own country. My mind and heart were on a teeter-totter, one winning out over the other at every move. The rich environment of Mexico that had made me feel so alive was completely absent now. I missed it terribly. I missed Carlos even more.

His letters became my weekly sustenance. My day-to-day life consisted of getting ready for work, going to work, coming home from work, looking to see if a letter had been pushed through the mail slot in the door, and then going out with friends, depending on the mood resulting from Carlos's letter (or from the *absence* of a letter). Carlos's words reinforced my hope and my self-esteem. They engendered in me a sense of belonging, not just to him but to Mexico. Part of the reason for my great need for his reassurance was that the States just did not provide a sense of belonging for me any longer. This was difficult for my family to understand. They were happy with their lives. I couldn't tell them the truth—that I felt more at home in Mexico.

The day came for me to move into the dorms. I did so with trepidation, my conflicted thoughts still ruling me. The only thing that propelled me forward was the fact that I could always withdraw if I couldn't take living here any longer. Meeting my roommates gave the relief of diversion, but I didn't really click with any one of the three, and so I just drew from the shallow reservoir of determination that I was fortunately able to find. I settled in, went over my class schedule, went to the cafeteria for a late lunch, and busied myself with making my bed and organizing my toiletries. I was anxious to turn the lights out and go to sleep. My roommates had gone out to a local restaurant/bar, but I just didn't have it in me to join them.

The next day, I received a letter from Carlos—typed, as usual, with his personal signature at the bottom. Carlos's words pulled at my heart like the earth's mass holds the moon in orbit. His words penetrated my soul and clanged inside my ears, and my body reacted as if a cataclysmic event was about to take place.

I lay on my bed, paralyzed with the struggle that was too large for me to endure. I had tossed and turned for weeks, going back and forth with the old "Ben Franklin" list—pros on one side of the page and cons on the other—until I was numb.

Pro: You love him. Go to him.

Con: Mexico's a difficult country for a woman (much less a gringa) seeking a career.

Pro: "You'll never be happy without him."

Con: You would be leaving your country of origin forever?

Pro: You're so happy and optimistic when you're with him.

Con: What if he disappoints you once you've moved there?

On and on and on my obsessive thoughts marched, day and night. No matter what I did, both the pro and con sides were equal. I'd thought the best way to break the string of conflicting thoughts was to make the decision to go back to school. But now, what I was experiencing in the dorm room trumped that thought.

In a rare moment of bravado, I made the bold decision to write a "Dear John" letter to Carlos. I simply couldn't cope with the internal battle I had been enduring. I tried to assure myself that it would give closure to my constant going back and forth. I had a few days before my classes started, and I took my education seriously (especially after my lackluster performance at UNAM).

I spent the whole night struggling with the perfect wording—not too many hurtful words, not too many wistful words, just the right conclusion, not too much fatalism. But no matter what I did, I found it impossible to make it palatable for him or me. I put it into the airmail envelope anyway, set it on my desk, and pressed a stamp on it as if to seal the deal. *Now! Go away haunting thoughts, harassment of my soul, indecision*, I thought. *I'm starting a new life.*

30

GOOD COUNSEL

My Dear John letter wasn't received well. Carlos called me (a big expense from Mexico), and his first words were, "Why are you doing this to us? Don't you trust me? Don't you see that I am breaking my back to make your life in Mexico beautiful? I love you, Collette. Don't do this to us. You are ruining the beautiful bond that we have. Venceremos!"

I wasn't able to talk. It hurt me as much as it hurt him. I was angry with myself for writing it; I was angry with myself for not being able to cut the cord; I was angry with myself for not being stronger. I was angry with myself one minute, for any one of those reasons, and then the next minute, I was proud of myself for resisting the almost overwhelming temptation to just stop everything in my life and move to Mexico. I was a wound-up ball of nerves, obsessing over which way to go and not finding a conscionable answer. Finally, after a long stretch of silence, I faced the truth and told him that I desperately needed to talk to someone about the conflicted thoughts I was having. I promised to call him the next day to confirm that I had made an appointment with a counselor and a real effort to move toward a decision for both our sakes. We ended with "I love you" and "I miss you."

The next morning, I walked to the reception desk at the dorm to inquire about student counseling. To my shock, displayed right in front of me was a folder of pamphlets titled "Need Counseling?" I nonchalantly reached for it, not wanting to appear desperate, and stuck it in a textbook I was carrying. I was full of excitement to think that *this* might be my way out of my self-terrorizing thoughts. As soon as I got to my room, I dropped on my bed, opened the pamphlet, and started reading it. It began with a friendly welcome and asked, "Do you need help with campus life?" It listed possible symptoms of those who might need to talk to a counselor. It further assured the student that the health insurance provided by the university covered the counseling 100 percent. It was free, and it was near campus. It was a veritable fountain of promise spouting right in front of me.

I picked up the phone and made an appointment with the soft-spoken receptionist. She told me that I would be meeting with Dr. Sonders. I didn't ask any questions. What mattered was that *hope* was in sight. She said, "If you'd like to come by to pick up a new patient form, you can have it filled out in time for your appointment." I said I'd be right over.

As I stepped up to the desk on the third floor of the building two mornings later, the receptionist kindly gestured for me to give my completed form to her and to sign my name on the roster designated for Dr. Sonders. I began shaking as I took a seat. I knew this was not just going to be a casual "help me with a little problem I'm having" counseling session. This was about *my life*. I knew I was on the brink of either disaster or exhilarating joy. Within a few minutes, a tall blonde woman, wearing a reassuring smile, stepped out from an office down the corridor to my left and called my first name. She took on the aura of an angel, and I immediately prayed that she would be my savior. She gestured for me to take a seat on her comfy sofa as she quietly shut the door behind her. I noticed the box of tissues thoughtfully placed on the side table as I sat down at that end of the sofa.

Dr. Sonders was about forty years old. As she began to ask questions, I realized that she was no one to fear. She was confident yet gentle, and her questions gave me an outlet for expressing the details of my life that I wanted her to ask. If she didn't know enough about my past, how could she talk to me about my future?

One question was, "What would make you happy right now, if no mental or physical obstacles stood in your way?"

Whoa! I was stunned. That was a question you didn't hear every day. There is always something in the way. That's why we go to counseling. I stammered a bit, saying something dumb like, "Uh, I've never thought in that way before … it doesn't seem to be a logical way to think."

She responded firmly, "That's exactly why I'm asking you this question. I want you to think outside of your normal paradigm."

I began to cry, not even knowing why I was crying at first. Then I realized that it was because I *knew* what would make me happy. It had been on the tip of my tongue for months now, but I couldn't dare voice it—or could I? The very thought that I was *going to* voice it caused me to break down and cry. I had wanted to tell someone for so long, but I felt I would receive nothing but laughter or comments like, "What? Are you crazy?"

After crying on and off and lots of talking back and forth, I was finally able to put words to my emotions and allow them to flow naturally out of my mind and mouth. I gave her the whole history of my trip to Mexico, my time with Carlos, my feelings for him, and the frustrating outcome. She paused for a while as I sat quietly, waiting for her response.

She essentially advised me that love doesn't come along in life every day and that there are risks in every relationship. She suggested that I had obviously wracked my brain long enough and that my misery quotient was such that I had to make a decision. She gave me a book to read about self-assertion and conflict resolution, as well as a questionnaire to complete after reading the book. It was a little paperback, easy to read, packed with exercises related to decision making, and I was to turn in my "homework" the following week.

In two more sessions, she confidently told me, I would be making some sound decisions about my dilemma. With that, our hour ended, and I walked out feeling that we had had a very comprehensive meeting. I was anxious to do the reading and homework to further the analysis of my dilemma.

During the next week of classes and homework, I made sure to read my book and assignment from Dr. Sonders as well. I gave much thought to this new world of psychology that I had entered into, and I wrote down my innermost, personal thoughts, as the book required. I showed up for my next appointment, and Dr. Sonders guided me through the first three chapters that she had assigned, asking me for my written responses as we progressed. There were fewer tears this time and a very productive discussion about everything from my desired career path to what I needed from a potential mate. The next appointment, she informed me, would be the last three chapters, which would focus on decisionmaking and resolution of conflict.

"This is going to be where the rubber meets the road," she said firmly.

I thanked her, feeling much more confident than I had a week ago, and left with book in hand, looking forward to the next week, when I would begin the revelation of my future.

The week went by at a snail's pace, with intermittent obsessive worrying, followed by a gradual return to more rational thinking. In between, I eagerly read the next three chapters of my book from Dr. Sonders. I forced myself to read the last chapter (and the scariest portion) of the book. It was riveting, it was demanding, and it brought my obsessive thinking to a halt.

What the book kept reiterating was that some decisions are life-changing. These are the decisions that often do not get made, as there is not enough difference between the positive consequences and the negative consequences. However, I remembered that the counselor had told me that nothing in life is certain and that it would be impossible for me to predict the outcome of every issue. She reminded me of the old adage: "Nothing ventured, nothing gained." The last part of the workbook required that I weigh the literal, tangible things, qualities, and opportunities of my current life against the same issues in my potential *new* life. Among them were the following:

➤ Sense of belonging (Would Carlos's family see me as friend or foe?)

> ➤ Reality of how often (or how seldom) I would be able to visit my family
>
> ➤ My everyday comfort with the culture I would live in (conveniences versus inconveniences)
>
> ➤ Access to education (length of time to be accepted, if at all, at a Mexican university)
>
> ➤ Whether my earned credits would be applied to my new foreign school
>
> ➤ Access to the economy (job availability and salary)
>
> ➤ Access to health care (How much would health insurance cost me, and what would I get for the price?)
>
> ➤ Exposure to legal entrapment (Would I have all the legal rights of a Mexican citizen, and if not, what liabilities might I face)

These were the most difficult mental and emotional exercises that I had ever experienced. I had never had to choose between my current life and an unknown life. How many people ever do? *Why me? Well, why not me?* I thought. But then, was it blame that I should consider, or was it fate? I never planned what happened. Sure, I made the choice to be driven home by a stranger from that party. But wasn't I without a way home? And didn't I ask to see their driver's licenses? Yes. And was it really a bad call on my part to accept a dance with that handsome Mexican guy? I didn't feel guilty; I felt compelled to discover what lay ahead. Did we really have the opportunity to stave off what seemed to be preordained? Or did we unknowingly fall into predicaments, just by ambling along in life?

The next counseling session was the capstone of my future. After the counselor intently read my heart and soul's intimate thoughts and my highest brain's attempt at cold logic, she looked at me and asked, "So what conclusions have you drawn from all that you have answered here?"

After a long pause, I said, "Uh, well, I was hoping that you would help me with that."

"Really? This is supposed to be your final exercise. You are to determine what your decision will be, from your own thoughts and feelings and from the pros and cons and all of the discussions we have had."

"Oh, well, I have only come to the conclusion that I am more confused than ever. Nothing truly wins out on one side or the other that helps me make a decision. Truthfully, the only terrible thought I keep having is not having Carlos. I just cannot imagine myself as a happy person ever again without him."

"Well," she responded, "I think you need to start making plans to move to Mexico."

My face lit up like a Christmas tree; this was exactly what I was desperate to hear! "Oh my God! I am so relieved that someone has given me *permission* to live out my desire! Thank you for saving me from the terrible stress I have been under!" I began to sob.

The counselor calmly replied, "This is what we call a no-brainer. You're in love, and your brain is not going to let it go. You need to proceed with a *plan,* and I want to see the plan in writing next week. Please do not take any action, other than to prepare the plan, until I see you next week. Especially do not tell Carlos, your parents, or your friends that you have decided to move to Mexico. I want the written plan to be your final exercise, and I want to see how comfortable you are with it after you've written it. Now go and have a good week. You don't need to keep mulling over things. Your job is to prepare the plan, not to go back and forth with 'Should I or shouldn't I?'"

31

A PLAN COMES
TOGETHER

Although I needed to study for exams and planned to go out with friends from the dorms that following weekend, I acknowledged that the counselor's advice was of the ultimate importance. I was focused on the job before me. *I'm going to figure out my life!* I shouted to the hollow space in my head that awaited clarity. Making a quick phone call, I bowed out of my Friday night plans and buckled down at my desk. I began an outline of "The Plan."

I started my outline without much effort. It seemed simple (the outline, not the challenge). It looked like this:

I. Getting Ready to Move
    A) Call Carlos and confirm
    B) Withdraw from school
    C) Try to get tuition and book refund
II. How to Move
    A) Book flight
    B) Get shipping information
    C) Pack

III. Tell Friends and Family
   A) Dinner with Dad
   B) Visit with Mom and Sis
   C) Visit (certain) friends; call others
IV. Ship Personal Items (Wedding Dress?)
V. Pack
VI. Leave

Of course, I knew this was simplistic, but if I got caught up in more details, I would never finalize my plan. It was funny how easily these steps rolled out of my brain, as if they were held hostage there for months, just waiting for permission to be expressed. Now, I felt a freedom unlike any I had ever felt before. In life, I realized, it was easy to go with the flow, as most people do, staying in the area of their birthplace, going to school there, marrying there, living out a career there. But you can also decide to challenge that flow by making a U-turn, swimming back upstream to a place or a special person that you experienced along the way. I was doing both of the latter.

I wrote details below each of the headings in my plan and knew that the most urgent thing on my agenda (aside from meeting with my counselor next Thursday) was to call Carlos. I was very worried that Carlos was starting to give up on me, and I had no reason to blame him for that. I had been on again/off again with him for so many months now that I was becoming worried about whether I still embodied his life's dream. I started obsessing about what his next letter would say because one was definitely due.

I walked into the main hall at the dorm and approached my mailbox. I was afraid to open it. I slowly pulled on the metal hook and opened it just enough to peek in. There was some mail, but it was too dark inside to see what it was. *Oh God, what if he has given up? Can I bear this?* My next thought was, *What can I do to salvage our relationship? I wish I had already called him! There has been such confusion and pain between us.*

Without separating the stack, I took the mail to my room. Luckily, only one roommate was there. She offered a brief "How ya doing?" as she looked up from her study session. I just threw out a "Good; how are you doing?" She replied with a requisite, "Good."

I knew it was safe to sort through my mail without interruption. I hoped to see a letter from Carlos—and I saw it in the third letter. I tore it open.

Dear Collette:

I am so distraught about your unwillingness to come to Mexico and then your decision that I shouldn't come to the US either. I feel like I have lost my life's dream, and I can't go on this way. I have not received a letter from you, and you never sent back the photos I sent to you of when you were here. I remember dancing with you so many times, listening to all those American songs.

I need to know if I should restart my life, and it is only fair for you to tell me one way or the other: are you coming or not? If you are in school, it is obvious that you will not be able to come to Mexico until the first of next year … clearly, three more months. I cannot take it unless you are ready to commit to me that you are coming.

If you can call me, I will be home on October 25, 26, and 27. This letter will get to you before those dates, so I will wait by the phone each night. Please, please call me! I don't want someone else to take your place, but you have pushed me away from you for so many months, and I am very distraught about it. So many days I feel weak and go out with my friends. I am around other girls, and it is difficult to convince myself that I have someone else who lives in another world and won't promise to come to me!

I will be waiting by the phone the 25th, 26th, and 27th. I pray to God you will call!

With doubt, but love,
Carlos

Of course, the dates he would be waiting by the phone were that night (Monday), Tuesday, and Wednesday—all before my appointment with my counselor on Thursday. "Oh Lord," I openly prayed, "help me!"

That night at seven o'clock, our dorm phone rang. "Oh, please don't answer it, you guys!" I yelled at everyone. I hadn't mentioned the possibility of Carlos calling. I just hunkered down and hoped he wouldn't.

"I'm expecting a call!" Marsha said. "I have to get it!" She picked it up. "Who is calling?" she asked, seeming puzzled. I knew that meant it was Carlos. "Oh, just a minute, please," she said, turning to me. "It's for you, Collette. It's a long-distance call from Mexico."

I had no choice, and I knew it. I sprang from my bed and took the receiver from Marsha's hand. Truthfully, an electric charge had hit me the minute the phone rang. "Hello?" I said, as if I had no idea who was on the other end.

Carlos's deep, melodious voice answered, "Hola, Collette." He sounded so subdued and sad.

I immediately experienced a deep pain shoot from my head to my toes. "Hola, Carlos," I responded, unable to add anything else.

"What are you going to do, Collette?" he asked in English.

"Oh, Carlos, I want you to know that I started going to a counselor, and she is helping me make a decision by this Thursday. I can't stop thinking about you. You know I love you!"

"You do?" he asked. "Then why haven't I heard from you? I'm telling you I have almost let go of the dream we had. How can you do this to me? I am going crazy without you! You cannot expect me to keep living in this lonely way, going out with my friends like a zombie, while they enjoy their lives!"

"If you will just wait for me until Thursday night, I will call you and give you my answer! Yes, my *answer*! I am suffering also, and I too cannot keep living in this limbo."

"Okay, then, I will wait for your call on Thursday night. I really hope I won't be disappointed again. I can't take this, Collette." He was brief, but I understood why. The call was expensive, and he wanted substance, not *talk* about my answer but my *answer*.

Thursday afternoon came, and I met with my counselor right on time. I had my plan in an envelope. I handed it to the counselor immediately, so proud of myself for doing my homework. She asked me how the week had gone, and I said that it had been very cathartic. I shared with her my absolute sense of freedom at choosing my own destiny. She gradually opened it up, and she looked very surprised to see that it was only two pages!

"It only took me an hour to put it together," I said.

"Yes," she said, "it seems very … well, *concise*. How do you feel about it? Do you feel confident about it?"

I answered her truthfully, although the doubts I had felt before began to crop up in me. "I want this plan to work. That is my answer. I have come to the conclusion that I cannot bear the alternative of going on as I have been, desiring to go to Mexico and to be with Carlos, yet prohibiting myself from going."

The counselor's face relaxed as she looked at me with deep regard and sincerity. "Collette, you are definitely in charge of your own destiny. No one else can make this decision for you. In fact, not many people will even understand the strong feelings you have, not just for Carlos but for Mexico. It is something that you alone can understand. I must tell you that you are a very brave young woman and that I respect your feelings and the intense struggle that you have gone through. It is time to, as they say, fish or cut bait. You must move to Mexico and get on with your life. And do it with confidence! Get your things in order talk with your parents about your emotional struggle all these months, our counseling sessions, and the plan. Then, let Carlos know your plan and make sure he is still 100 percent in support of your moving to Mexico and that he still has accommodations for you at his parents' home. You have played with his emotions for so long that it is fairly predictable that he has had every reason to seek out another relationship.

"If Carlos is still desirous of your coming and making a life together, take time to consider the quality of your relationship with Carlos before making a decision to get married. Take time to live the culture; get to know his parents very well; participate in his friends' lives; and slowly draw your final conclusion. Is this the life you want to live? Is this the person you want to live it with? Is this where you want to live? You still have time for these thought processes. Take advantage of them. I wish you all of the very best. I wish you a deeply meaningful and *successful* life with Carlos and a life in Mexico! May God be with you."

I was ecstatic. I couldn't wait to leave her office, as I felt confident now that she had validated my plan.

I ran back to my dorm room to call Carlos and tell him the news. I prepared myself beforehand with a prayer: "Lord, please be with me. I am a pilgrim about to take a journey that is unpredictable. Please make me aware of anything I have overlooked, and guide me through this. Amen."

I waited for my roommate to leave, as she had a night class that started at five o'clock. As soon as she left, I arranged a blanket on the floor under the wall-mounted dorm phone we all shared. I carried my big corduroy bedrest over to the blanket and set it against the wall. I wanted to be comfortable for this all-important call. In an additional attempt to add a sense of warmth and calm, I pulled my quilt off my bed and wrapped it around my shoulders. It was a gift from my grandmother that had been with me for many years.

I knew I had to be ready for any emotion—good, bad, or indifferent. I knew that Carlos had felt used and played. I wasn't at all sure if he would receive my news with joy or if he would tell me he couldn't trust my dedication any longer.

I walked to the little fridge we had in the room and took out an ice-cold bottle of Diet Pepsi. It felt good to have something for fortification. I walked to my little nest and crouched down on the floor against my bedrest. I dialed Carlos's number. On the third ring, he answered.

"Bueno?" This was the Spanish greeting when answered the phone, equivalent to hello in English.

"Carlos, it's Collette," I said.

There was a long pause before he said, "Sí, Collette?" It was as if he was asking a question.

"I'm calling you to apologize for all the frustration I've caused you over all these months."

"Pues, he estado muy desilusionado, Collette." He admitted his disillusionment.

"I know," I said, "but I'm calling with news—good news!" I said hastily.

"Dime, Collette." He prodded me to tell him.

"I, uh, I told you I've been seeing a counselor. She has helped me to evaluate my feelings and work through my indecision."

Again, Carlos said, "Dime, Collette." His tone was tenuous, as if expecting doom.

I felt a lump in my throat. "Well, I've decided that I want to move to Mexico. And I am sure of my decision. I hope you are as happy as I am about it."

"Hay, Collette. Estás segura?" (Oh, Collette. Are you sure?)

"Yes, I am sure!"

Carlos sounded exasperated when he said, "Pues, estoy muy sorprendido, pero necesito saber que esto es el fin de todos los meses de indecisión." (Well, I am very surprised, but I need to know that this is the end of all the months of indecision.)

"Yes, those months are behind us now. I promise you. But I need to hear from you that this is what you want now, in spite of what we've been through."

Carlos responded immediately with *yes*, using English to emphasize his delight. "I am very anxious to make this happen, Collette. I have thought through so many things for so many months for our future, and I am very relieved to hear this from you. We have a lot to do!"

Knowing the cost of the phone call, I told Carlos that I would call him again two nights later. "I love you, Carlos, with all my heart and soul. I can't wait to make it happen! Good night, mi amor!"

"Buenas noches, mi novia!" Carlos said good night to me as his fiancé.

32

THE ANNOUNCEMENT

I made the announcement to my father first. I asked if we could get together for dinner on Thursday of that week.

"Sure, honey. Just decide on a place, and I'll pick you up about six."

"Thanks, Dad. You don't know how much this means to me. I love you. I'll see you then."

"See you then, honey. Nighty-night."

He always said that to me, followed by "sweet dreams" when I was younger. Oh, he was so precious to me. How could I leave him? I gave myself some self-talk, as Dr. Sonders had coached me: "Stop! Just stop!" This exercise was supposed to make my obsessive thoughts stop and move me on to another topic. If it didn't work, I was to start walking away from wherever I was—to a different area of my dorm room or campus, for example. I was to metaphorically "walk away" from my thoughts, putting them in the subservient role. Shortly, I found myself focused on my English 201 textbook, reading the remainder of a chapter, and then segueing to a study session in preparation for my exam the next day. It had worked!

Thursday came. I was eager to meet with my father. I was painfully aware of how hard my news was going to be for him to hear. But I also knew that he had truly enjoyed meeting Carlos and had even mentioned that if I were to move to Mexico (if Carlos and I were to get married), he could fly down to see us without much difficulty since he had his own light plane. He had urged Carlos to complete his studies here so that he could qualify for a job in the US. Thus, the conversation had a foundation. It wasn't out of the blue. My dad knew how I felt about Carlos, and he had a good idea that our relationship was going to have to find a country.

Dad pulled up next to my apartment right on time. I hurried down the stairs and greeted him as I opened the passenger side of his new Dodge Monaco coupe. I sat down and reached across the seat to give him a big hug.

Dad had always been meticulous about his collection of cars. His friends were a mixture of white-collar and blue-collar people, and his best friend had his own auto mechanics business. Dad called on him for his opinion about prospective car purchases my dad made from time to time. In this case, Dad had opted for a brand-new car for nice occasions. This was definitely a nice occasion. Just being with my father was heaven on earth. He was my idol, the person I looked up to in life, my stability. I knew that meeting with him was the best experience I could have right now. It was the right thing to do … and, of course, without his blessing, I would be miserable.

"Where to, sweetie?" he asked, giving me his beautiful, white-toothed smile.

"I was hoping you would choose."

"How about Trapper's?" He knew I loved that restaurant.

"Mmm, that sounds perfect!" I responded with pleasure. Trapper's was located in the town where Dad had worked for the past eight years. He had a thriving business—his own car dealership. He was the president of an international charity organization at that point, and I admired his achievement and generosity in contributing to his working community. He was well liked by so many, and he was loyal to those friendships. We arrived at Trapper's and walked together to the door. We were greeted by the hostess, who was also the owner. "Hello, John!"

"Good to see you, Helen. This is my daughter, Collette," he said proudly.

"She's a beautiful young woman, and I'm sure she's proud of her father!"

My dad blushed a bit but kept his composure. "Not as proud as I am of her," he said.

"I know you didn't come here just for compliments, so let's get you seated in a nice booth so you can enjoy each other's company and have a great dinner." She led us to a softly lit booth. The spirit of the restaurant was upbeat, with plenty of conversations going around us, so our intimate discussion could, thankfully, be private.

"Let's take a look at the menu, sweetie," Dad recommended.

"Good idea; I'm hungry," I replied.

Dad suggested I try the delicious prime rib that he had enjoyed here so many times with my stepmother. I was more than happy to oblige him. We both loved beef, barbecued or roasted; it seemed to be our favorite for as long as I could remember. In no time, our server came and took our orders. The first phase of the night had been easy.

"So, Dad, I bet you'd like to know why I asked you to dinner," I said.

"I'm guessing you have something to tell me," he said.

"Yes, I do. And more important, I need your advice and thoughts." I took a deep breath and exhaled slowly. "You know that Carlos and I are still trying to figure out how to make our relationship work. We've both experienced each other's country, and we've been writing and calling each other, but we're very conflicted about what to do."

Dad gave me a sentimental look, knowing I was struggling and knowing that, ultimately, no matter what we decided, his relationship with me was going to be affected by my decision. "What are you two thinking of doing?" he asked.

"That's the problem, Dad. I have to confess to you that I am not only in love with Carlos, but I am also in love with Mexico." *There, I got it out*, I thought. The real dilemma had been divulged.

"Boy, that's really a tough one," he volleyed back to me.

"I know; that's why we're here. I haven't told you, but I've been so frustrated that I started seeing a counselor at the university. It's free, and so I availed myself of it."

Dad looked puzzled. With his hardscrabble background, he likely had never heard the term. I could tell that he was worried that maybe I was mentally ill.

"Dad, counseling isn't just for people with mental illness. It's also for people—in this case, students—who are having difficulty with an area of their lives that could use some sorting out." I said.

Dad looked relieved, and he managed to eke out a slight smile, which comforted me.

"I have had many discussions about how to solve this dilemma, and the counselor has helped me to work through it all," I said. "She has concluded that I need to—and I quote—*follow my dream*. She has heard all of my desires, complaints, worries, and concerns, and her take on it is that I am in love, and I can't erase that fact. The obstacle is deciding where to live when Carlos and I get married."

Our meal came, and it was just in time; we both needed to breath awhile.

"Let's just enjoy our meal now, Dad," I suggested. "We have plenty of time for this discussion after we eat. Let's catch up with what's going on with everyone in the family and just take our time. Does that sound good?"

"I think you've got a good idea. We can digest our thoughts as well as our food."

I loved the pleasing way my father made everything seem all right. He had seen such hard times in his life, and from that he had a perspective that many people never gain. He knew how to joke at just the right time to tamp down anxiety. I knew right then that his greatest joy was seeing that I was enjoying my life. He had provided for me for twenty years now and had been by my side as I wandered down my life's path. He was always there. Steady and strong. My rock.

We talked about everything from Dad's business to his recent travels with my stepmother to Hawaii. They had only been married a year at this point, but I felt like she had always belonged in my father's life, and therefore, in mine. I loved her and knew that she could have been sitting right there with us tonight and that it would have been fine. But

I needed one-on-one time with Dad for this life-changing decision, and I was confident that she understood.

The last bite of prime rib was taken prisoner by my fork, and I moaned as I chewed it, feeling my stomach's rebellion at the amount of food I had forced on it. "That was so good, Dad. Thank you so much for the wonderful dinner."

"You're welcome, sweetie. My pleasure. And now, how about that discussion we were having?"

"Well, I'm ready if you are," I gently replied.

"I'm ready." He met my smile.

I wiggled a bit in my seat, trying to give my stomach a new position that might make room for my ambitious meal. "I just need to know one thing, Dad. Will you honestly be able to fly down to visit me if I move to Mexico? I mean, at least a few times each year?"

He looked quizzical. "That question leads me to believe that you've already made your decision."

"I'm leaning that way, Dad," I responded. "I just don't think I can give up my love of Mexico, and that's what has really been weighing heavily on my mind."

"Yes, I could fly down to visit. But to be practical, Barbara and I would probably just take a commercial flight. I'm sure it's not that expensive, and the weather wouldn't be a problem as it is for light planes. You would fly here also, wouldn't you? Your old dad wouldn't be too happy if you didn't."

I was relieved to see my father's attempt to absorb so quickly the reality of his little girl getting married and moving fifteen hundred miles away. I was, as always, amazed at his resolve and confidence in the face of obstacles. I was overtaken by emotion, now that I knew this was really going to happen. I began to cry and reached my hand across to my father's.

He took my hand and softly said, "I love you, sweetie. You need to follow your dream. If you don't, you will probably regret it. I don't want that for you. Let's just make sure that all the right steps are taken to put you in the best position possible for a good life in Mexico. And remember you can always move back here. There's nothing stopping you from that. There are many things that I don't know about Mexico, and maybe you can go over some things with me and Barbara this Sunday when you come over. That would be a good idea. I think we'll all feel better about things when we have some more details. Would you do that for me?"

"Of course I will, Dad. I want nothing more than to go into this together, so there are no looming questions or uncertainties between us."

Dad took care of the bill, and we scooted out of our booth. We walked out to the car and enjoyed small talk on the drive back to my apartment. Now that the most difficult task of telling my father was taken care of, I looked forward to Sunday, to taking time with Dad and Barbara to talk in detail about the practical things, knowing there would be sentimental tears cropping up off and on during our time together. It would be valuable time, preparing our minds and hearts for my avant-garde future. Now, to tell my mother …

My call to my mother went as smoothly as I'd hoped it would. Being an adventurous and very independent-minded woman all her adult life, she related to my dream. She had loved her time with Carlos and had heard more about our hopes for a future together in Mexico than I had previously divulged to my father. After all, we were both women and talked more comfortably when it came to matters of the heart.

As I told her the decision I had reached and how the counseling had gone, we settled into an agreeable conversation about the things that I would need to do in order to move myself to Mexico. She laughed at one point and said she would have to learn more Spanish words before our wedding. She was truly not afraid of enjoying life, in spite of the risks.

33

MY PLAN TAKES FLIGHT

Carlos looked up the information about the best flight for me and gave me all the information I needed. I called the travel agent and made the reservation, thanks to my father's generosity. In those days, there were no computers. You had to call (or go to the travel agency) to talk to a travel agent, who would then make the reservation over the phone with the airline company. If you went to the agent in person and wrote a check, the reservation could be made, and your tickets would be expedited back to the travel agent as soon as the check was received from the agent. You would then go back to the agent in about a week and pick up your tickets.

While I waited for my ticket, I gathered together different outfits I could wear in Mexico, remembering the dress code. I loved this part of my adventure, as I imagined myself in every outfit and which pants and tops I could interchange to expand my wardrobe. I was (and still am) a clothes horse. I was sewing my own clothes at that time, so I had a wide range of colors and printed fabrics that I could mix and match. Eventually, I packed everything I could into my college trunk and one full suitcase.

My carry-on bag was a big duffel bag, which I would use to bring a thoughtful gift for Carlos's parents, as well as the things I couldn't fit in my trunk and suitcase (another pair of shoes, my very important makeup kit, toiletries, and my trusty Spanish vocabulary book from Señor Valadez's class in high school). "What was I thinking?" I asked myself, as I practiced lugging the behemoth bag over my shoulder.

On October 10, I left for Mexico City. I didn't know what awaited me, specifically, but I knew it was a whole *new* life! I knew I was in for adventure. This time, I knew that the breadth and depth of my relationship with Carlos would eclipse my previous experience.

As soon as the plane crossed the Mexican-American border, I was keenly aware of the gravity of my decision. This was not only the anniversary of my first trip to Mexico, but it was, more accurately, my "engagement" trip. I toasted my relationship with Carlos with my glass of water, as if he were there next to me. Under my breath, I said, "Here's to the most exciting life I could have ever imagined!"

After I ate the breakfast the flight attendant had brought, I basked in the certainty of love, security, and cultural charm that awaited me. Shortly after, I fell into a deep, much-needed sleep.

When I awoke, with my head comfortably against the window, I realized there was only one hour left in the flight. I decided it was the perfect time to practice my Spanish (which would also keep my adrenaline down). *How do I say "I had a great flight"? How do I say "I missed you so much"? Or "I am so eager to start our new life together"? Oh, never mind; Carlos speaks English!* I obviously couldn't concentrate, so I just gazed out at the beautiful, foamy clouds and blue sky and let my mind float. For the rest of the trip, I focused on loving arms, which would soon encircle me, and the man that I adored. Besides, I *knew* how to say "Te quiero!" (I love you!). That was all I really needed that day

I felt the captain cut the power ever so slightly. Adrenaline shot out to every nerve in my body. *If I were neon, I would be glowing like a fireball*, I thought. My next thought was, *Hurry; check your makeup*, followed by, *Go to the bathroom*. I took care of both quickly and then smoothed my clothes before sitting down for the final time. The next time I got up would be to reunite with Carlos—in less than an hour. I knew he was already anticipating my arrival and. Just thinking of him standing there waiting for me caused my face to flush and my body to tremble. Containing my excitement wasn't easy now, but contained it would have to be!

The captain cut back the power again. He came on the intercom, first in Spanish and then in English, advising us that we would be landing in fifteen minutes. With my face pasted against the window, I caught a glimpse of the neighborhood where Carlos lived (my future home). It was easy to identify, as it was so close to Chapultepec Park, which had caught my eye just moments before. The sprawling, grassy-green park was huge and took minutes to pass by, even in a fast-moving plane. I was gawking at it and realized that I could trace the route to Carlos's parents' house easily since I had traveled the freeway so often with Carlos. I knew the off-ramps and streets within a one-mile radius so well that it led me right to the street and house where my dreams were being kept safe. It was surreal! I could see the roof, the backyard—wow!

Another decline of the engine lifted my stomach up to my rib cage as we descended toward the runway. Now it was a matter of five minutes before I would be on Mexican soil. It was so hard to keep from shouting, *"Finally!"*

The landing was as smooth as licking an ice cream cone and just as sweet! I unleashed my body from the seatbelt and tried not to jump up and run to the door. I restrained myself until the plane came to a full stop, and then I popped up like a jack-in-the-box. Since I was in the middle of the plane, just behind the wing, there would be a wait. I had just enough strength to hold myself back. I nudged the woman sitting in the aisle seat in my row, motioning that I wanted to get my carry-on out of the overhead cabinet. She moved with the same indifference she had maintained during the whole flight, which was fine with me; I just wanted to be ready to go!

Finally, the crowd began to deplane. I tested the viability of my legs as I stepped into the aisle and started my trek down the aisle—what a perfect analogy to what I would be doing soon! As quickly as I could move, I juggled my duffel bag and purse between the seats until I reached the cabin door. Fresh air! Mexico! Carlos! I paused to scan the crowd that was waiting outside on the tarmac, and there he was! *Oh Lord, keep me from tripping all over myself!*

I maneuvered the stairs, and now my steps were faster as I rushed across the tarmac to my target. *Yes! Oh God! I'm holding him now! He's holding me now! He's smiling at me now. I'm crying now! We're weeping together now! Now we're* one*!*

34

MY NEW HOME

Carlos and I could hardly stop embracing as we slowly made our way to the baggage claim area. Quick affirmations—like "I can't believe I'm here!" or "Oh God I have missed you!"—were repeated over and over as we walked a few yards and then stopped and stared into each other's eyes to dispel our doubts that this was real.

We were like one person with four arms and legs, almost tripping over each other on the way to his car. Finally reaching it, Carlos quickly put my bags inside. Again, once inside the car, we turned to each other and held each other with an invisible fire engulfing us. How could we contain the untamable magnetism that welled up so quickly between us? I looked forward to the challenge!

Carlos drove straight to his parents' house. They were waiting for us. Since I had arrived at three o'clock at the airport, it was time for la comida, the most substantial meal of the day. His father would be home, taking his two-hour break from work, and his mother would be preparing the meal.

"Oh Lord, the US is totally missing the point!" I whispered to myself. Nothing could be more innately meaningful than joining together with your family for two hours each day, not at the end of the day but during the day, when you are still alert and have the energy to contribute your best to your most sacred relationships. Such an event deserved your all.

When Carlos opened the door to the house that I had held in my heart all these months, Marisa, his brother's wife, was standing just a few feet away. She was holding their sleeping daughter in her arms and swaying back and forth to soothe her. I was overjoyed. I had met Marisa when I visited Carlos's parents before I left Mexico the prior December. She and her husband, Martín, had moved into his parents' home. Their baby girl was just eleven months old. Her name was also Marisa, but as is customary in Mexico, they called her Marisita. The feminine "ita" or masculine "ito" is added to children's names to indicate that they are a "little version of" their mother or father.

"Que preciosa!" I whispered with enthusiasm. Marisita's thick, long black lashes were so striking, extending out from her closed eyes against her ivory cheeks.

"Remember, I speak English," Marisa said with a kind smile.

"Oh, I forgot! How wonderful that I can speak to you in English!"

Marisa spoke English with the same ease as an American, so clear and precise. I would learn that she had become proficient in English while attending high school in Boston. Her parents had sent her there to live with an aunt and uncle for her junior and senior years. She was a few years older than me, a beautiful small-framed woman with fair skin and natural blonde hair. Her eyes were a beautiful blue-green, and as she spoke to me, they almost seemed to be searching my soul. Yet I wasn't uncomfortable. I had a *knowing*, an inexplicable *knowing*. It was as if we had been friends for millennia. I was in awe and found it hard not to say, *I remember you. I have always known you.*

Still holding the sleeping Marisita, Marisa motioned for us to come into the house, knowing that Carlos needed to carry my luggage to the room they had designated for me. It was unoccupied now, since Carlos's sister had left just months prior to be married. She and her husband lived across town in a small apartment now.

The spare bedroom was the first one on the right. Carlos took my hand and led me in, while Marisa carried Marisita down the hall to put her down for her nap. He set my suitcase on the double bed so I could unpack. He walked over to a standard-sized closet door across from the bed and opened it to show me that it was bigger than the door portrayed. It would be ample for my clothes and most of the other things I had packed in my trunk that would be arriving any day.

The bed was framed by a large window that looked out to the yard behind the house. Carlos took my hand and held me close to him as we looked out the window. He whispered in my ear, "What a happy man I am, at last. To have you here with me is the beginning of my happiness. I love you, Collette. Never leave me again. It was a very bad time in my life."

I returned his gesture with a hug and whispered in his ear, "I am here with you for the rest of our lives. Never doubt that again."

We kissed and then released our embrace and walked out of the bedroom to check on Marisa's progress in getting the baby to sleep. We passed Carlos's parents' room on the way, and I again noticed the crucifix over their bed. *What a devoted couple they are*, I thought. *I hope that Carlos and I will honor our marriage as they do.*

Marisa had laid Marisita on her stomach in her crib and covered her with a light blanket. It was the end of the rainy season in Mexico, which began in June. The breeze that was sweeping across the cloudy sky was refreshing, not cold. Marisa pulled the curtains to darken the room a bit, knowing it would help Marisita to enjoy a long nap. What a precious scene the room presented, with their matrimonial bed next to the crib. A young couple, starting out in life, full of love for each other, and now blessed with a sweet little daughter. I was enamored with the whole idea.

I felt so whole, so content, so blessed. I was right where I wanted to be. And I was with the person I was helplessly in love with. Life was blooming!

35

MARISA AND MARISITA

The prospect of another meal with Carlos's father (whom I referred to as Señor Herrera) enchanted me. Again, I was honored to sit at the table across from this hardworking patriarch of the family. Carlos sat to my right. Theresa scuttled about, placing food-laden plates in front of each of us. I was politely told that no help was needed, that I could perhaps be of assistance at the next meal. "This is your welcome meal," Theresa said in her attempt at English. Her voice was so sweet and light. I was the guest of honor!

Marisa came downstairs and took the seat to Señor Herrera's left. Marisa's husband, Martín, wasn't able to make it home for lunch. His job required him to travel all over the city, and his last appointment was about an hour away. As Theresa finished serving the plates, she sat down at the right end of the table. I felt that we were a closely knit *family*, sitting together as if I had always been one of the fundamental strands of familial yarn. The sound of the Spanish language encircling me and the interaction between Carlos, his mother, and his father engendered a nascent memory in me that I couldn't locate in the folds of my brain.

"Yes, Collette, this is your family," Marisa said in English, as if she knew what I was thinking. "We are so glad to have you here in Mexico. This is your home."

Theresa smiled and held up her glass of lemonade. "Bienvenidos! Esta es tu familia!" (Welcome! This is your family!)

The goodness of these capable, loving people brought out goose bumps all over my body. I felt like I should pinch myself to confirm the reality I was living. I knew that they were sincere, that they had accepted me as one of their own. *You are the luckiest person in the world! Now begins your new life in Mexico, in full force*! I silently proclaimed to myself.

The meal was delicious and would prove to be one of my favorite dishes over the years—pollo con mole (*mow*-lay). Mole is a very special sauce, thicker than gravy, and laden with finely ground almonds or peanuts, chocolate, dry chiles, and cinnamon as a starter. These ingredients vary, depending on the region in which the mole is made. The thick mixture is then seasoned with chicken broth and simmered over a low flame until the right consistency is reached, and it is hot and ready to grace the meat, which is usually chicken breast and thighs. The mole can be either red, brown, or black, depending mostly upon the color of the dried chiles used. For example, mole from Oaxaca, a state southeast of Mexico City, is black.

As side dishes, Theresa served rice and creamed *chayotes*, that wonderful, light-green squash so similar to the pale green variety of our American summer squash.

After much laughter, mixed with serious talk about our wedding plans and the future apartments to be built behind the house, it was time for Carlos and his father to return to work. It had been a wonderful experience, a great start to my new life. I was more than ready to start living an authentic, everyday life in Mexico.

Marisita made us aware that she had awakened right when the dishes were done, and we had sat down in the living room to have coffee. Our faces brimmed with excited smiles, just to know that we were going to be interacting with little Marisita. It was obvious that her grandmother Theresa was as delighted as any grandmother would be to hear the sound of a new baby in the house.

"Why don't you come upstairs with me?" Marisa suggested to me. "Marisita needs to start getting acquainted with you."

I was ecstatic. I hadn't had much experience with babies. My sister's first child was born when I was busy working in the summer, and then I left for college in San Diego. So my visits were infrequent, and I didn't really participate in his life. This was going to be a precious opportunity for me to learn all about the details of childrearing. Even though I was only twenty, it wasn't unusual in the 1960s to get married at age eighteen and start a family right away. I hadn't been interested in an early marriage before I met Carlos, but now that we were virtually engaged, I thought it was the perfect time to at least prepare for the future.

As we entered the bedroom, little Marisita was standing in her crib, holding on to the railing, a tear still clinging to her cheek. She wanted to be with Mommy! Marisa gently lifted her out of the crib and held her close. She kissed her cheek and calmly told her, "Hola, mi niña, como dormiste? Bien?" (Hello, my little one, how did you sleep? Well?) She turned to me and said, "I will change her, and then you can hold her."

I nodded with pleasure. All of the necessary things had been laid out on the bed—baby powder, diapers, baby lotion, Q-tips, and various articles of clothing for quick changes. It was a precious manifestation of a well-organized, doting mother, ready at any moment to care for her daughter. I took careful note of the scene.

Little Marisita smiled as her mother lovingly cleaned her and powdered her, smoothed her hair and put a fresh top and pants set on her. A little lotion on her arms and face and a *beso* (kiss) concluded the operation. She was ready now to pass her to my arms. I put my arms in a cradle position and smiled as if I was going to receive a wonderful gift. Calmly, confidently, Marisa passed her precious daughter to me, assuring her with a smile and sweet *ah-ah-ah* that she was being put in the loving, safe arms of a trusted friend.

As Marisa withdrew her hands, leaving Marisita in my arms, I felt a magical sense of wonder. Her precious, smiling face looked up at me, with those twinkling black eyes contrasted against her porcelain skin, and I fell in love with her. This was a very potent moment in my life. It would never be forgotten. I spoke softly to her as I pulled her close to me, telling her in English that she was precious to me and beautiful.

She seemed fascinated with my face, as it was, of course, new to her. But best of all, she seemed so at ease with me and trusting. She smiled, as if to say, "Yes, I will accept you as my *tía* [aunt] Collette."

Marisa and I sat on the bed, with Marisa still in my arms, and talked about everyday life in Mexico, a sort of introduction for me. I wanted to know so many things, and she was the perfect teacher. I knew her judgment was impeccable. I was the student at the teacher's feet, ready to absorb her knowledge. She covered topics such as how she managed everyday errands and how she got around in the city (taxi, walking, buses, and by car). She explained how the household tasks were planned so that she and Theresa shared in the cooking and other various necessities. She told me which tasks the maid took care of.

Of course, the mention of a maid was so familiar to me, since I had enjoyed the help of our maid in Roma when I was in school.

"Every household is different," Marisa told me. "It is up to the woman of the home to determine what the maid will be asked to do."

Marisa did her own family's laundry, shared in the grocery shopping, and cooked the meals that were her own favorites. The maid did all of the other cleaning and did whatever shopping or cooking she was asked to do. This sounded like a very workable arrangement, but I offered to do whatever I could to ease the burden for the whole family.

"Just tell me what, and I'll do it!" I insisted. "I don't want to be waited on. I like helping with anything I can."

After we discussed the basics, I couldn't restrain a yawn. I was very tired from getting up at five in the morning in California, and I still needed to unpack and arrange my things so that I could start my role as a member of my new family. Marisa graciously took Marisita from my arms, suggesting that tomorrow we should go on a shopping trip together.

"We'll walk," she told me, "and take the baby with us. You can get to know the immediate neighborhood and learn your way around."

I was so delighted that she took such an interest in me, as I hadn't expected such hospitality. Our friendship was firmly established; I knew that. It was clear to me that we had an uncanny compatibility and that we both felt completely comfortable with each other. What a blessing!

I spent at least two hours in my new room, unpacking, reorganizing my clothes, trying to divide them between what would be hung in the closet and what would be folded in the chest of drawers. The big window was such a welcome touch. Even though it was five o'clock, early evening, the east-facing window still allowed enough sunlight to fill the entire room. I kept thinking how similar the weather was to Southern California. Even though it was close to the equator, the mile-high region was graced with brisk arid winds that dried up any lingering humidity and manufactured puffy white clouds out of the remainder. I watched the chalky, billowing clouds race against the periwinkle sky, which was a stunning backdrop. I mused that I was in a romantic play and that in less than an hour, the curtain would gently bring the last act to its end. The clouds would be absorbed into the darkness, and Carlos and I would applaud the finale.

I could hear Marisita playing in her playpen in the living room. She was chattering and her grandmother was laughing and saying endearing things to her. I carried a small box of toiletries across the hallway to the big bathroom that we would all share. It was very large, with a sink and vanity to the immediate right of the entrance and a large bathtub to the left. Adjacent to the tub was a large tiled shower stall, and across from it was the toilet. The tiled floor was a bit cold on my feet, as I was still in my pantyhose and dress that I had worn on the plane. Having no forced-air heater or air conditioner in the house, I knew that I would be using the small electric heaters that I noticed in strategic positions around the house. The tile was probably a blessing in the summer, but in the late fall and winter, it would be close to the outside temperature. I would have to start relying on my clothing for comfort, rather than just setting a thermostat at seventy-two degrees.

36

FIESTA!

Carlos arrived from work at seven that night. He announced his arrival with a shout from the front door—"Hola, hola!"—and then in English, "Where is my Collette?"

I was in my new bedroom, primping for his arrival. Theresa was in their bedroom, getting ready to go out to dinner with Señor Herrera when he arrived home.

"Estoy aquí, en mi recámara!" (I'm here, in my bedroom!)

"Ven!" he called to me. "Ven aquí! Tengo algo para tí!" (Come here! I have something for you!)

I couldn't walk down the stairs fast enough. There he was, with a bouquet of beautiful long-stemmed roses in his hand—red, yellow, and pink. He held them up with one arm and reached out to me with the other. "These are for my beautiful *novia*!" he proudly announced as he embraced me around my waist and kissed me. *Novia* was a beautiful word for me to hear. It was what I had been dreaming of—being his fiancée; it was what I had resisted for so long and now had embraced with all my being.

"Gracias!" I responded with another kiss. "These are gorgeous!"

"Well, this is your welcome bouquet from Mexico. Tonight, we are having a reunion—a party—with your friends from last year! And a few new ones—Raphael, both Jaimes, Antonio, and Chacho are coming. They want to welcome you back to Mexico. They are very excited to see you. I made all the arrangements from work."

"I can't believe it! What a tremendous surprise! What can I do to get the house ready for them?" I offered eagerly.

"You don't need to do anything. They are bringing chicharrones, salsa, and some antojitos, and I am providing the tequila and music. They are bringing their girlfriends—well, those who have one. We can dance and enjoy the occasion for which we have waited for so long. It will be so nice to be together again, all of us!"

This reunion was clearly a sincere call to others to join in our happiness as a couple. We knew our friends embraced our relationship, and they were happy to celebrate it with us.

Carlos went up to shower, and I decided to change clothes. I knew exactly what I was going to wear—a new outfit I had bought for a night out or, in this case, a party at home. The pants were black, zippered at the back, and the top was sleeveless with a scoop neck. The color was what we referred to in the '60s as "hot pink." I was so glad there was a full-length mirror inside the closet door that allowed me to check myself before seeing everyone. This was a big event, and I could not have been more excited. It was like New Year's Eve for me. Here I was, pinching myself again.

"You are in Mexico. You are with the love of your life. You are in the house you adore, with the people you adore! This has really happened!" I was floating.

Only fifteen minutes later, Carlos again called for me from down the hall in his little bedroom. "Are you ready Collette?"

"Almost!"

"Okay, I am going to go buy the tequila and limes, so I'll be back in a little while. Come downstairs when you're ready. My parents are going out tonight—they know we're having a reunion. I talked to my mother this morning before I left for work."

I was touched by the fact that Theresa hadn't said anything to me during the day, nor had Marisa. They knew it was a surprise party. Marisa and Martín were preparing to leave, taking little Marisita to her other grandmother's home for the evening. They advised me that they would be back around nine. I was glad to know that they would enjoy some time with us when they returned.

"Okay, I'll see you when you get back!" I shouted back through a crack in my bedroom door.

All I really had to do to finish my primping was to choose a pair of shoes and spray some perfume on my shoulders. My hair was perfectly coiffed, since the style was manipulated into place by tight teasing (referred to as "ratting" with a comb in those days) and then smoothing over the teased mess with a brush to shape it into a smooth globe with straight bangs. A little hairspray, and what was holding up the globe would never be seen.

Carlos was back shortly with the tequila and limes. He asked me to help him set up the dining room table and chairs for the party. We needed space to dance, so we were going to move the table against the window at one end of the dining room. The chairs could flank one wall of the living room, and the couches would allow for the rest of the group. The table would hold all the antojitos, and Carlos set up the bar on the buffet.

"It's so sweet of you to put this party together for me, Carlos. I want you to know how much I appreciate it. I'm so excited to see your friends again. I have to keep pinching myself to accept that what we struggled for so much has come true. I'm here, in Mexico, and we have our lives ahead of us."

"Well," he reminded me, as a teacher would a student, "life is a struggle, but if you make up your mind, you can do anything. And they are not just my friends, Collette. They are *your* friends too."

I smiled a smile of grateful joy, and my shoulders dropped into their natural position of calm. I knew what I had wanted all along; it just took time for me to make up my mind to follow through with this move. I had kept Carlos captive for so many months, but the moment I said yes, nothing stood in our way. As Carlos had written in several of his letters to me in the previous months, "Venceremos!" (We will overcome this!)

Within seconds, the doorbell rang. I walked with Carlos to answer the door. As he approached it, whoever was on the other side called out, "Hola, compadre!"

Carlos opened the door and greeted Raphael.

"Felicidades!" Raphael said. "Donde está Collette?"

I peeped out from Carlos's side and threw out my arms. "Raphael! Que honor! Ha pasado demasiado tiempo! Hola, hola!" (Raphael! What an honor! Too much time has passed! Hello, hello!)

We hugged and laughed out of the sheer pleasure of seeing each other again. It conjured up all the wonderful memories we had had over the months that I had known him. We had laughed, cried, talked politics, pondered the idea of love—all as a group of young men and women full of life ... and with a little help from a little tequila. Now we were picking up where we had left off, and it was a miraculous feeling.

Raphael turned to his side, his arm reaching back for someone. "Pasele," he gently said, telling someone to come in. Raphael's reaction to us, coupled with his height, had completely distracted us from noticing that he had someone with him. "I would like to present Micha to you. She is my girlfriend." (He struggled with English, but did a good job of it.)

Carlos responded quickly, welcoming Micha and introducing her to me in Spanish so that she could understand him. Her smile was so kind and sweet.

"Nice to meet you," she said, also in English. It was obvious that the two of them had practiced what they were going to say when they arrived. Of course, they were familiar with English, as it was taught in all levels of their schooling. But using it in daily conversation outside of school was a very different experience. I appreciated their effort.

"It's nice to meet you also," I reciprocated.

Carlos settled them into the living room and made them a drink. He brought one to me as well, and then he joined us. No sooner had he sat down than the doorbell rang again. The fun was really starting to build.

"Hola!" Carlos said jovially, opening the door. "Como estás? Collette, it's Antonio!"

I jumped up and was at the door in two steps. I grabbed him, hugging him tightly. He was such an amiable person. We had really bonded during our times together last year. He was the storyteller, giving away secrets about Carlos's past and all the antics of their crowd before they reached adulthood. He quietly held his forefinger over his lips and then jokingly said, "I promise not to tell any more stories about Carlos tonight!"

Carlos laughed and retorted "Well, I can tell some stories about you, then, just to get even!"

Antonio also had someone with him. "Me gusta presenter mi novia, Alicia." His small-framed, fair-skinned girlfriend stepped alongside Antonio. She reached out her hand and shook mine.

"I am very glad to meet you," she said almost perfectly in English. "I am glad to be able to practice my English with you!"

I was stunned that she was serious about practicing English. "I would be honored to speak English with you, if you will forgive my clumsiness with my Spanish!" We laughed with an accepting spirit, and I motioned for them to come take a seat in the living room.

The pace of the arrival of friends continued until everyone had arrived who was on the invitation list. We greeted each other with the same heartfelt joy and laughter as before, and soon the whole bottom floor of the house was resounding with '60s rock and roll and enough tequila to fill a child's swimming pool. Marisa, Martín, and Marisita arrived about eight o'clock and joined in the fun, full of conversation with all of Carlos's friends, whom they had known since childhood. Marisita was sleepy but managed to dance for us, with a lot of help from her mommy. We applauded as she moved her not-so-steady legs to the music and then plopped her bottom down on the floor and proudly looked at all of us, obviously satisfied with her achievement. With their daughter's performance topping off their social time, Martín and Marisa slowly said their good nights and were off to bed with their sleepy little girl.

We continued to eat and dance until ten o'clock, when Señor Herrera and Theresa arrived from their night out. They had come in from the interior garage door right into the hallway that flanked the party room we had set up. With smiles on their faces, they were greeted by each of the guests, obviously with great respect. Carlos turned down the music a bit out of consideration of his parents, and they wished everyone a good night and ascended the stairs to their bedroom.

37

SHOPPING, REBOZOS, AND CHICKEN FEET

The next morning, as promised, I went shopping with Marisa and Marisita. She asked if I would be comfortable helping her carry the baby.

"Of course!" I jumped at the chance.

"I want to show you how we carry our babies in Mexico," she said in her very accomplished English. "It is different than in the US. We don't use strollers as much because we make quick trips to the local market and other shops in the *colonia* [small neighborhood] and because the sidewalks are often cracked, and the streets are full of traffic. So this is what we do." She picked up her large, oblong shawl, or *rebozo*, and placed it across my shoulders. Then she gathered up Marisita and placed her in my arms. "Now," she said calmly, "I'm going to wrap you and Marisita together!"

"Well, okay, that sounds like fun!" I smiled, intrigued.

Marisa confidently and quickly wrapped Marisa up in an intricate "hammock," using my body as the "trees." The wrapping wove its way under Marisita, then up across my shoulder, then back down to my waist, where Marisa deftly pulled the two ends of the shawl together and tied a fat knot. I felt as if I had become pregnant, only inside out.

Marisa inspected her work and gave it an approving wink. "You're ready to go now!" she said. It was such a simple process, yet the tension of the shawl, pressing the baby's weight against my body, coupled with the nice big knot, was a well-engineered support system.

"Necessity is the mother of invention," I said to Marisa. "That's an American saying that fits this situation to a T, especially since mothers invented it!" I marveled at the probability that this manner of baby wrapping had been practiced for many thousands of years by as many women.

Off we marched, with Marisa holding the enormous, woven plastic shopping bag that I had seen carried by hundreds of people on the streets during my semester in Mexico. They were serious bags, not for the weak or frail of the population. Empty, they were as light as a feather. But they could hold about ten kilos (equal to 2.2 pounds) of goods, which was wonderful. The only problem was that they had to be carried home.

"We are just going to buy some chicken, but before that, I want to see if I can find some new shoes for Marisita, now that she has started walking," Marisa explained.

"I realize that whatever we buy, only one of us can carry the bag home, so I'm glad our shopping will be light!" I joked.

We walked a few blocks and found the shoe store that Marisa had in mind. I was glad to get there so I could sit down and relieve myself of Marisita's weight. She'd just had her first birthday, and I remembered Marisa telling me that she weighed roughly twenty-five pounds! Seeing my heavy breathing, Marisa said she would exchange "cargo" with me as soon as she picked out the shoes. I was content to just sit with Marisita sleeping on my lap. It was a tender moment, feeling her warmth and projecting my own life as a mother onto the screen of my future.

"These are perfect!" I heard Marisa say. As the clerk went to search for a box for Marisita's new walking shoes, Marisa went to the small counter and gathered the correct number of pesos to complete the purchase. The clerk came out from the storage room behind the curtain with the box, and the first item on our shopping agenda was taken care of.

Marisa put the shoes in the big shopping tote and came over to me to unwrap Marisita. "Hold her carefully because I'm going to be unwinding you both," she whispered. Effortlessly, she maneuvered the shawl over her own shoulders, leaving Marisita sound asleep in my arms. On Marisa's cue, I passed Marisita to her, and before I could ask what I could do to help, Marisa had Marisita wrapped up and was ready to go. It was so humbling to see what women could do without all the baby equipment we relied on in the US.

Heading home, we stopped at a *polleria* (chicken shop). It was just a tiny opening in the middle of the stucco facades on a street about three blocks from home. An old woman offered every cut of chicken from behind the big white display counter that edged the sidewalk. When she saw Marisa's face, she smiled with familiarity. "Hola. Como está, Señora Herrera? Como le sirvo este dia?" (Hello, Mrs. Herrera. How can I serve you today?)

"Buenos días, Señora Alvarez," Marisa replied. She gave her order to the kind merchant.

Peering through the glass window of the counter, I noticed something that startled me: a big pile of chicken feet, displayed as if they were something of value!

I asked, "Porqué tienen patas de pollo, Marisa?" (Why do they have chicken feet?)

Marisa looked amused and giggled as she explained that in Mexico, mothers pluck out their claws, boil them and then tie them around the necks of their teething babies. "They are better than pacifiers that you buy in the supermarket," she said. "They are just the right consistency. Like rubber!"

I looked away, as my mouth was hanging open, and I didn't want the little old woman to be offended by my reaction.

Marisa had asked for "seis piernas y seis pechos, por favor"—six chicken legs and six breasts. As the owner chose the perfect chicken pieces, an amiable conversation commenced between the two women; they obviously enjoyed the back-and-forth of how things were going in the neighborhood. Their smiles and laughter reinforced my perspective that in Mexico, life is about people, not *things*. As a rule, I never noticed any impatience between people, whether in the markets, restaurants, businesses, or on the street, just kindness and interest in others.

Marisa gestured to the direction we would walk home. "Tonight, Martín and I are going over to some friends. We will be taking Marisita," she informed me. "I hope that you and Carlos enjoy your evening. Maybe you can go out to a nice restaurant! You need to have time together, and I think you would enjoy getting to know some of the small but wonderful restaurants and interesting places that are not too far from our colonia."

"Yes, that sounds great," I said eagerly. "It would feel like old times ... I remember a few places Carlos and I went last year that were really amazing. We'll see how he feels when he gets home."

We ambled home, Marisa carrying Marisita, and I carrying the big multicolored bag with the shoes and the chicken in it. Our shopping trip had been short but sweet, just venturing out to do some otherwise ordinary shopping. The only thing I had shopped for last year was jewelry and clothing.

When we arrived home, Marisa prepared some cooked vegetables for Marisita. She ate heartily. It was definitely time for play now, after being wrapped up like a taco for a couple of hours. Marisa carried her up to their bedroom, where she kept her books and toys. I went to my room to do some additional organizing (and resting). But the tiny room adjacent to my room beckoned me. There was a door that had remained opened while I was unpacking yesterday. I had ventured in to see what was inside. There was a large wooden desk and chair on the right wall, and a big window to the left that looked out over the backyard. A wooden file cabinet was positioned next to the window. Directly across from the entrance door was a heavy, industrial-style door. I assumed it led to an exterior stairway, but it was apparently locked with a big lever that secured it. Curious beyond my own good, I imagined that Señor Herrera's writings were kept in the big roll-top desk. Oh, if I could just rummage around and dig into his writings, it would be ecstasy! I worked very hard, talking to my conscience, telling it that it was headed for disaster and, more than that, deceitful behavior. I paused there, wishing I could shove my conscience aside, waiting for the urge to dissipate. But I found my moral code, turned toward my room, and stepped out of the "secret" room. To keep my focus where it should be, I closed the door and vowed never to open it again.

38

STREET VENDORS AND THE TIÁNGUIS

As Carlos ran errands for his mother, he took me along to introduce me to the various owners of shops in the neighborhood. I felt integrated into the village culture without any effort, thanks to Carlos and Marisa. Now I felt confident to walk alone, if necessary, to find whatever service or product I needed. I had a great time memorizing where the *tortillería* (tortilla shop) was, the produce store, the *farmacia* (pharmacy), and the stationery shop (for stamps and notepaper). On Thursdays, we went together to the open farmer's market, known in Mexico as the *tiánguis* (tee-*ahn*-geese). It was at least a block long, with merchants and their tarps set up, with their products proudly displayed—lettuce, mangos, papaya, bananas, tomatoes, limes, a large selection of herbs (many indigenous to Mexico that I had never seen), walnuts, pecans, spices, medicinal herbs, and on and on the displays beckoned. Each merchant learned who you were and which area of the colonia you lived in. Next time you visited, you were recognized, and a familiar smile welcomed you. "Como está usted?) Bienvenidos!"

What I especially loved were the sounds of the street vendors who provided snacks, specialty items, and services to the neighborhoods, usually by bicycle. All of these vendors brought me back to my childhood experience in California: We had a corner store in our neighborhood, and people stopped and visited with each other on the way to and from the store. In those days, there were also the biweekly visits in our neighborhood of the bakery truck (the Helms Bakery company's beautiful "woody" station wagon with the deep, deep drawers filled with fragrant doughnuts and rolls). There was the ice cream man, known as "Harky," whose recorded organ music sent a joyful chill down our spines, anticipating a delicious ice cream sandwich or Popsicle. The fresh-produce man, "Marcelo," who was born in the US to a first-generation Italian mother and father, graced our street twice a week as well. We knew his signature whistle that he blew into his horn as he slowly crawled along the street, attracting many housewives to his crispy lettuce and savory, fat red tomatoes.

Mexico's burgeoning lower economic class has always survived on entrepreneurial mastery. The street vendors earned a living by developing a keen sense of what the needs of the people were. They studied the colonias surrounding the area where they lived. They knew the inner workings of each street like the back of their hands. They knew what economic class lived where and which services and products they wanted. Then, these entrepreneurs staked out their territory, and, in the hubbub of activity, they capitalized on these needs.

One day, while at home, I heard the call of a vendor, shouting, "Chi-char-ron-es! Tortillas! Pan dulce!" I opened an upstairs window and was struck by what my eyes beheld. A young man was peddling a customized bike with chicharrones piled high in a basket affixed to the front of his bike. Behind him was another basket affixed over his back wheel, full of tortillas and Mexican sweet breads. Other vendors would come along and shout different announcements: "Tacos de carne asada, or tamales!" Maids and mothers came out of their houses automatically, knowing the call of this vendor and knowing his goods were fresh and tasty.

Every week a young man came down our street, peddling a very large tricycle that was brimming with fresh chicharrones, tortillas fresh off the *comal* (flat round grill), or *tacos de canasta* (a basket full of tacos) or tamales (steamed, fine cornmeal slabs filled with chicken, pork, beef, or cheese—or raisins and a pineapple, for those with a sweet tooth. In all of the neighborhoods, these bicyclists drew attention by shouting in strange ways, or whistling or ringing bells to attract attention to their goods. One of my favorite treats was *camotes* (sweet yams). When I heard a steam whistle screaming, I always stuck my head out the window to spot the tall pot fastened to the back of a vendor's tricycle. Underneath was a flame fed by a portable propane burner. I learned to identify which product was being sold just by the sound I heard.

Another notable vendor was the knife sharpener. Ringing a little bell and smiling as if he was enjoying the attention, he stopped when beckoned by someone in her doorway and pulled up at the curb. He got off of his bike and faced his client. She handed him several tools, mostly scissors and knives. He took the scissors and knives and put them the metal basket that was mounted in front of his handlebars. Then he got off of his bike and lifted the whole bike off the ground while he unhooked a sturdy metal kickstand with one foot. The stand dropped into a locked position. His bike was now suspended on the stand. He remounted the bike and, with his right arm, unlatched a stone wheel that was hanging over the front wheel of his bike, held firmly by a steel pulley. The stone dropped about two inches, allowing it to meet the front wheel of his bike.

The young man began peddling slowly. The stone wheel started spinning. He held one of the knives in his left hand against the spinning stone as he held the bicycle handlebar with his right. The shrill scream of a blade being sanded by a rough stone pierced the muddled sounds of the neighborhood. Before five minutes had passed, he had sharpened the maid's tools, taken ten pesos, handed the tools back to her, reattached the stone wheel to the pulley, flipped the kickstand back into its folded position, and began peddling away. Off he went, ringing his bell again. I shook my head and said, "Only in Mexico!"

Some vendors would ring your doorbell. They might be selling *sopapillas* (hot filled tortillas, sealed on the edges) or *meringues* (meringue injected into an ice cream cone), or a few might be "selling" religion—Mormons (in their white business shirts and black ties) or Jehovah's Witnesses, passing out their booklets.

The most annoying sound from vendors on the street was the clanking bell of the trash truck, with its timbre that sounded like a fire alarm in the US. It was the size of a large cowbell, on a stick. *Clang, clang, clang!* The worker would alert the neighborhood. People (or maids, for those with that luxury) came out of the houses to take their bags of trash to the truck. There were no garbage disposals in the kitchens of Mexico, except in the homes of the *very* upper crust.

Some vendors just found places in heavy traffic to resell their wares. For example, at a stoplight, in the midst of four lanes of traffic, you may be approached by a young man urging you to buy two or three colorful toys he held anxiously in his hands, hoping a parent would succumb to the children's cries for something new. Or another young man or woman would yell, "Chicles," simply holding boxes of chewing gum high in the air to catch your attention. I saw everything from plastic containers (Tupperware facsimiles) to flowers being sold on the streets. In other enterprises, men and women offered purses, soft drinks, wooden spoons—the list went on. The vendors proudly stood at your car window with a big smile, hoping you'd smile back and ask, "Cuanto cuesta?" (How much is it?) They promptly would begin an enthusiastic discussion with you if you were thinking it over. "These are very useful," or "I'll give you two for one," or "I'll lower the price." If you said yes, they would they put the goods in your back seat (for example, a set of bowls) take your money, and off you'd both go, happy with your purchase at the stoplight!

When I looked for a parking space at the supermarket, there would be at least two parking security employees (sometimes self-appointed) with a whistle in their mouths, calling my attention to a parking space. Of course, there was a small price for this service. There were others whose sole (often self-selected) job was to watch your car for you as you shopped (two pesos were gladly accepted, about twenty cents at that time). If you parked in the rain, kind entrepreneurs would shield you with their umbrella all the way to the front door of the store and back to your car, one peso per trip. That was the only income they received, as the supermarkets simply gave them authorization to work there.

Inside the busy supermarkets, marketing was just as imaginative. Wearing aprons, costumes, or trademarked uniforms, young, industrious workers offered samples of various branded products—bread, milk, soft drinks, etcetera. On many of my shopping excursions, I was overcome with excessively loud rock music playing on a big speaker. A vendor's representative was trying to draw attention to the product being promoted. On one of my visits, a young man wearing a sequined shirt was set up under a tarp inside the store. He was working a turntable, with loud speakers pounding as he shouted on his microphone offering shoppers a sample of the beverage he had on display. As they came for a taste, they were asked to write their (hopefully) positive opinion and phone number on a raffle ticket to win a big radio or a tape player that sat atop the stack of beverages. Conservatism seemed to have no place in advertising in Mexico!

39

A PALATIAL START

Just as I decided to start on my closet organization, I heard Carlos come in the front door with his usual "Hola! Hola! Quien está?" (Hello, hello! Who's home)? His mother answered with her sweet lilting voice from the kitchen, "Aquí estoy!" (Here I am!) I heard Carlos greet his mother, and within seconds, he was on his way up the stairs. "Collette? Collette? Where are you?"

I opened the door to my room and jumped out, just to startle him. "Here I am!"

He laughed at my attempt to surprise him and looked me straight in the eyes. "I have something planned for us for tonight. Can you get ready in a few minutes while change my clothes?"

"Of course!" I said. "Where are we going?"

"It's a surprise!" He disappeared into his bedroom.

In less than fifteen minutes, Carlos was knocking on my door and greeted me with a kiss on my cheek when I opened it. "You're really going to enjoy this!" he said.

We started down the steps, and I followed him into the kitchen. "Mamá, Collette and I are going to get some dinner," he said in Spanish.

"Está bien," she responded with a ready smile. "Que bonita que van a disfrutar de algún tiempo solos!" (How nice that you are going to enjoy some time alone!)

Carlos always had an agenda! Now, he said, "I thought it would be fun to have dinner and then do some dancing afterward. What do you think?"

"That sounds fantastic!" I responded. "I'd love to pick up where we left off last year. Remember that nightclub we went to in Polanco? It was so fun, and remember the lounge act? That Elvis impersonator?"

"Of course I do!" Carlos said. "Don't you remember him singing 'I Can't Stop Falling in Love with You'?"

I laughed so hard, remembering how Carlos had paid the entertainer in the lounge that night to play that very song so that Carlos could sing it to me and the audience in English. People had applauded him and seemed amazed that a Mexican guy knew all the English words to the song. I, of course, fell deeper in love with him.

"I have something a little different in mind to start off the evening," Carlos advised me with a grin.

"Where are we going?" I nudged his arm coyly.

"We've been there before, but tonight we're going to take a better look at it," he said, purposely vague.

"What is it?"

"*It* is a building."

I pouted. "That's not enough information!"

"You'll see in about ten minutes. Be patient, Collette!"

Sure enough, in about ten minutes, we arrived at the National Palace of Mexico at the Zócolo, the downtown plaza of Mexico City. It was dusk, and I wondered what on earth we were doing there. We couldn't eat or dance there ... and the workday was still in session. There was a museum there, but we had seen that last year. I remembered studying about the palace in my Mexican history class. It had been the site of the ruling class of Mexico since Moctezuma II ruled the Aztecs from here. Although it was rebuilt, many of the materials from the original Aztecan palace were used in the new construction. As I was recounting my history lesson, the whole palace lit up!

"What just happened?" I gasped.

"They light the whole palace up at night, as it is a national treasure and very much visited by tourists. Doesn't it look majestic?"

"Yes! I feel like we're at the Palace of Versailles!" I said, mesmerized.

"I have a reason for bringing you here, Collette." Carlos turned the car off and turned to me.

"What reason?" I asked, puzzled.

"Let's get out of the car and take a walk along the front of the palace. I'll show you the reason," he assured me.

"Okay." Intrigued, I accepted his invitation.

Carlos came to my door and opened it, making a gesture with his arm toward the palace to indicate that he was personally presenting it to me. He took my hand, and we walked over to the sidewalk that edged the palace lawn.

We stood together for a moment, looking up at the bright lights, and the coolness of the early evening air brought our bodies together. Holding me, Carlos said, "I have something to ask you."

"What is it?"

He gently stepped back from me and kneeled on the sidewalk on one knee. I almost fell backward, realizing the position that he had taken was *definitely* meaningful "Will you marry me, Collette? I am very serious and very committed to this proposal."

"Oh my gosh!" I almost scared both of us with my loud response. "Oh, this is so sweet! I can't believe this is happening!" I swallowed anxiously, every nerve in my body fired. I managed to gather my wits after several deep breaths. Finally, I regained my voice. "Yes, without any doubt or reservations. Yes! I will marry you!"

Still on his knee, Carlos reached in his pocket and brought out a tiny jewelry box. Without opening it, he said, "I have loved you from the first moment my eyes met yours. I will love you always and be faithful to you if you will accept this ring." His words were so spontaneous and sincere. He slowly opened the gift box and turned it for me to see.

"Oh my God, Carlos! You bought this for me?" It was a beautiful princess-style diamond in a white-gold Tiffany setting. I reached out my left hand to him, and he slipped it on my finger. It fit perfectly.

As he withdrew his hand, the reflection of the lights from the palace penetrated the facets of the diamond and danced on its surface. "It is absolutely stunning! Yes, I accept *again* with all my heart. You are my soul mate for life, Carlos!"

"I love you, Collette," he now said more informally and stood up to embrace me. He held me and kissed me more tenderly than I could ever remember being kissed. I felt in that moment that our souls were absorbed into one, encircled by our huddled bodies.

"I love you so much, Carlos. You are my life."

We withdrew slowly from our embrace and walked arm in arm along the front of the glowing palace. I felt like a princess every step of the way.

We walked together to the car in a daze. Both of us agreed that a nice dinner with champagne was the most appropriate way to end our evening. We wanted to talk about our plans, and dancing now took a back seat. I felt so confirmed in my belief that together we had overcome all the obstacles that our relationship had presented to us thus far. The new ring on my finger erased any doubt that my future with Carlos was out of reach. Two countries had come together in us. Both of us would make sacrifices from this point on, but being with him, knowing how confidently he conducted himself, his mastery of two languages, his solid judgment, and his analytical approach to our future made me feel that I was truly in the perfect place.

40

BREAKFAST, BLESSINGS, AND PLANS

The next morning, I began to awake, but my eyes were still closed. A sweet awareness came over me as I reached for the ring on my left hand, turning it around on my finger, thinking, *I didn't dream that! This is my future, and I can't believe it's come true!* I slowly opened my eyes, eager to be surprised all over again. There it was, glistening in the early morning light. It wasn't a fairy tale. It was as beautiful as I remembered it. I, like so many millions of other women in the world, was wearing a symbol of love and commitment. My future with Carlos was sealed by its official placement on my finger.

I knew that Carlos and his brother had already left for work, as the clock on my nightstand pointed straight up seven o'clock. I could hear little Marisita down the hall, obviously just waking in her crib. Her mother would be waking right along with her, as the day would begin at Marisita's beckoning to her. "Mamá! Mamá!" She found her morning voice.

I stretched my arms and yawned, full of contentment just to be in this sweet house, so full of family caring for family. There seemed to be no greater purpose than the assurance by each member of the family that the others were well fed, comfortable, and happy. *This is heaven on earth,* I thought.

I pulled my body out of bed, needing to use the bathroom. Slowly opening my door, I crept down the hall and quietly closed the door behind me. As I went about my business, I could hear Marisita saying, "Tía! Tía!" It was such a sweet sound, for the first time to hear Marisita voluntarily calling for me. Her mother had been teaching her to call me "Aunt." My heart lit up. I could hardly wait to greet her.

As I finished washing my hands, I heard Marisita again. "Tía!"

Her mother said, "Just a minute, my precious. We will see Tía Collette after I change you and get you dressed."

As soon as I'd dried my hands, I quietly opened the bathroom door and knocked gently on Marisa's bedroom door, just a few feet across the hall. "Are you awake?"

"Yes, yes!" she answered.

"Do you mind if I come in?"

"Of course not. Come in and see your niece. She's calling for you!"

I peeked inside the door, and little Marisita turned her head away from her mother. "Tía Collette!" she shouted in her sweet little voice, with a big wide smile.

"Yes! I am here, sweetheart," I said in English (as her mother encouraged me to do with her). "Good morning!" She reached out her arms to me as I gathered her into mine with anticipation. She smelled so sweet; her skin so soft and warm. "Oh, how I love you!" I told her softly in her ear. I hugged her and turned around slowly, pretending to dance with her. She was so comfortable with me. It was as if we had been together since she was born. I felt wholly in love with her, an official auntie now.

"How did you sleep?" Marisa asked.

"Very well, surprisingly," I answered.

"Why are you surprised?"

"Well y … look what is on my finger!"

She was absolutely shocked and could hardly respond. Taking my hand, she lifted it slowly toward her, focusing her eyes on my ring. "It's beautiful! Did he propose to you last night?"

"Yes!" I blurted out, almost before she could finish her sentence. "Yes! In front of the National Palace, just as all the lights went on." I grinned, trying to contain my excitement.

"That Carlos! He is full of surprises." She shook her head back and forth. "I am very happy for you. I am so proud to have you in our family and in our lives! I wish you the very best life possible, and I will do all I can to help you make it so. You have my blessings."

We hugged, with Marisita between us. Marisa's official blessing was what I yearned for when I opened her door. Her character and judgment were so confirming and such a vital part of what I needed to make my new life complete. I felt abundantly blessed with someone I thought the world of.

"Speaking of engagements," Marisa mentioned, "my cousin is getting married in Vera Cruz this coming weekend. I have been planning on going, but Martín cannot go. I know that Carlos has to work on Saturday, and I wondered if you would like to go with me. We would be taking Marisita, and the bus ride is really nice. You would see some of the country on the ride, and I would love for you to meet my Aunt Beatrice! Her daughter, Angelica, my cousin is the one who is getting married. It will be a very nice wedding, if my aunt has anything to do with the arrangements. She is a very wealthy woman, owning many properties. She would love for you to come. I have already talked to her."

I was immediately a willing companion. "I would love to go! Are you sure there is enough room?"

"Oh yes," Marisa responded. "My aunt has a huge home. We will be very well accommodated!"

"Then let me talk to Carlos; in fact, I will call him at work today and see how he feels about it."

"Sounds good," Marisa quickly responded. "Let me know as soon as you talk with him, okay?"

In agreement, I left mother and baby to go to my room and get dressed for the day.

Theresa was busy in the kitchen as I came down downstairs. She was using the blender, and I wondered what on earth she would be making so early in the morning. "Buenos días," I said to her and gave her a tender hug.

She was dropping little green tomatillos into the blender, obviously making a salsa. "Buenos días, Collette!" She turned her head and greeted me. "Estoy preparando salsa verde Vamos almozar chilaquiles esta mañana" (I am preparing green salsa. We are going to eat *chilaquiles* for breakfast this morning) *Chilaquiles* was a mixture of scrambled eggs, cheese, tortilla chips, and salsa.

"Pues, huele rica!" I enthusiastically told her it smelled wonderful. I had eaten chilaquiles in Maria's kitchen, but I knew these were going to be superior. Almost anything was superior to Maria's cooking.

"Si quieres, puedes informar a Marisa que el almuerzo está listo." (If you'd like, you can tell Marisa that breakfast is ready).

"Gracias, Theresa. Sí! Tengo hambre!" (Thank you, Theresa. Yes, I'm really hungry!) I made a beeline up the stairs toward Marisa's room, hoping she was as hungry as I was. She was already walking out of her bedroom with Marisita.

"I heard! I'm hungry too!"

"Oh, good!" I responded and walked with her and Marisita downstairs to the dining room. I went into the kitchen and offered to help Theresa with serving the breakfast while Marisa settled Marisita in her high chair. The aroma of fresh fried corn tortillas mixed with the tangy scent of the hot, citrusy green tomato salsa filled my senses.

The warmth of the kitchen and the smiling, contented face of Theresa made for a sweet, peaceful atmosphere. Patiently, she scooped up a pile of the egg mixture and carefully placed it onto the first plate. I carried it to the table and continued carrying the next platefuls to the table until we were all seated together, with Marisita in her high chair.

"This looks and smells wonderful," I said in Spanish. I took my first bite of the delicate dish. "Mmm" was all I could utter, as my mouth was too involved in its indulgent pleasure to offer anything more. I said nothing between the first few bites and then was able to come up for air. "Thank you for all your efforts, Theresa. You are a wonderful chef!"

"Did you notice Collette's ring, Theresa?" Marisa winked at me.

Theresa was sitting to my right. She immediately looked at my rather obvious left hand. "Que hermoso!" (How beautiful) She reached for my hand to study it more closely. "Ahora está' realidad! Son novios!" (Now it is a reality! You are engaged.)

"Yes!" I smiled proudly. "We are!"

"I have invited Collette to go with me to Anjelica's wedding," Marisa interjected. "I think she would really enjoy meeting our family in Vera Cruz."

Theresa looked surprised but delighted. "That would be a wonderful opportunity for her! I am sure that Tía Beatrice will be excited to meet her. And she can meet all the cousins and see a real Mexican wedding!" Theresa snickered a bit as she mentioned my witnessing a Mexican wedding. "She can learn some of our wedding traditions and gather ideas for her own wedding." The gratified look on her face told me that she was indeed content about our wedding plans.

After finishing our breakfast and conversation, I gathered our plates and rinsed them in the kitchen sink as Marisa cleaned the egg off of Marisita's face and hands. Theresa followed me into the kitchen and, as usual, shooed me away from helping.

"No, please!" I responded. "If I'm going to be part of this family, I want to act like a member." I smiled, easing the otherwise brusque approach. "Really, I am so happy to help." I softened my tone. "It makes me feel so much more comfortable. Will you please allow me?"

Theresa gently put her hand on my shoulder and replied, "Sí, mija." (Yes, of course, daughter.)

I was more than delighted with her calling me *daughter*. I finally felt at ease about household duties. Now I was officially a part of the household support system.

I called Carlos once we were finished in the kitchen. He was surprised at the idea of my leaving him so soon after arriving. "Are you sure you want to do this?" he asked.

"Yes, I think it would be good for me to have time with Marisa and Marisita and to meet your mother's side of the family. I don't think I will have this opportunity again."

"Well, if you're really sure, I will be okay with it. I, of course, don't want you to go, but I guess I have to agree with you." Carlos sounded a bit disappointed, and my heart dipped a little, hearing his reluctance. But the adventurous side of me trumped his reaction, as I reminded him that it was just a short time, and then I would be back. He accepted the idea, confirming that he had to work all weekend anyway.

"Okay, then. I will see you tonight, and we will have time together to make up for the weekend," I reassured him.

That night, we had a cozy time, staying home and enjoying the immediate family. Martín had returned home a little early from work, and he and I had a chance to get to know each other. He was such a gentle spirit, yet bright and ambitious. He was so handsome and tall. His eyes were penetrating, always wanting to know the details of every subject we talked about. I appreciated his interest and was impressed by the authenticity of his heart. He seemed to want everyone in the family to be content and all things in order. I decided that he was the rock of the siblings, never veering from his moorings. *What a vital member of the family*, I thought. Carlos was the opposite, always wanting adventure, like me. I knew I would need Martín in the future for his sage advice on many different matters.

Carlos arrived about an hour later and joined Martín and me in the living room. Theresa began to serve us *café de olla* (coffee boiled in water with piloncillo and cinnamon). I, of course, helped her, reminding her of our earlier conversation. She opened a paper bag full of pan dulce and placed them on a platter. She motioned for me to take them to the living room. As she followed, Marisa arrived from upstairs with Marisita. Now we were all sitting in the living room together—the coffee table full of our cups and goodies, and our faces full of contentment. Marisa allowed Marisita to toddle over to me, and I pulled her up to my lap and hugged her. She lay her head on my shoulder, and I felt the most endearing feeling.

"Now I am completely content!" I exclaimed to everyone.

"Collette loves children," Carlos informed his family. "Everywhere we go, she pays attention to the children, giving them centavos, whether on the sidewalks or in the parks."

"Well, that is a very wonderful trait, I think," Theresa said. "She will be a wonderful mother!"

My face instantly heated up, and I knew it was glowing like a red Christmas bulb.

"We will wait for that time!" Carlos said.

"Yes, you have plenty of time for that," Martín agreed.

When I awoke the next morning, I lay in my bed, reminiscing about the night before. We were all so compatible. We were so at ease with each other and on the same intelligence level. Señor Herrera had arrived late, since his job at the restaurant required his devotion almost twelve hours a day. The evenings were an essential time, as they were the most lucrative, and the cash income had to be well monitored and managed. He joined us at about 8:30, taking a one-hour break before he had to return.

With the whole family together, there was a lively synergy as we conversed about how our days had gone and about various family-related matters. I shared in their innermost thoughts about various subjects, including other family members and their situations and possible solutions to certain problems, both economic and social. I had become more and more a part of the family, and it was such a natural, comfortable progression. I trusted this family as my own.

Carlos and I had ended the evening at the dining room table, talking, just the two of us. He told me that when I returned from Vera Cruz, he would arrange for his father to talk to us about finding an apartment for us. I was excited to know that he was such a forward thinker, and that he took such a serious interest in laying out our life's plan. He walked me up to my room, as he was exhausted from a long day. We embraced outside my door, savoring lingering kisses until another one would be too emotionally overwhelming to both of us. "Good night, *mi amor*," he softly said in my ear.

"I love you so much," I gently responded. He edged the door open for me and allowed me to step in as he reluctantly closed the door behind me. *My life is so sweet!* I shouted silently to myself. I heard his footsteps going down the hall. I was so eager for us to be together in one room! But that could wait for now. I started to pack for Vera Cruz.

41

VERA CRUZ

Marisa and I decided that we would prepare the food for our trip early in the morning. We were in the kitchen by six o'clock, dressed and preparing quesadillas for breakfast and sandwiches for our lunch. We finished by 6:45. Marisita was happy in her high chair, eating little scraps of cheese and ham. I had just filled our thermos with hot coffee when the cab arrived at seven o'clock. No one was up yet, so we quietly left the house. The cab driver carried our suitcases to the car and packed them carefully in the trunk. I carried our breakfast and lunch bag and Marisita's diaper bag. Marisa carried Marisita to the back seat and set her in the middle. "Ya! Ya! Coche!") Marisita's sweet little voice announced to us all. (Oh boy! Car!)

Smiling at her adorable spirit, I got in next to her. She was so excited, knowing she was going somewhere, and the *where* didn't really matter. She knew she was loved and had two virtual mothers on each side of her to attend to her every need. Of course, we started out with patty-cake (something I had taught her in English).

Marisa gave Marisita the warm bottle of milk she had prepared just before we left, and before we knew it, we arrived at the bus station. I tipped the cab driver and then took hold of my suitcase with one hand and proudly stood with Marisita, whom I had wrapped in my very own rebozo (like an experienced Mexican mother). Marisa lugged the diaper bag and our food bag over one shoulder and took her suitcase in her other hand. We were forty-five minutes ahead of time—a good fortune, since there was a huge line to the ticket window to retrieve our tickets.

By 8:30 we had settled into the deluxe bus toward the back, with Marisita nestled between us, chewing on a quesadilla I had wrapped in aluminum foil just before we left the house to keep it warm. I knew the soft Oaxacan cheese inside was a comfort to her. Marisa and I arranged our bags under the seats in front of us. We used our rebozos to cover all three of us.

"These will keep us nice and warm," she announced. "Together, our body heat will make us—how do you say?—snug as bugs in a rug."

I chuckled. "You are picking up all my American *dichos* [sayings] faster than I am picking up yours!" Within minutes, we were on the highway, knowing we had a long trek ahead of us but not caring. Between the three of us, we had all the conversation and entertainment we wanted.

We passed the morning hours chatting, eating our quesadillas, sipping our hot coffee, and picking at the papaya that I had cut up earlier that morning. We had sandwiches for later, in addition to grapes, cookies, and some chicharrones we could snack on. We knew we would be fine until we arrived for dinner at Tía Beatrice's.

The bus made its first of two stops prior to arriving in Vera Cruz. The bus station was not as large as I thought it would bet, but there were shops and taquerias adjacent to it, so we had a chance to get off the bus and do some looking around. Fortunately, the bathroom at the back of the bus was adequate and clean. Somehow, Marisa had managed to change Marisita in that little room while we ambled down the road. We were in good shape to spend a half hour browsing during the rest stop. Marisa took Marisita's hand and let her toddle down the aisle of the bus with her. Her little legs were still a bit untested on stairs and sidewalks, but Marisa felt it was best for her to get some exercise, and she was certainly excited to cooperate. I followed close behind her, soon noticing that the stairs down to the street were too steep for her to navigate. I picked her up and set her down on the very last step where her mother was waiting to ferry her to the ground. She giggled as she tried to make the big step, knowing Mommy would protect her from falling. Into her mother's arms she went from there, and we were off on our little tour of the tiny town just off the main highway.

Souvenirs and straw hats and baskets abounded. There were carnitas cooking over an open fire on a large iron grid. They smelled wonderful, but both Marisa and I knew that we were already prepared for lunch. Still, savoring all the smells, including the fresh tortillas cooking on a huge round steel disk, was an enchanting experience. I spotted a coloring book that I thought Marisita would enjoy helping me color. I asked, "Cuanto questa?" and, the vendor asked for ten pesos (a dollar in US money). I bought a small bag of crayons to go with it for another ten pesos and looked forward to passing some time teaching Marisita her colors and letting her hold the crayons as "we" colored some miles away.

Having stretched our legs and sharing a sweet *churro* (warm Mexican funnel cake), we boarded the bus right on time. The driver announced that we would have another stop in two more hours. After that, it would take one hour to arrive in Vera Cruz.

"Well," I said to Marisa, "at least we've covered more than a third of the trip."

Soon after boarding, Marisita fell asleep, and Marisa and I joined her. It was more than an hour before I awoke. Too droopy-eyed to make conversation, I decided to lay my head against the diaper bag, and before I knew it, I was back asleep. Finally awaking in a less foggy state, I asked Marisa for the time.

"We just have a half hour to go until we make our next stop!"

"Oh, I'm so glad," I lazily responded. "I need to breathe some fresh air and walk awhile. All I've done is sleep since our last stop!"

In less than a half hour, the bus came to a slow stop at a little town much like the one we had stopped in before. Again, we got out and stretched our legs, and this time we spread our napkin-wrapped sandwiches on an unoccupied picnic table. I noticed that an indigenous woman was stirring something in a huge pot on top of a nearby table. I walked over to her and bought a cup of her frijoles de olla (beans cooked in a pot). Her blue-black braids hung like heavy chain links over her shoulders, contrasting with her white pinafore. I thought of Diego Rivera's iconic mural paintings that depicted peasant scenes he often saw and loved. She would have been the quintessential model.

Finishing our picnic spread a la Spanish style, again we boarded the bus. In one hour, we would actually reach our destination. We were more than ready to be retrieved by Aunt Beatrice and to enjoy the comfort of her home. Thankfully, the bus would be stopping at an intersection as a first stop before the train station. We would get off there, where Aunt Beatrice would be waiting for us.

Marisa and I talked and talked, as usual, about every subject of life, and nothing seemed to be outside our comfort zone. Our friendship was becoming deep, and we seemed to know each other's hearts like a book. We were straightforward, yet kind and loving toward each other. I thanked God for her, as I had no expectation that, in my coming to Mexico, I would be gifted with such a rare person to come alongside of me.

As the bus stopped at our drop-off place, I noticed a big Dalmatian standing on the corner. "Do you have Dalmatians in Mexico?" I asked lamely.

"Of course. Why?"

"I don't know. This just seems so odd to see something that I thought was strictly American. I guess this is yet another reminder for me that we in America are *not* as unique as I thought. I'm glad I'm getting a taste of the world. The more I see of it, the more I realize how similar we all are."

Fortunately for us, Aunt Beatrice pulled up to the curb right then. Marisa recognized her and her gigantic Chevrolet. A young girl jumped out of the passenger's side.

"Hola, hola, Marisa!" she shouted. "Aye! Que linda!" she said as she saw Marisita.

Marisita was smiling, knowing that she was among people who loved her. Marisa picked up Marisita and put her in the young girl's arms. "Aquí es tu prima segunda, Breatricita!" (Here is your second cousin!). Then, Marisa said, "Collette, I would like you to meet Beatricita, my cousin. Of course, my aunt has the same name, Beatrice, so her daughter is called Beatricita."

Marisa and I put our luggage into the trunk and got ourselves situated inside the car, where Beatrice was waiting anxiously. "Hola! Bienvenidos!" she shouted. She was a large, jovial woman, obviously excited to have us join in as part of the family gathering. As she saw Marisa and Marisita in the back seat, she cheered, "Que milagro! Y Marisita, que lindos los ojos! Que preciosa es! [What a miracle! Her eyes are so beautiful! She is so precious!] Well, when we get to my house, I am going to hug her all night long! And who is this beautiful young woman you have with you?" she half-jokingly asked.

Marisa didn't hesitate. "This is Collette. She is Carlos's fiancée! I asked her to come with me to meet my wonderful family."

"I am very happy to meet you, Collette! We are so glad that Marisa brought you. It is our honor to host you. Please call me Tía Beatrice!"

She said everything in Spanish, and I proudly caught it all. I thanked her in Spanish to show my best intent and told her that I was excited to meet her and the whole family. With introductions out of the way, she pulled away from the curb, and we were on our way to what I surely expected to be a bigger-than-life experience.

Tía Beatrice's driving was as freewheeling as she talked. By the time we arrived at her house, she had described the dress her other daughter, Angelica's wedding dress, every detail of the bridesmaids' dresses, and every detail of the relationship each of the bridesmaids had with the bride-to-be as well as with each other. She went on with biographical sketches of what seemed like endless boyfriends and each relationship to the girls in the whole bridal party. By the time we turned down the dirt road leading to her house (which she abruptly swerved onto without taking her foot off the gas), she had begun to cover every detail of what was left to do before the bride could walk down the aisle. I personally felt like I had already *been* to the wedding. I wondered what was left to experience.

As the car pulled up to Tía Beatrice's house, we gathered our various bags and purses. Her maid came running out to help us. Tía Beatrice gave orders for her to carry everything to our bedroom and then told us, "Ven ustedes! No necesitan llevar a nada! Déjala arreglar a todo!" (Don't lift a thing! Just let her take care of everything!) With that, I took Marisita's little hand and walked behind Marisa and Tía Beatrice, with Beatricita flanking us, sweetly engaging Marisita in conversation.

Aunt Beatrice's home was a grand, monolithic two-story building. A collection of various tropical trees shouldered it, giving it an even grander impression. Except for the trees and the fact that it was painted hot pink, it would have looked at home in any tract of modern homes in California at the time. But the outside belied the fabulously ornate interior of the house. Entering the front door, we were surrounded by what could only be described as a ballroom-sized formal living room. The grand ten-by-twenty-foot windows encircled the entire left wall, which jutted out from the house, forming a huge, curved alcove. Under each window was an identical tan suede overstuffed sofa with burgundy pillows. The windows were framed by golden drapes with burgundy cords that gathered them to the sides of each window. The spacious beige tile floor was accented with a centerpiece of inlaid tile that was inscribed with the initials of Tía Beatrice and her husband in burgundy. *Very impressive!*

A massive wooden table was placed to one side of the room, each side occupied with four cackling young women. They were obviously the bridesmaids and the bride-to-be. Each girl had an *estética* (beautician) attending to her. Tía Beatrice explained that she had hired the beauticians to give the girls manicures and pedicures and to create elaborate hairstyles. As was common in the sixties, the more formal the event, the bigger the hairdo. It was fascinating to watch, as this was nothing I would expect to see in the US. No parents I had known would hire beauticians to come to their daughter's home to treat them like princesses, but that was being done right here in Mexico. The girls were in various stages of their makeovers, from getting their nails painted (all the same burgundy), to having their makeup gently (but heavily) applied. Using a deep black mascara and matching eye pencil, faces were transformed from the naïve look of youth to sexy, ready-for-dancing young women.

Only one of the bridesmaids was close to a complete makeover, and her bouffant hairstyle easily measured ten inches from the top of her head. A French roll graced the back of her head, with the teased hair on top smoothed over to form a dome that was then worked into the top of the roll. It looked more like a sculpture than a hairdo. Long black curly locks finished the hairdo, hanging from her crown down onto the sides of her face. The hairdresser had placed a miniature tiara, about four inches above her hairline at the top of her head. It was made of garnet-colored rhinestones. This was an anomaly for me, as such a hair accessory in the US would only be worn by the bride (and it would be made of pearls or rhinestones). All I could think was, *What are their dresses going to look like?* With the garnet-colored crystal crowns and deep cranberry-red nail polish, would they wear red dresses? Now, that would *really* be different.

Marisa motioned for me to follow her upstairs. She suggested that we get our dresses out of our suitcases so they could hang for a while, and she could put Marisita down for a nap. Tía Beatrice had arranged for a sister of one of the bridesmaids to watch over Marisita while we joined all of the girls for the meal being served in the dining room. We scurried about in the big bedroom that was designated for us, pulling our dresses out of our suitcases and getting our jewelry, toiletries, and shoes laid out, as Marisita calmed down and fell asleep. We freshened up quickly, washed our hands and faces, and went to join the girls in the dining room.

It was obvious that Tía Beatrice did not do things in a small way. She had a beautiful dining table set with Majolica dishes. I knew the name of this beautiful pottery from my trips to the California border town of Tijuana. I had admired it as a teenager when my parents took my sister and me to Tijuana to buy souvenirs on several weekends. I remembered buying a rustic leather coin purse during one of those trips, and my mother bought a set of Majolica bowls that she admired. We enjoyed those bowls for years, until all had been broken but one.

A whole bevy of maids were consigned to the task of serving each of us and pampering our every need. The meal was elaborate: A plump chicken breast surrounded by black mole, and rice with onion and *nopales* (peeled, chopped, and cooked pear cactus). I recalled that this was the same dish that Carlos's mother had prepared for me when I first met her. I hovered over my plate until every morsel of the mole-smothered chicken was savored.

Satisfied with our long, wonderful lunch, Marisa brought Marisita down for a little plate of chicken and rice and then some fresh air (which we also needed). The girls were going to get dressed now, so it was a good time to leave the scene so they could have their privacy.

Tía Beatrice came out to the front porch shortly afterward and shouted for us to come into the house. "Ven! Están listas las chicas!" (Come! The girls are ready!)

I picked up Marisita, who had just picked a little pink flower from the ground. Allowing her to hold it, Marisa and I scuttled along as fast as we could to our room to prepare ourselves for the wedding. Marisa dressed Marisita in the sweet little dress that she had brought for her, while I freshened up and smoothed out the wrinkles in my dress. Marisa did the same, and soon we were dressed and ready to go.

As we entered the living room, we beheld a dramatically dressed group of young women, with plumes of yellow ostrich feathers stuck into the top of their French rolls. Their dresses were floor-length burgundy satin. Their arms, covered in long burgundy gloves, held long-stemmed white calla lilies with yellow stamens that matched the ostrich feathers. I was puzzled at the combination of colors … but then I thought again, *This is Mexico!*

We came downstairs, and Tía Beatrice's son, Hernando, told us that he would be driving us to the wedding in his car. He was in his early twenties, a very handsome escort. He was going to be one of the ushers, so we would be at the church about thirty minutes before the wedding started. I was looking forward to some good front-row seats.

Nestled in the second row of pews, Marisa, Marisita, and I were ready for the big event. Finally, the crowd of people were all seated, and the music started. A beautiful song (that I couldn't fully understand) was sung by a gifted soprano, high above us at the back of the church. Goose bumps rose on my arms. I could imagine Carlos and me, waiting at the back of the church, separated from each other, ready to make our debut in our magnificent wedding attire. Just then, another song began, "Ave Maria," sung a cappella by a baritone vocalista. Now I was completely floating on a cloud and imagined the fairy tale that awaited Carlos and me.

Just then, the plucking of a Spanish guitar was audible, playing a gentle ballad for the wedding ensemble to begin their procession down the aisle. The entire room stood and all turned to look for the first person in the bridal party to appear. A beautifully dressed little girl, about six years old, came ambling down the aisle from the back, a big smile on her face, with ringlets of dark silky hair cascading from the crown of her head. She was obviously enjoying her job, showering the carpet with white rose petals from her little basket as she made her way up the aisle. About twenty feet behind her, the ring bearer walked like a little soldier, protecting the treasure that had been carefully affixed to the burgundy pillow he was carrying. The little black box, which would soon be opened by the groom, was in his safe little hands. He had been coached, it was obvious, to be very stoic and keep his pace very exact.

The first bridesmaid began her trek down the aisle now, joined on her left by a handsome groomsman; together, she looked like a plumed Las Vegas dancer (albeit a modest one) with her date. After seven of these pairs made it to the front of the church, they were all in their places and ready to receive the bride and groom.

The standard yet startling organ chords of *dah-dah-dah-dah dah dah dah* grabbed the attention of the entire church. Eyes became more focused now, as the bride's appearance was imminent. And appear she did. In an elaborate, long white gown, wearing an intricate lace veil, she was joined by her father, and they began their trip to the altar.

With a beautiful array of young women and men standing in front of us, and now the bride joining the handsome groom. I was completely full of joy. *What will my wedding party look like? What will I look like?* I thought. I felt a wave of electricity shoot straight down my spine to my feet, and my shoulders quivered. The sermon, along with many rituals I didn't understand, lasted about thirty minutes. The bride and groom were given permission to kiss, and I melted as I watched the crescendo of an event that I knew had been a year in the planning. As the bride passed us, we could see the train of her dress float by, seemingly endless. It was also the *beginning* of a new kind of relationship for this couple—a *married* relationship. It wasn't lost on me.

After the congregation of about two hundred people had filed outside, Hernando came and found us and escorted us back to his car. The reception was just down the street at what in Mexico is called a "salon." It has the same meaning as a reception hall in the States. Shortly, we pulled into the enormous parking lot. Marisita needed some time to practice her walking for a bit. Marisa and I were "bus-lagged" at this point, but we knew that soon we would be having a nice glass of champagne and would be able to sit back and just watch all the partying.

Finally, all of the tables in the huge hall were occupied. People were shouting over the music and getting up to greet each family member and friend. Marisita was very popular at the reception. It seemed that almost every attendee picked her up and loved her. It was such a warm experience for me to watch the interaction among grandparents, aunts, uncles, cousins, brothers, sisters, sons, and daughters. A comfort enveloped the whole crowd, as each responded to the other with such graciousness and understanding. I felt that I was part of the whole—accepted without question or hesitation as Marisa introduced me to one friend or family member after another.

It was a lively, joyous celebration. All kinds of antics were dreamed up by the groomsmen, and the bridesmaids performed a lip-sync skit to a popular Mexican song. I didn't recognize it, but the words were sentimental and showed the obvious affection the girls felt for their friend, now a bride.

Thanks to Hernando, we arrived home near eleven o'clock. The wedding festivities were still going strong, but Marisita was asleep, and we needed to do the same. Numb and ready for bed, we blindly got ready and, without any memory of hitting the sheets, all three of us slept like babies.

The next morning was such a treat. As we quietly stepped down the stairs, we could hear Tía Beatrice in the kitchen, giving orders to the maid. As we approached the kitchen door, we found Tía Beatrice sipping a very large glass full of pale-yellow liquid. I asked what it was, and she responded, "Just a minute, and you will see!" Before I knew it, the maid was making one for me. "Now, try it!" Tía Beatrice kindly commanded me.

I took her orders gladly. "Mmm, this is delicious!" I exclaimed.

"It is a banana shake with cinnamon," she told me.

"I love it!"

Marisa took a sip as well. "I'll have one of those," she teased. Soon, we were all sipping banana shakes, with coffee on the side. Marisita was enjoying a strained version of our shakes in her bottle.

Next, Tia Beatrice ordered *juevos enfrijolados con pan tostado* for us (fried eggs with the "gravy" of cooked, ranch-style beans poured over them, with warm corn tortillas) As we gladly received the next course, we lapped it up, and here and there added a little of the delicious (and hot!) salsa, which was on the table in a little wooden bowl, a mainstay of Mexican meals. We were as happy as little pigs. After discussing every single event of the night before, and after thanking Tía Beatrice and Hernando for all they had done for us, we went upstairs to take showers and get ready for our trip home.

About an hour later, we hugged and thanked Tía Beatrice and Hernando many times again, boarded the bus, and bid goodbye to one of the sweetest adventures of my life.

42

THE MESSENGER

Our trip to Vera Cruz had been an enormous delight for me, and I knew Marisa and Marisita both thoroughly enjoyed it. It had given us a rare chance to separate ourselves from the rest of the family, allowing us to become closer in a much more accelerated way than we would have had while living among the others. This wonderful bonding would quickly reveal itself as a very timely blessing.

It was near midnight when the taxi delivered us from the bus depot. Weary-eyed and a bit sore from the cramped bus ride, Marisa and I managed to get our suitcases inside the door. Everyone was obviously asleep, given their busy schedules. Marisa carried Marisita up to their room, while I slowly towed my own suitcase up to my room. I went back to retrieve Marisa's suitcase. As I reached her bedroom, I thanked her profusely for giving me a memory that I knew I would never forget.

"It was my pleasure, Collette. It was a wonderful trip. I so enjoyed being with you, and I know Marisita and the whole family did too. We all love you. Good night. Sleep well."

I slipped into my room, opened my suitcase, and pulled my pajamas out of my bag. Oh, yes, sweet sleep, "Where is thy sting?" I went down to the bathroom and brushed my teeth and washed my face. I knew I would fall asleep the minute my head hit the pillow.

When the morning light protruded through my bedroom window, I slowly came out of the dream I was having. Carlos was standing in front of me, begging me to get married. It was surreal, and somehow there was an urgency that I didn't understand. I was apprehensive and wondering why he decided to move the wedding date. I was wandering around, deep in my unconscious mind, asking friends of the family for their help in order to expedite the wedding. Favors for the reception, a group of mariachis, table centerpieces—I was overwhelmed! This was enough to rouse me from my almost anesthetized mind and body after the long, exhausting day we'd had yesterday. Due to the travel on the bus and my disquieting dream, I felt a reluctance to allow myself to fully awake. But little by little, my body and mind responded to the sunlight, and I came back to life.

I gradually opened my eyes. Almost immediately, someone knocked on my door. "Who is it?" I asked, still groggy.

"It's Marisa. Can I come in please?"

"Of course!"

She opened the door slowly, holding Marisita in her left arm. "We wanted to visit you and see how you are doing," she said sweetly. Marisita's darling little smile brought me to complete consciousness, and I sat up to receive her.

"Come here, sweetheart!" I gestured to her. "How are you this morning?" I asked as I pulled her close to me and kissed her little cheek. I then repeated the same question to Marisa.

"We are fine ... so far," she responded.

I thought that was odd. "Why do you say 'so far'?" I asked.

"Well, I have something to talk to you about." Her voice took on an ominous tone. "Martín and Carlos have left for work, and I wondered if you could come down to our room while I get Marisita ready for the day."

"Of course," I said with a sense of concern.

After passing Marisita back to Marisa, I pushed through the paralyzing feeling that started to invade my body. I managed to get my arms into the sleeves of my robe, but for some reason, I felt robotic, not in tune with my own self. I felt the doom of a giant question mark settle on my shoulders. I knew something of a serious nature was awaiting me.

Marisa took a seat on the bed, with pillows positioned behind her, as if she was going to remain there for some time. She had placed Marisita in her playpen with toys and her warmed bottle of milk. Marisita was content and lighthearted. Marisa was *not*.

"I have made a comfortable place for you here next to me," she said as she reached to her right, making me aware of the pillows she had gathered for my comfort. I walked around the bed, smiling at Marisita on my way, and sat down. "Make yourself comfortable," she said calmly and lovingly. "I wanted to tell you again how wonderful it was to be with you on our trip to Vera Cruz. Marisita, Martín, Señor Herrera, Theresa, and I love you so much. Now, a big part of our family in Vera Cruz loves you too. You have made a very meaningful and lasting impression on our family, Collette. I love you, and you know that. There is no question about how I feel for you and that my friendship with you is a treasure that is forever."

I was started feeling an increase in my heartbeat. I knew she was gently leading me to something painful, something that was not of her making.

"Collette, do you remember when you went back to the States last Christmas?"

"Of course," I answered, as if to hurry up the process.

"Well, Carlos was very tormented during those months that you were trying to decide whether you would ever come back to Mexico. I know he went to visit you, and I know he had a wonderful time. But after he returned home, he became despondent when he read your letters. He had told Martín that the last letter you wrote was a Dear John letter. He didn't think you were coming back to Mexico."

I knew all of this, of course, but I answered her with a hesitant "Yes?"

"Well," she gently continued, "Carlos was very depressed and didn't trust your intentions after so many negative letters. He was, as you say in English, on the rebound. He went back to his old high school girlfriend for comfort. She lives in this neighborhood." She tried to maintain a matter-of-fact coolness. "Her name is Montserrat, and she has known Carlos since they were two years old. She lives three streets away. Martín woke me this morning to tell me that yesterday, while we were traveling back from Vera Cruz, Montserrat's grandmother came to our house. She asked for Theresa—they are acquaintances. She was invited in, and she told Theresa that her granddaughter is pregnant and that Carlos is the father."

Dead calm. Dead eyes. Dead weight on the bed. Paralyzed tongue. No feeling. A marshmallow sitting on the bed. Deaf.

I don't know how much time passed before I was conscious again. All I knew was that Marisa's face was hovering above mine, troubled, desperate, begging me to speak, while she hesitantly swatted at my cheeks, trying to get me to breathe deep, to respond to her. But I had no feeling.

I was lying in a fog, not knowing where the fog ended and my body began. "I'm overwhelmed," I uttered.

"You are here, Collette. With me, Marisa," she responded lovingly but firmly. "You must be strong, Collette. I won't leave your side. If you need help, I will call the doctor."

"I don't know what I need. ... Let me breathe for a ... few ... minutes," I stammered. I just could not make my tongue or my mouth move, not even my mind.

At some point, I was able to move my feet to the side of the bed and slowly sit up. "Can you please take me to my room?" I mumbled.

"Okay, take hold of my arm," Marisa offered. She was holding Marisita in her other arm.

I was able to slowly come to a standing position. "Thank you," I managed to say. "I think I can walk now." Carefully, Marisa moved with me down the hall, questioning me about whether I felt dizzy or if my legs felt strong enough. We made it to my bedroom, where she led me straight to my bed.

"I want you to lie down while I get you some soup. Stay here and don't do anything," she said in a firm, loving tone. She covered me up gently and left to organize Marisita and bring some soup to me.

I heard her call to Carlos's mother. "Theresa, me puedes ayudar?" (Theresa, can you help me?)

And sweet Theresa answered, "Sí, voy!" (Yes, I'm coming.)

Shortly, Marisa came into my room with the soup. "Everything is going to be all right. I promise you," Marisa assured me. "Just rest for twenty minutes, and I will be back to be with you, and we will talk, okay?"

"Yes, sure. Thank you," I vaguely responded. "I just need to absorb what you told me, okay?"

"Of course you do, but don't think for a minute that you are alone! I am with you! I understand, believe me. We will come to a calm conclusion about what to do when I come back. I love you, Collette. You are my sister."

Thirty minutes later, Marisa gently knocked on the door and came in. "I am so worried about you, and so heartbroken for all of us. Theresa is sobbing; she considers you her own daughter. Carlos came home from work early, as he hardly slept all night. He is so distraught. He went to see Monserrat to make her tell him the truth—whether she is sure this is his baby or not. He wants to end his life if it means losing you. But we all know that this is not the solution. If this is his child, he is responsible."

"Why did I keep changing my mind when Carlos called me over and over in the States? Why has God turned his back on me, now that I have made a decision? Why can't the love between Carlos and me remain in its sacred place? Why? Why? Why?" I started crying convulsively. "I don't want to see him or anyone, please. I need to be alone in here for the rest of the day and all of the night before I can overcome this tragedy. Please keep Carlos and everyone away from me! I'm begging you!"

Marisa promised me that she would convince Carlos not to disturb me.

I had never fallen so low in my entire life. No disappointment compared with this one. My life had been invaded by a hideous cancer! I was ashamed. I was livid. I was hurt. I was lost.

I woke at ten the next morning, although I had slept off and on all night. The only interruption in my solitude had been Theresa, delivering cooked oatmeal and orange juice to me. We had no words for each other except the utilitarian, "Here is some breakfast for you," and, from my mouth, "Thank you."

I knew what I had to do. I had done nothing but ruminate for the past few hours. I had looked at my wedding dress and laughed at it. I had looked at my ring and laughed at it too. What a cruel joke! I had taken it off and placed it back in its black gift box. I had written terrible words to Carlos. I had torn up everything I wrote. I had closed my eyes and pretended that this was just a nightmare. I had tried everything not to face what loomed in front of me. *"You need to go home."* That was all I could see now.

I called Carlos, who was at work. My only words were, "I'm leaving." I hung up.

He called back. "I will never love her. I never have. I will always love you."

"I don't have anything to say to you, Carlos!" I was a seething lightning rod, absorbing a million watts of searing hot pain. I hung up again.

I called Maria. She was a friend of the family who had a car and three children at home. I didn't want *any* family member to be a party to my leaving. I couldn't face anyone. I just needed a trustworthy ride. Maria answered my call, not asking any questions. (I knew that Theresa had already told her about the situation, as she was one of her best friends.)

At one o'clock, Maria pulled up in front of the house with her three children in the back seat. I had packed my bag in solitude, Marisa staying down the hall with Marisita. The pain was too tortuous, too fresh for either of us to touch. I had been transformed once again into a robot. I needed to push my "forward" button, descend the stairs, walk to the car, insert my suitcase, and take a seat. That was it.

We pulled away from the curb, but Maria needed to make a small U-turn at our dead-end street. As we turned around in the cul-de-sac, I saw Theresa, Marisa, and Marisita standing in the doorway, sobbing and doing their best to wave. It was crippling. I could barely raise my arm to reciprocate.

The trip to the airport was completely silent. I was beholden to Maria for doing what was an unsavory task.

I was in line at the ticket counter at 1:30. Carlos spotted me and caught up with me. He reached for my hand; I withdrew. He asked me to look at him; I turned away.

Finally, he said, "Collette, I will regret this the rest of my life. I will love you the rest of my life, and there is not going to be any happiness for me." He began to cry, embarrassed but losing control of his pride. He wrapped his arms around me, and pathetically, we both sobbed and sobbed. I pulled away, without looking at Carlos, and walked to the gate.

The truth and the corresponding pain that were visited upon me that fateful day in Mexico had changed me, mentally and emotionally, forever. The Cinderella story that I had embraced through my American culture—books, songs, movies, and the enchantment with that butterfly my loving mother had nurtured—had been crushed forever. Those beautiful Spanish songs that serenaded me in Mexico had been scrapped. My hope would never be naïve and simplistic again. It would forever be tempered by that day. Reality—that *harsh* reality that is never welcomed by any human soul—had engraved my tender heart with a painful memory that would affect my attitude and every step I took in life from that point forward.

43

NEW YEAR'S EVE 2018

(Fifty-Two Years Later)

I knew that this seed
I had cultivated for so long
Would grow and transform me
As I made announcements
Of its sprouting, I felt a great
Stirring in my mind
I doted on it, and spent
Countless hours trying to
Imagine its final form
Tonight, when the timing is right
I will reveal it to others, and celebrate it
On this New Year's Eve of 2018
The clock arrives at twelve o'clock …
And as I release it to the world
I pray that it will be as big a blessing as it has been to me
200-plus online pages and thirty-eight chapters full of colorful characters

COLLETTE SOMMERS

Glorious memories and, yes, tragedies
Have culminated in this book I bore today
Welcome to the world!

—Collette Sommers
2018

44

THEN AND NOW

Carlos aside, I have remained in communication over all these years with his family and the friends that I came to know during my time in Mexico City. They sustain my soul. In recent years I have traveled many times over that life-changing border to spend time with my Mexican family, as I call them. They are always eager to welcome me.

Looking back to 1966 when I first came to Mexico, I have come to realize that the ultimate purpose for my life was not just to attend school there and not just to meet Carlos. The purpose was to bless me with the discovery of a beautiful culture and, more importantly, with the devotion of so many deep and sincere friendships. Carlos was my introduction to that culture and those friendships. For this, I thank him.

Today is New Year's Eve. Tomorrow will be January 1, 2018. As so many times before, I have planned a trip to visit my Mexican family in the next few months. It has been three years since I visited them, and I miss them terribly.

In a few months, I will once again board a plane that will lift its burden of passengers up and away from the Los Angeles airport and slowly set its course for Mexico City. Once we reach the circumference of the city, I will look out from my standard window seat, from which I can see Carlos's parents' house. My heart will skip a beat, but it will go on ticking.

From the air, the city is just a mass of concrete buildings. Nothing hints at the warmth of its people and their culture that thrives within those walls, nor the events that shaped my life.

45

FAVORITE RECIPES

Gabi's Potatoes and Chiles
(Receta de Papas con Rajas de Gabi)

Gabi was Marisa's maid and cook. She was from the mountains of Michoacán, which she described as an area that was abundant with flowers and fruits of all kinds. She loved her home state, but there were no jobs there, she explained. Although she spoke a native dialect, she had learned enough Spanish to manage her day-to-day interactions with Marisa and Martín and the shop owners nearby.

Gabi was only seventeen, a diminutive natural beauty with long blue-black hair that shone brilliantly in the sun. Most of the time, she was smiling. But on one occasion I noticed her sadness about leaving her native state. I asked about her parents. Though stoic, her eyes welled with tears as she spoke of them. Her father was blind, she explained, and so her mother had no money. Her work in Mexico City provided enough for Gabi to share half of it with her parents. Since she ate all of her meals at Marisa and Martín's home, six days a week, her food budget was minor, and her rent was a very small amount, since she only paid for one day a week to stay at a rustic apartment with three other women outside of the city. As Gabi cooked, I asked her to explain each step of her preparation of this delicious side dish that I came to love over the time I stayed with Marisa and Martín.

Cook four potatoes in boiling water until al dente. Drain and set aside. Pour vegetable oil over two poblano chiles to coat them slightly. Hold one at a time over the stove-top flame until the skin blackens and breaks down in cracks. Place in a plastic bag and let sit 15 minutes.

Peel chiles by rubbing them gently with a paring knife blade. (Do this with gloves on, or if without gloves, wash hands thoroughly in dish detergent and rinse well afterward.) Cut open along sides, lengthwise. Open and lay skin side down. Remove vein. Cut in lengthwise strips about 1/4 inch wide. (You can keep the strips long or cut them in half to make them shorter.) Cut half of one yellow or white onion in 1/4-inch slices. Cut the slices into half rounds. Sauté until they start to become translucent. Cut potatoes in one-inch cubes, then add to pan along with the rajas (strips of Poblano chiles). Add 1/3 cup chicken or vegetable broth. Simmer and stir until heated thoroughly. Cover and let rest five minutes.

Serve, and top with Mexican cream (crema). Enjoy as a side dish with tacos, or use as the filling for the tacos.

Posole de Marisa
(Hominy Soup with Pork and Chicken)
(A labor of love)

During one of Marisa's visits with me in the US, I accompanied her to a Mexican market to buy the ingredients for her posole. I wrote down the recipe as I tried to help her with this big production. My family loved it so much; I wish I had the confidence to make it on my own.

one gallon can of white hominy
eight filets of pork shoulder the size of your palm
four chicken breasts
one yellow onion
one head of garlic
two bay leaves
one bunch of cilantro
one tablespoon each of cumino (cumin) and salt
white vinegar
four tomatillos (small, green tomatoes sold in Mexican markets)
eight of each of the following chiles: guajillo chiles (wah-*hee*-yo—red, long dry chiles); chiles de arbol (red, dried); chiles cascabel (shaped like bell peppers but smaller and deeper red)

Ingredients for Toppings for the Posole: chopped onion, shredded lettuce, sliced radishes, dry oregano, lime slices, avocado slices, sour cream

Set a very large, tall pot on stove, filled halfway with water. Bring to a boil. Place the pork filets into the water along with half the onion, whole tomatillos, and a pierced head of garlic (not cut or crushed; left whole). When meat starts getting tender, remove everything but the meat. Set aside in a colander.

Add all of hominy and let cook until hominy bursts open. Then, add the chicken breasts. Let boil.

Wash and pat dry all dried peppers. Hold a cloth over your nose as you sauté them and turn them in a large frying pan, about fifteen minutes. Turn off heat. Let cool. Remove seeds and stems with gloves on. Place in a separate smaller pot and cover them with water. Cover and cook until soft. Set aside all but four of the guajillo chiles.

For the Salsa: Pour two cups of the hot chile water into a blender, and put the four guajillo chiles inside with two cloves of garlic, a small slice of onion, and blend. Pour the mixture over a colander into the posole pot. Dip the colander into the posole water a few times to capture the essence of the flavors. Add cumin and salt to the pot.

Salsa: Put the remaining peppers in the blender with two palms of cooked hominy. Add a tablespoon of sesame seeds to a fry pan. Toast with a lid on loosely so they don't pop out. Stir like popcorn. Add the sesame to the blender with a little white vinegar and water, but keep the mixture thick. Add salt and blend.

Serve posole in very large crock, and place little bowls and plates with the toppings and salsa around it. Serve with toasted corn tortillas (toasted just before serving and put in a stack on the table, covered with a festive cloth).

Enjoy your friends and family!
They are everything you need!

Photos from My Travels in Mexico

Printed in the United States
By Bookmasters